THE NEW GERMAN ARCHITECTURE

THE TENTH MUSE   THE TENTH MU

ROOF CITY

THE NEW
GERMAN ARCHITECTURE

Gerhard G. Feldmeyer

Introduction by Manfred Sack

With an essay by Casey C. M. Mathewson

Rizzoli
NEW YORK

First published in the United States of America in 1993 by
Rizzoli International Publications, Inc.
300 Park Avenue South, New York, NY 10010

Copyright © 1993 Rizzoli International Publications, Inc.

All rights reserved.
No part of this publication may be reproduced in any manner whatsoever without permission in writing from Rizzoli International Publications, Inc.

Library of Congress Cataloging-in-Publication Data

Feldmeyer, Gerhard.
   The new German architecture / Gerhard Feldmeyer ; essays by Manfred Sack and Casey C. M. Mathewson.
     p. cm.
     ISBN 0-8478-1672-9. — ISBN 0-8478-1673-7 (paper).
   1. Architecture, Modern—20th century—Germany.
2. Architecture—Germany. 3. Architecture and society—Germany. I. Sack, Manfred, 1928– . II. Mathewson, Casey C. M. III. Title.
NA1068.F36 1993
720'.943'09048—dc20   92-32826
                                                  CIP

Series designer: Paul Chevannes
Designer: Mary McBride
Translations from the German by Mark Wilch

Printed and bound in Singapore

Front cover photograph: Kauffmann and Theilig, Office Complex, Ostfildern-Kemnat, 1988–90
Front cover drawing: Rüdiger Kramm, Public Housing Project, Frankfurt-Bonames, 1989
Frontispiece: Daniel Libeskind, The Tenth Muse, Wiesbaden, 1992
Back cover (hardcover only): Behnisch and Partner, German Postal Museum, Frankfurt am Main, 1984–90

Illustration Credits

Numbers in roman refer to page numbers. Numbers in italics refer to illustration numbers.

© Bauwelt: *54;* A. Beck: *6;* © Dirk Bleicker: 130; Böhlau Verlag: *35, 36;* Peter Bonfig: 112; © Richard Bryant/Arcaid: 103, 109, 110, 111; © Gert Elsner: 179; Susanne Elsner: *3;* Gerhard Feldmeyer: *2;* German Architecture Museum: *47;* © Hans Georg Göllner: *63;* Reinhard Görner: *44,* 65 middle and bottom; Hatje Stuttgart: *48;* Christian Kandzia: 66, 67, 71, 72, 75; © Atelier Kinold: 193, 196, 197, 199; © Wilmar Koenig: 172, 174, 175; Stefan Koppelkamm: *12;* © Waltraud Krase: 131 top, 133 top; © Heiner Leiska: 76, 77, 79, 104; © Dieter Leistner: 80, 83, 84, 85, 86–87, 114–115, 116, 126, 127 bottom, 160, 162, 163, 164, 167, 218, 222, 223; © Luftbildverlag Hans Bertram: *45;* Thomas Lüttge: *27;* Casey C. M. Mathewson: *42;* Norbert Michalke/octopus: *17;* © Studio Ivan Nemec: 124, 125, 128, 154, 155; © Monika Nikolic: 89, 133 bottom; © Uwe Rau: *49,* 90; © Tomas Riehle: *30;* Stadtarchiv Ulm/HfG-Archiv: *15;* Reger Studios: 54–55; Barbara Schneider: *43;* © Philipp Schönborn: 119; Senatsverwaltung für Bau- und Wohnungswesen: *41;* G. Stöckmann: *7;* © Wilfried Täubner: 202, 203, 205; Ullstein Bilderdienst: *31, 40;* Ullstein Bilderdienst/Fritz Eschen: *32;* Ullstein Bilderdienst/Klaus Lehnartz: *38, 39;* VEB Verlag für Bauwesen: *37;* Vieweg und Sohn: *33, 34;* Ingrid Voth-Amslinger: *25;* © Jens Weber: 118, 120; Wolfgang Wiese: *13;* © Valentin Wormbs: 136, 138 bottom, 139 bottom

To my wife Yong Sun

Acknowledgments

I would like to acknowledge with great appreciation all the help I received from the architects and their office colleagues in the preparation of this book. In addition, the photographers supplied me with excellent material, as did the various archives, especially the Ullstein Bilderdienst.

My secretaries Petra Domnick and Marion Kröger were particularly helpful. Thank you for adjusting to the rhythm of my work. Without your enthusiasm and systematic approach this project would not have been possible. Also, thanks to everybody in the Hamburg and Düsseldorf offices of HPP for their support in this extra challenge. I hope that I have met everybody's expectations.

I wish to acknowledge Dr. Manfred Sack for graciously agreeing to write the introduction to this book. Thank you for letting me share your knowledge and wisdom; your criticism and input were essential for the book. Special thanks to Casey Mathewson, not only for his essay but also for our inspiring discussions throughout the process. I look forward to working together on another project. I would also like to express my gratitude to Mark Wilch in San Diego, California, for doing most of the translation work and accepting my tight schedule.

Without the confidence, encouragement, patience, and substantial help of David Morton, senior editor at Rizzoli, this project would not have been possible. The same applies to Andrea Monfried, associate editor at Rizzoli. Thank you for your great spirit and deep engagement in this project; you made me feel a part of it until the very last moment.

Lastly I would like to thank my wife for her understanding throughout the last year. I know what I have to make up for. *G.F.*

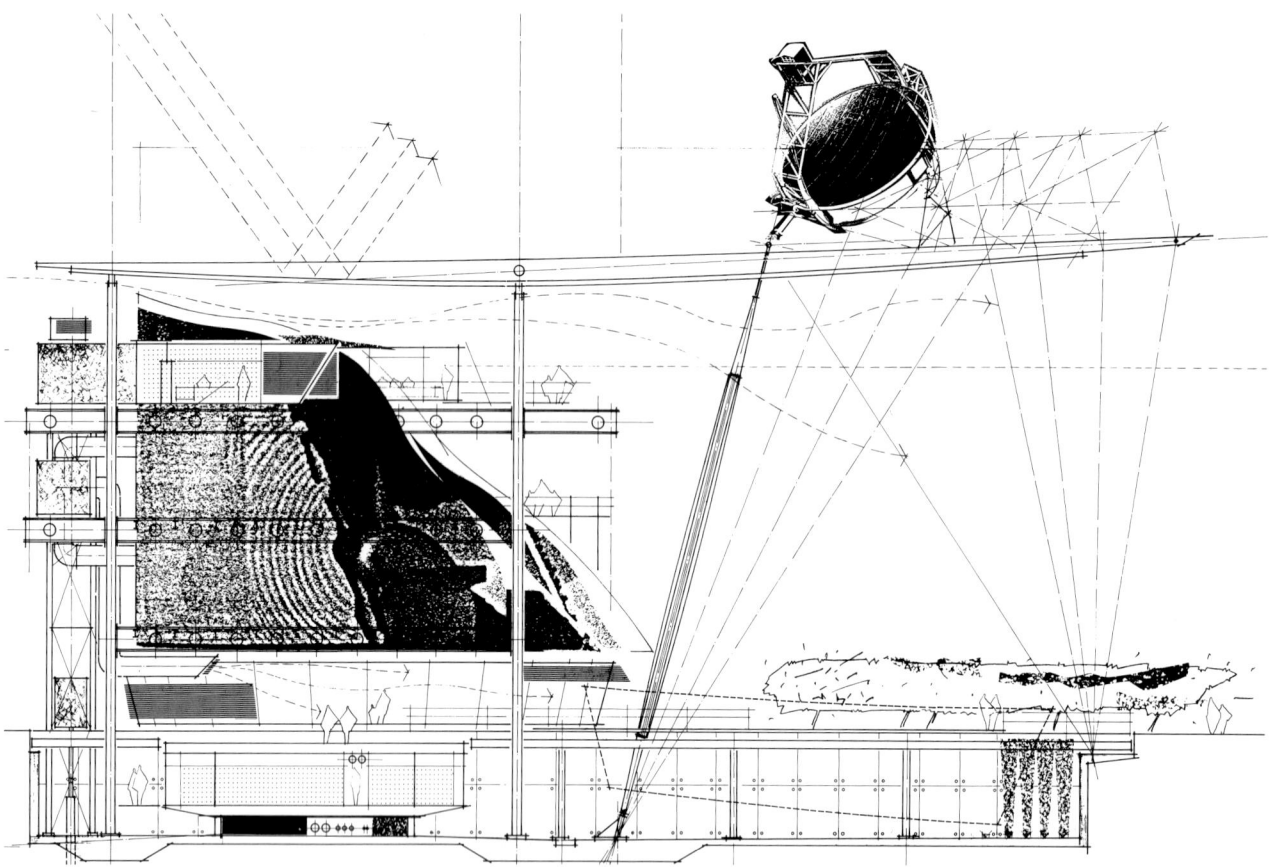

Auer and Weber, German Exhibition Pavilion, Seville, 1990

Contents

Architects' Biographies 8
Preface
  by Gerhard G. Feldmeyer 10
Introduction
  by Manfred Sack 17
From City Planning to Urban Design: Rebuilding Germany 1945–1992
  by Casey C. M. Mathewson 32

The Architects
  Auer and Weber 54
  Bangert and Scholz 60
  Behnisch and Partner 66
  Böge and Lindner 76
  Gottfried Böhm 80
  Andreas Brandt and Rudolph Böttcher 88
  Eisele and Fritz 94
  Meinhard von Gerkan 100
  Thomas Herzog 112
  Hilmer and Sattler 118
  Jochem Jourdan and Bernhard Müller 124
  Kauffmann and Theilig 134
  Uwe Kiessler 140
  Josef Paul Kleihues 144
  Hans Kollhoff 154
  Rüdiger Kramm 160
  Christoph Langhof 170
  Arno Lederer and Jorunn Ragnarsdottir 176
  Daniel Libeskind 182
  Karljosef Schattner 192
  Axel Schultes 202
  Otto Steidle 208
  Otto Steidle and Uwe Kiessler 212
  O. M. Ungers 216

Architects' Biographies

AUER AND WEBER
Fritz Auer and Karlheinz Weber opened their office in 1980.
Fritz Auer
- Born in 1933
- Graduated Stuttgart University, 1962
- Scholarship, Cranbrook Academy of Art, 1958–59
- Employed in the offices of Behnisch and Lambart, and Yamasaki and Associates, 1959–66
- Partner in Behnisch and Partner, 1966–79
- Professor of Architecture, 1984–present

Karlheinz Weber
- Born in 1934
- Graduated Stuttgart University, 1961
- Scholarship, Ecole Nationale Supérieure des Beaux Arts, Paris, 1959–60
- Employed in the offices of Behnisch and Lambart, and Les Frères Arséne-Henry and Prof. Louis Arretche, 1960–66
- Partner in Behnisch and Partner, 1966–79
- Professor, Dresden University, 1992–present

BANGERT AND SCHOLZ
Dietrich Bangert and Stefan Scholz opened their office in 1992.
Dietrich Bangert
- Born in 1942
- Graduated Technical University of Berlin, 1969
- Own practice, 1969–71
- Partnership with Ganz Müller and Rolfes, 1971–73
- Partnership with Bernd Jansen, Stefan Scholz, and Axel Schultes, 1974–91

Stefan Scholz
- Born in 1938
- Student at Technical University of Krakow, 1961–65
- Graduated Technical University of Berlin, 1969
- Own practice, 1970–71
- Partnership with W. Pohl and U. Ringleben, 1971–74
- Partnership with Dietrich Bangert, Bernd Jansen, and Axel Schultes, 1974–91

BEHNISCH AND PARTNER
Günter Behnisch
- Born in 1922
- Graduated Stuttgart University, 1951
- Employed in the office of Prof. Rolf Gutbrod, 1951–52
- Own office, 1952–66
- Established Behnisch and Partner, 1966
- Professor of Architecture, Technical University of Darmstadt, 1967–present
- Member, Academy of Arts, Berlin, 1982
- Member, International Academy of Architecture, Sofia, 1990
- Honorary Member, Royal Incorporation of Architects in Scotland, 1992

BÖGE AND LINDNER
Jürgen Böge and Ingeborg Lindner-Böge opened their office in 1986.
Jürgen Böge
- Born in 1950
- Graduated Stuttgart University, 1975
- Employed in the office of Wolske and Erler, 1978
- Own office, 1980
- Partner in Böge, Friedrich, Lindner, 1981–86

Ingeborg Lindner-Böge
- Born in 1951
- Graduated Stuttgart University, 1973
- Employed in the office of APB, 1978
- Own office, 1980
- Partner in Böge, Friedrich, Lindner, 1981–86

GOTTFRIED BÖHM
- Born in 1920
- Studied architecture and sculpture, Munich University and Academy of Art, 1942–47
- Employed in the office of Dominicus Böhm, 1948–50
- Employed in the office of Rudolph Schwartz, 1950–55
- Took over office of Dominicus Böhm, 1955–present
- Professor of Architecture, University of Aachen, 1963
- Member, Academy of Arts, Berlin, 1968
- Honorary Fellow, American Institute of Architects, 1982
- Member, Académie d'Architecture, Paris, 1983
- Professor, University of Pennsylvania, 1985–86
- Visiting lecturer and professor, Massachusetts Institute of Technology, University of Pennsylvania, Washington University, 1985–90
- Pritzker Architecture Prize, 1986
- Honorary Fellow, Royal Institute of British Architects, 1991

ANDREAS BRANDT AND RUDOLPH BÖTTCHER
Andreas Brandt and Rudolph Böttcher opened their office in 1979.
Andreas Brandt
- Born in 1937
- Graduated Arts Academy, Düsseldorf, 1964
- Own practice, 1964, 1968–79
- Visiting professor, University of California, Berkeley, 1967
- Professor of Architecture, University of Darmstadt, 1991

Rudolph Böttcher
- Born in 1938
- Graduated Arts Academy, Düsseldorf, 1962
- Employed in several offices, 1962–70
- Own office, 1970–79

EISELE AND FRITZ
Johann Eisele
- Born in 1948
- Studied civil engineering, Technical University of Darmstadt, 1970–71
- Studied architecture, Technical University of Darmstadt, 1971–78
- Academy collaborator, Technical University of Darmstadt, 1979–84
- Visiting professor, colleges in Bremen, Darmstadt, and Braunschweig, 1987–89
- Professor of Planning and Construction Design, Technical University of Darmstadt, 1990

Nicolas Fritz
- Born in 1948
- Studied architecture, Technical University of Darmstadt, 1967–73
- Employed in the office of Behnisch and Partner, 1974–75
- Employed by Chandilis, 1975–77
- Academy collaborator, Technical University of Darmstadt, 1978–83
- Guest professor, College for Arts and Music, Bremen, 1987–88
- Professor, Technical University of Karlsruhe, 1989–90

MEINHARD VON GERKAN
- Born in 1935
- Studied physics and law, Hamburg, 1954–55
- Graduated University of Braunschweig, 1964
- Own office in association with Volkwin Marg, 1965–present
- Board member, Hamburg Chamber of Architects, 1971
- Appointed Free Academy of Arts, Hamburg, 1972
- Professor of Architectural Design, Technical University of Braunschweig, 1974–present
- Received 200 prizes in national and international competitions, delivered lectures, wrote publications, acted as professional juror, 1965–92
- Visiting Professor, Nihon University, Tokyo, 1988

THOMAS HERZOG
- Born in 1941
- Graduated Technical University of Munich, 1965
- Employed in the office of Prof. P. C. von Seidlein, 1965–69
- Assistant Professor, University of Stuttgart, 1969–71
- Rome Award, Villa Massimo, 1971
- Own office, 1971–present
- Received doctorate, University of Rome, 1972
- Professor, University of Kassel, 1973
- Visiting Professor, University of Lausanne, 1979
- Mies van der Rohe Award, Architecture Guild Award, 1981
- "Deutscher Werkbund" Award, 1982
- Guest of Honor, German Academy, Villa Massimo, 1985
- Professor, University of Darmstadt, 1987

HILMER AND SATTLER
Heinz Hilmer and Christoph Sattler opened their office in 1974.
Heinz Hilmer
- Born in 1936
- Graduated Technical University of Munich, 1963

Christoph Sattler
- Born in 1938
- Graduated Technical University of Munich, 1963
- Employed in the office of Rudolph Schwarz, 1960
- Employed in the office of Prof. P. C. von Seidlein, 1962
- Studies at Illinois Institute of Technology, 1963–65
- Worked in the office of Mies van der Rohe, 1965
- Received Master of Sciences degree, Illinois Institute of Technology, 1965

JOCHEM JOURDAN AND BERNHARD MÜLLER
Jochem Jourdan
- Born in 1937
- Graduated Technical University of Darmstadt, 1965
- Professor of Architecture, University of Kassel, 1978–present

Bernhard Müller
- Born in 1941
- Graduated Technical University of Darmstadt, 1969
- Lecturer, Technical University of Darmstadt, 1974–present
- Member, Deutscher Werkbund, BDA, SRL
- Own office, 1980–present

KAUFFMANN AND THEILIG
Dieter Ben Kauffmann and Andreas G. Theilig opened their office in 1988.

Dieter Ben Kauffmann
- Born in 1954
- Graduated Augsburg Polytechnic, 1978
- Project architect, Behnisch and Parter, 1980–84
- Project architect, Heinle, Wischer and Partner, 1984–88

Andreas G. Theilig
- Born in 1951
- Graduated Technical University of Darmstadt, 1978
- Project architect, partner, Behnisch and Partner, 1979–88
- Professor, Biberach Polytechnic, 1987–present

UWE KIESSLER
- Born in 1937
- Graduated Technical University of Munich, 1961
- Own office in partnership with Hermann Schultz, 1962–present
- Professor of Architecture, Technical University of Munich
- Member, Academy of Arts, Berlin

JOSEF PAUL KLEIHUES
- Born in 1933
- Graduated Technical University of Berlin, 1959
- Scholarship, Ecole Nationale Supérieure des Beaux Arts, Paris, 1960
- Own office, 1963–present
- Professor of Architectural Design and Theory, Dortmund University, 1973–present
- Professor of Architectural and Urban Design, Dortmund University, 1984–present
- Initiated "Dortmund Architectural Days"; served as director 1975–80
- Director of Planning, new construction, IBA, 1979–87
- Irwin S. Chanin Distinguished International Professorship, The Cooper Union, 1986–90
- Visiting Professor, Eero Saarinen Chair, Yale University, 1987

HANS KOLLHOFF
- Born in 1946
- Graduated Karlsruhe University, 1975
- DAAD Grant, Cornell University, 1975–78
- Reseach Assistant, Faculty of Architecture and Design, Technical University of Berlin, 1978–83
- Own office, 1978–present
- Visiting Professor for Architecture and Construction, HdK, Berlin, 1983–85
- Acting Chair of Urban Development and Industrial Construction, Dortmund University, 1986–87
- Visiting Professor, ETH, Zürich, 1987–88
- Exhibitions in Paris, London, Lausanne, 1989
- Professor of Architecture and Construction, ETH, Zürich, 1990–present

RÜDIGER KRAMM
- Born in 1945
- Own practice, 1971–73
- Graduated University of Darmstadt, 1972
- Diploma in Urbanization in Developing Countries, DAAD Grant, University College, London, 1973–74
- Worked with Behnisch and Partner, 1973
- Own office, 1977–present
- Professor, Faculty for Graphic Art, University of Mainz, 1981–88
- Professor, Institute for Building Construction, Construction Design and Planning, University of Karlsruhe, 1990
- Partnership with Axel Strigl, 1990–present

CHRISTOPH LANGHOF
- Born in 1948
- Studies at Technical University and Academy of Applied Arts, Vienna, and Arts Academy, Düsseldorf
- Postgraduate studies at the Academy for Graphic Arts, Berlin
- Own office, 1978
- Partnership with Thomas Hänni and Herbert Meerstein, 1981–87
- Professor, Architectural Association, London, 1987–89
- Visiting Professor, College for Graphic Arts, Frankfurt, 1990–91
- Exhibitions and lectures in Berlin, London, Los Angeles, Milan, Moscow, New York, Paris, Rome, San Francisco

ARNO LEDERER AND JORUNN RAGNARSDOTTIR
Arno Lederer and Jorunn Ragnarsdottir formed their partnership in 1985.

Arno Lederer
- Born in 1947
- Studied architecture, Stuttgart and Vienna; received degree in 1976
- Employed in the office of Ernst Gisel
- Own office, 1979–present
- Professor of Construction and Design, Stuttgart Polytechnic, 1985
- Professor of Architecture, University of Karlsruhe, 1990–present

Jorunn Ragnarsdottir
- Born in 1957
- Graduated Stuttgart University, 1983
- Employed in the office of Arno Lederer, 1983–85

DANIEL LIBESKIND
- Born in 1946
- Graduated The Cooper Union, New York
- Received a graduate degree in History and Theory of Architecture, Essex University
- Head, Department of Architecture, Cranbrook Academy of Art, 1979–85
- Visiting Professor, Harvard University, Ohio State University, University of Naples; Louis Sullivan Professorship, University of Illinois at Chicago; Lee Chair, University of California, Los Angeles; Bannister Fletcher Professorship, University of London
- Founder and Director, Architecture Intermundium, Milan, 1986–89
- Own practice, 1989–present
- Visiting Professor, Danish Academy of Art, Copenhagen, 1992
- Davenport Chair, Yale University, 1992
- Senior Scholar, Getty Center for the History of Arts and the Humanities, 1992

KARLJOSEF SCHATTNER
- Born in 1924
- Graduated Technical University of Munich, 1953
- Employed in the office of Franz Hart, 1953–54
- Own office, 1956–57
- Director, Diocese Board of Works, Eichstätt, 1957–present
- Honorary Professor, Technical University of Darmstadt, 1983–present
- Heinrich Tessenow Medal, Fritz Schumacher Foundation, 1986
- Visiting Professor, Technical University of Munich, 1987–88
- Visiting Professor, ETH Zürich, 1989–91

AXEL SCHULTES
- Born in 1943
- Graduated Technical University of Berlin, 1969
- Partnership with Dietrich Bangert, Bernd Jansen, and Stefan Scholz, 1974–91
- Own office, 1992–present

OTTO STEIDLE
- Born in 1943
- Studies at Governmental School of Building, 1962–65
- Graduated Academy of Art, Munich, 1969
- Principal, Muhr and Steidle, 1966
- Principal, Steidle and Partner, 1969
- Professor of Design, University of Kassel, 1979
- Professor of Design and Construction, Technical University of Berlin, 1981
- Visiting Professor, Massachusetts Institute of Technology, 1991
- Visiting Professor, Berlage School, Amsterdam, 1991
- Professor of Architecture, Academy of Art, Munich, 1991–present

O. M. UNGERS
- Born in 1926
- Graduated Technical University of Karlsruhe, 1950
- Lecturer, Technical University of Berlin, 1963–68
- Head, Department of Architecture, Cornell University, 1969–75
- Visiting Professor, Harvard University, University of California, Los Angeles

PREFACE
Gerhard G. Feldmeyer

THE SEARCH FOR works that would justify the title of this book was anything but easy in a country that, lacking a true metropolis, tends to scatter its architectural potential widely. In France or Japan, for example, the architectural oeuvre of the nation is concentrated in Paris or Tokyo; in Germany, focusing on Berlin or Frankfurt is not enough. Many other cities—Stuttgart, Bonn, or Hamburg, even towns like Eichstätt or Bremerhaven (1)—have buildings essential to an accurate picture of contemporary German architecture. This is just one of the characteristics crucial to an understanding of the larger historical and contemporary German architectural and cultural community.

German architecture, for decades better known for its craftsmanship than for its visionary, conceptual, or experimental elements, is at long last seeing the return of avant-gardist trends. It would be premature to try to categorize them and, in fact, counterproductive to their survival. But one thing can be said: contemporary architecture in Germany is characterized by individualism and pluralism, by uncertainty and contradiction, by faith and the search for new beginnings in urban planning, and by "grand architecture."

Yet this new vitality springs from a profession that is emerging from, and in some senses trying to negate, a disheartening postwar era. In recent decades, the scope of activity and influence of architects have shrunk even while architecture itself has become a favorite topic of conversation. To meet the technological, ecological, economic, and functional needs of a project, a host of specialized experts is brought in, and simultaneously, general contractors are tending to carry out more and more of the planning in construction projects themselves. The choices made end by having more to do with the personality of the chooser and prevailing trends than with the task at hand. Architects have let the tools of their metier slip out of their grasp, tools only they can use to create projects with a value that transcends the present to be integrated into the architectural tradition. Architects have protested too little, mustered too little resistance to a basic societal attitude that does not recognize the worth of architecture.

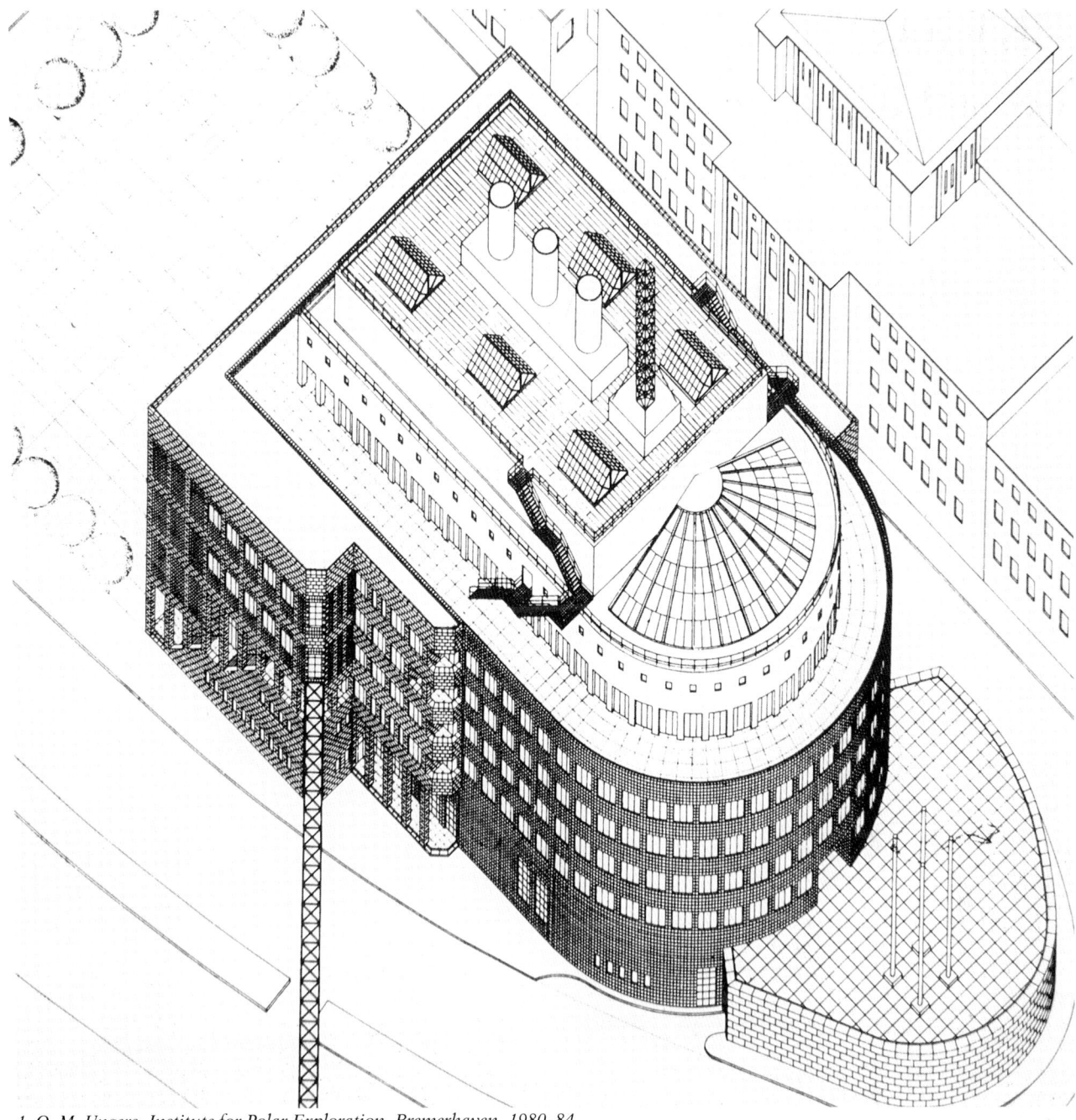

1. O. M. Ungers, Institute for Polar Exploration, Bremerhaven, 1980–84

Architectural Theory in Modern Germany

In the 1920s, in fact during the first third of this century, architects and aficionados all looked to Germany. The German architectural scene was a driving force for design developments and left its mark internationally. By contrast, despite the incredible number of buildings erected in West Germany after World War II, the country was far from having anything resembling an architectural culture until very recently. Even in the 1950s, when there was an attempt to pick up, at least externally, where the ideals of modernism had left off, its visionary and utopian powers were sorely missed. There was little thought or reflection; in the end, ideals were squelched by the dissimilar goals of the booming economy.

The 1960s were both climax and temporary end of that economic miracle, as the extreme fixation on progress and growth finally manifested its limits. The concentration on one-dimensional social processes led architecture,

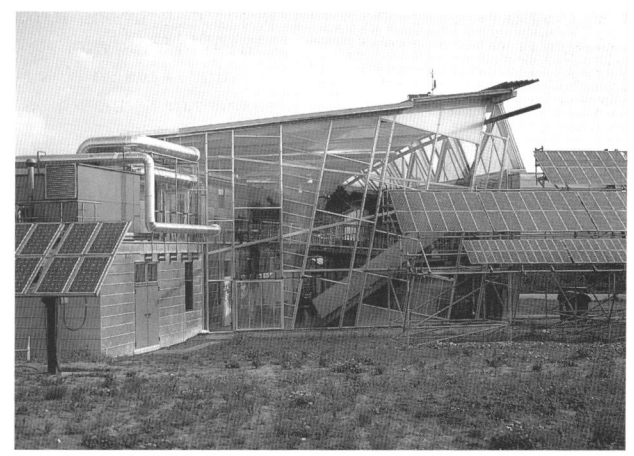

2. Günter Behnisch, Hysolar Institute, Stuttgart, 1987

3. Hans Hollein, Museum of Modern Art, Frankfurt am Main, 1992

4. Richard Meier, Museum for the Decorative Arts, Frankfurt am Main, 1979–85

5. Architektursalon Elvira, parking lot superstructure, Berlin, 1985

6. Formalhaut, Cow Project, Vogelsberg, 1985

7. Formalhaut, Rendezvous, 1986

too, to become merely a utilitarian discipline with its own optimized functionality. As a result, architecture could no longer live up to its multi-faceted social responsibility; it had become empty, devoid of meaning, a gridded, prefab monster greedily gorging itself on city and country alike.

This situation, recognized in part by the student movement of the late 1960s and early 1970s, brought about an awareness of the theoretical poverty implicit in focusing unconditionally on the aesthetic positions developed during the heroic phase of modernism while passively surrendering everything else to the empty functionalism of the construction industry. It is no surprise that as early as the late 1970s the demands for autonomy for architecture, for the restoration of architecture to an art form, were growing ever louder. These demands were largely, though not exclusively, responsible for the precipitous conversion to postmodernism, and the justification for returning to a kind of second historicism, to an apparent freedom to help oneself without reflection to history's teeming smorgasbord of architectural accomplishments.

Significantly, postmodernism's roots are not in Europe. It was only after its popularization by Charles Jencks that the word even entered into German parlance. This epoch, so characterized by an absence of theory and by a thoughtless, artless pragmatism, provoked polemic and exaggerated reaction in its wake, culminating, perhaps, in James Stirling's masterful Neue Staatsgalerie in Stuttgart, one of the clearest responses to the stylistic chaos that had preceded it.

Buildings like this exemplify an architecture which relies not on the abstraction of purely stereometric forms but on the diversity of form inherent in pictures and images, decoration and ornament, symbols and signs. With wit, irony, and playful lightness, Stirling brought an impressive architectural vocabulary to bear without seeming superficial or banal and without forgetting the true essence of architecture: to create space, to define space. The balance sheet is unfortunately sobering; the quality of the Neue Staatsgalerie was never again attained.

However, postmodernism, or postmodern classicism, is not so much a departure as a reaction to the corporate co-optation—and simultaneous failure—of modernism. Postmodernism dispensed with theoretical underpinnings and operated for the most part on an emotional, intuitive level. Just the opposite was a new buzzword making the rounds in the second half of the 1980s: deconstructivism. It influenced, confused, and seduced an entire generation of students; the publications of such architects as Bernard Tschumi and Rem Koolhaas were virtually devoured.

The deconstructivists pursue architecture as if it were a mix of the humanities and conceptual art. They involve the work of deconstructionist theoreticians like Jacques Derrida in their design process and thus distinguish themselves very decidedly from the postmodernists. While Koolhaas celebrated the dissolution of the urban fabric, fashioning from it his aesthetic principle for the city (as in *Delirious New York*'s City of the Captive Globe), Tschumi analyzed the urban landscape by dissecting it, as one might a sequence of images in a film. He tried to intertwine patterns, sequences of actions, and building plans so closely that a space would be created that was not defined by its unchanging boundaries but by its very dynamism.

The structures Koolhaas and Tschumi built in an attempt to realize their theories suffer from an innate problem: the intellectual design process is so closely linked to the end product (itself seen as an intermediate result) that the actual building cannot be understood on its own merits. Tschumi's follies in the Parc de la Villette in Paris, for example, a matchless example of deconstructivist architecture, ultimately seem somewhat shallow when one considers the complex design process from which they stem.

Architects such as Günter Behnisch in Germany or Coop Himmelblau in Austria were erroneously categorized as deconstructivists. Behnisch and his team actually celebrated the joy of doing the doable (2). A column did not have to be vertical, did not have to be straight; a support could very well be staggered. Their architecture is not elevated or transformed into a pseudoscience; it needs no verbal explanation. It mirrors a society that is coming apart at the seams and poignantly documents the energy with which this process of disintegration is proceeding.

The Profession in Germany

In the 1950s, architects drew inspiration from Scandinavia; in the late 1960s and 1970s, from Italy; and in the 1980s, from Japan, France, and Spain. The 1990s appear to belong to Germany, not only because of the German architects but because of the international group of practitioners that has a large number of projects there.

Germany's internationalism is fostered by special competitions which are staged to award contracts for any project felt to have an impact on the public realm. In addition to supporting a large number of talented young German architects, this mechanism has allowed cities like Frankfurt and Berlin to sponsor many modern architectural gems by designers like Richard Meier (4), Hans Hollein (3), James Stirling, and Toyo Ito.

The foreign competition has had a positive effect on architectural creativity within Germany. Unfortunately, it has also opened the doors for an increasing number of large, established foreign architectural firms—known as "factories"—which with foreign capital are pushing their way into German markets, their lack of independence and of an awareness of local problems notwithstanding. This is also a result of the current vitality of Germany's construction market, on the rise since the mid-1980s and driven even higher by reunification, and now at a scale reminiscent of the post–World War II reconstruction period.

The overall effects of reunification on the German architectural profession cannot be overestimated, especially in eastern Germany. In this part of the country, the point of departure was architecture as it had been at the end of World War II. Given the missing infrastructure and

8. Stefan Tschavgov, parking garage, Bad Kreuznach, 1988

the pitiful state of existing buildings, the term "reconstruction" does appear to be appropriate to describe the situation. East Germany had virtually stopped training architects; the standardized architecture dictated by the government made the profession superfluous. As a result, western German architects and their hastily opened branch offices in eastern Germany now have the majority of pending contracts. Further exacerbating the situation of the handful of eastern German architects is the lack of local real estate developers and the tendency of out-of-town ones to import their own architects. The established architectural offices in western Germany have in some cases more than doubled their number of employees, and new offices have been springing up in record numbers. Young, talented architects are now in a position to break from their mentors and make independent contributions while still supporting their schools.

Finally, even the physical geography of Germany, with its great number of smaller, historical urban centers, has influenced the practice. Though the intellectual and material potential of a metropolis may be missed by architects who practice in smaller cities, the federal system has enabled more subdued regional features to be retained and developed. It is an exaggeration to call this "regionalism," but a distinct stylistic division between north and south Germany cannot be denied.

The Next Generation

Two young German architects, Elisabeth Lux and Martin Wiedemann, who have joined forces under the name Architektursalon Elvira, did try to implement the theoret-

9. Eisele and Fritz, letter sorting facility, Hamburg, 1987

ical concepts of practitioners like Bernard Tschumi. Their project for a superstructure over a Berlin parking lot *(5)* is based on neither an aesthetic nor a conceptual pattern. Rather, it attempts to embody the process of movement as both function and form. Thus they did not seek to invent the single form appropriate for various functions but instead attempted in their design process to retain the phenomenological character of the function: the necessary, unfinished, and therefore dynamic aspects of an urban square shaped by a multiplicity of functions. It is not

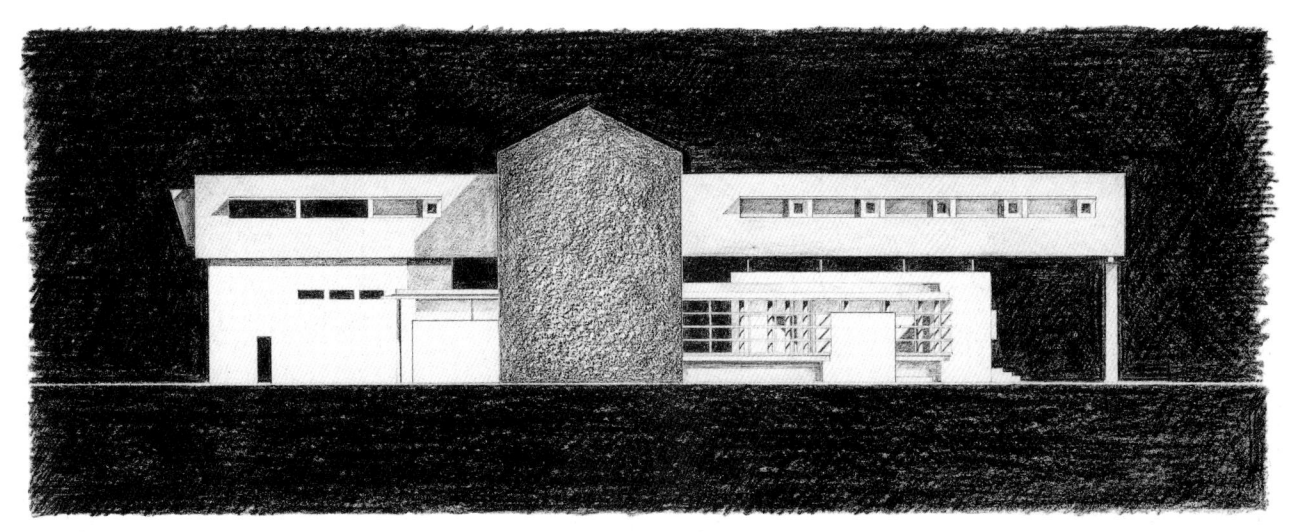

10. Christoph Mäckler, West German mission to East Germany, East Berlin, 1985–90

what is physically present that is of interest, but what is absent, between, fragmentary. The contradiction between the permanence of the individual object and the instability of the overall fabric can be resolved only if the various artistic media join forces.

The Frankfurt group Formalhaut, too, is experimenting with transgressing the boundaries between disciplines. Two architects and a sculptor work together on experimental projects that test one of architecture's principal concerns: architecture as a means of communication. Formalhaut focuses primarily on the sensual aspects of the spaces we live in and the societal strictures informing them. The 1985 "Cow Project" *(6)* and the 1986 installation "Rendezvous" *(7)* vividly illustrate the mutual influences of architecture and sculpture. In both proposals, the living being is at the center of attention. The transparent, nearly immaterial character of this sculptural architecture dramatizes the ambivalence between spatial delimitation and complete dissolution, exploring concepts of space without limits.

Despite its widely divergent formal manifestations, a trend is emerging in which architecture is understood as the result of situations, of moments, of intermediate hues, of movements and states of tension. The concept of ephemerality is key here, as paradoxical as that may be. It is in this context that we should examine the work of Stefan Tschavgov, an architect educated in Graz and currently working in Frankfurt. His project for a parking garage *(8)* is admittedly radical and aggressive, its technoid character expressing a belief in progress and a penchant for utopia. A traffic structure in the garage implies movement through its function; its design principle is space acting as a path. Tschavgov demonstrates formal possibilities in his buildings. He creates an interrelated structure out of geometric shapes, which are arrayed not according to the tenets of modernism but in response to his own emotions.

In the same vein, but under a different guise, is the design of the Darmstadt architects Eisele and Fritz for a letter sorting facility in Hamburg for the German Federal Post Office *(9)*. In 1987 the scheme won first prize in an architectural competition but unfortunately was never realized. A break with pure formalism is the hallmark of this design. A container, almost completely enclosed due to the functional requirements of the building and the site's island setting, takes its organic shape solely from the streets around the property.

There are also architects who celebrate the solid wall. Christoph Mäckler's design for the West German mission to East Germany *(10)*, for instance, illustrates the power of architecture to create space, along with demonstrating an underlying dialectic between the dynamic and the static. His works express the harmony of scale, number, and proportion, and therefore bear unmistakably classicist features. And his attitude toward urban chaos is a clear departure from that of architects like Architektursalon Elvira and Formalhaut. Mäckler highlights certain architectural accents—points of crystallization—to bring cohesion to diverse spatial situations.

Focusing on other issues are the projects of Max Dudler. Their claim to be public representational buildings is articulated by a break from their context. Endlessly long blocks of buildings cut an almost brutal slash through the urban fabric. Oversized primary shapes recall the architecture of the French Revolution. Nevertheless Dudler, too, is interested in offering a qualitative improvement in the utilization of open space. He is also interested in imbuing public spaces with social, communicative, and aesthetic meaning. The monumentality of his sports center in St. Gallen (its oval plan is not the only feature that harks back to the arenas of antiquity) simply seems out of place in a small city *(11)*. Regardless, it is in principle the continuation of an urban planning tradition: a group of anonymous utilitarian structures serves as backdrop for a building that is architecturally and conceptually unique, a building that offers architectural stimulation while fostering a sense of community.

11. Karl Dudler, Max Dudler, and Peter Welbergen, sports center, St. Gallen, 1987

It appears that architecture has returned to a point where architects are given the opportunity to develop large-scale plans that affect the entire cityscape. The large-scale building is, after many setbacks, no longer taboo. In the prevailing climate of stylistic pluralism, formal concepts almost taken for granted are being broken down and questioned in a variety of ways. The time of mere accommodation appears to be over, giving way to the realization that a spatial structure, an urban organism, comes to life only when innovative accents and contrasts are consciously set within it. Only then can a new self-confidence about planning emerge, a self-confidence that is sure to leave its mark on our cities, especially those in the eastern part of the country.

The Architects

The selection of architects in this book is subjective and does not claim to be complete. Though their share in overall construction may be quantitatively small, the influence exerted by these architects is inversely proportional. Many of these practitioners embody whole architectural schools (O. M. Ungers, Günter Behnisch, Josef Paul Kleihues); others, though trained in these schools, have now formulated their own design approaches (Hans Kollhoff, Kauffmann and Theilig). There are also the independents, who nevertheless do stand along a cultural and historical continuum (Gottfried Böhm, Karljosef Schattner), and those who exemplify today's zeitgeist (Christoph Langhof). While all the architects featured could be categorized, it is far more worthwhile—and in their interests—that they stand on their own merits.

All of these practitioners have already built projects or will do so in the near future. They have laid to rest the myth of the purity of an architect who only theorizes or designs, and so do not have to rely on critics to create a public, at least within the profession, for their work. Instead, they can expect more than a mere reaction from a much wider public if they live up to their social responsibility with their architecture: their art.

INTRODUCTION
Manfred Sack

Since Germany was reunified people can no longer talk, as they have for the past forty years, of West Germany (officially named the Federal Republic of Germany, a designation that today covers the whole country) and of East Germany (which insidiously enough called itself the German Democratic Republic, although it punished even the faintest stirrings of democracy). The story of one architect will help clarify the difference between the two.

Born in 1905, Hermann Henselmann was a very talented Bauhaus architect. His skill is evident in a villa he designed in Geneva in the 1920s *(12)*, which was recently restored. It is an elegant home, a blend of Gropius with a touch of Le Corbusier. After World War II he was among the few architects who emerged ideologically unscathed: he had not been declared a Nazi. And so immediately following the war he became the director of the Hochschule für Baukunst (School of Architecture) in Weimar, in the building which Henry van de Velde had designed and in which the Bauhaus first began before it moved to Dessau in response to political developments within Germany.

Needless to say, Henselmann was still an absolute modernist—a "Bauhaus man"—when he became the chief architect of East Berlin a few years later, a post he held for many years. He attempted to reestablish the tradition of high modernism which had been interrupted during the Hitler years. He felt an affinity with the Russian architects following the October Revolution of 1918: for him, too, it was a new era in which radical new buildings had to be built for a new type of human being. But in the Soviet Union, Stalin had long since sent the constructivists packing, reinstating in their stead designers of a traditional architecture loaded down with the trappings of bourgeois history, a quasi-neoclassical architecture. In Germany it was called "pastry cook's architecture."

And that was precisely what the communists demanded in East Berlin. They rejected the International Style with vehemence, declaring the so-called cosmopolitans enemies of the people and advocating a new national style, a popular mixture to be socialist in content, nationalist in form. Henselmann balked at this policy but then consulted the poet Bertolt Brecht who said: If the people

12. Hermann Henselmann, Villa Kenwin, Geneva, 1929–32

want kitsch, you must build them kitsch. An entire people, Henselmann later maintained, couldn't be wrong. So he reversed his stand and built the supposedly socialist Stalin Allee: a pseudo-urban boulevard, very broad, explicitly monumental, designed with "workers' palace" facades, but with standard interior floor plans. With it he won a peculiar type of international fame: he was considered a renegade of the people, one might say. (Due to postmodernism, the buildings are praised today by people like Leon Krier and Philip Johnson, who see them as impressive, big-city architectural gestures.)

Scarcely was Stalin dead when his successor Khrushchev began, at the end of the 1950s, to advocate a new simplicity: functionalism from the factory, an industrialized architecture for the masses whose characteristic feature was to be the wall-sized, reinforced concrete slab. The resulting residential projects, huge, monumental, and depressing, were similarly ugly and monotonous in all the countries behind the Iron Curtain, including East Germany. It was a misanthropic architecture, based solely on principles of economics and production technologies: poorly built standardized apartments for standardized people. Barely ten years later they had already begun to fall apart, and are now being restored with difficulty, for the housing shortage is acute. This kind of mass architecture originated almost completely without the involvement of architects. It was produced by one of the omnipotent state apparatuses of the GDR, the Deutsche Bauakademie (German Building Academy), which issued binding orders on design and production. The architects employed there were asked, at most, to develop superficial, cosmetic decoration, to match the architectural particularities of old cities, for example. The profession of architecture had ceased to exist in the GDR.

Even those few who tried to revitalize the discipline were discouraged. In 1979, for example, West Berlin was in the midst of preparing for what was in every respect a hyperbolic (and therefore typical) event for the city: the IBA, unique in its scope, methods, and pretensions, the Internationale Bauausstellung (International Building Exhibition). Its avowed task was to recapture "the city as a residence." Attention was also, of course, to be directed toward other prominent projects, one of which was to develop a worthy design for the Prinz Albrecht Gelände where the S.S. and the Gestapo had maintained their headquarters: the administrative center of the Holocaust.

In 1983 two young East Berliners also chose to participate in this competition, which was open to all German architects, and in doing so, acted against the recommendation of their professional association, the Association of East German Architects. Although the GDR was constituted as an antifascist state, and the competition was certainly in keeping with that spirit, the state took the two architects to court and had them sentenced to two-

and-a-half years in prison. Their crime: tarnishing the reputation of the GDR. This suit was undertaken with the express approval of Henselmann, a diehard communist to this day, who still considers his courageous young colleagues traitors to the party and to the state.

And so Hermann Henselmann remained the only East German architect whose name was known in the West. With a few isolated exceptions—the Palace of the Republic in East Berlin, which covers half the square where the Prussian city palace once stood, and the New Gewandhaus with its concert hall for the famous Leipzig Gewandhaus Orchestra were both designed by architects—the next forty years saw no architecture in East Germany worthy of the designation.

As a result, new architectural history has been written only to the west of the Berlin Wall—in America, Japan, and western Europe. Consequently, when someone speaks of German architecture the reference is to the West German variety, between Berlin in the east and Bonn in the west, Hamburg in the north and Munich in the south. Even though the focus is only on two-thirds of Germany, the architectural tradition is nevertheless singular.

German Architecture of the Twentieth Century

It is important to remember that there were two forays into modern architecture in Germany: the first after World War I, launched in 1918 with tremendous revolutionary élan, and the second after World War II, in a country devastated by war, littered with ruins. The 1920s and the 1950s were similar in many respects. Both were postwar decades, poor, indeed wretched times with shortages of everything from bread to stone. Scarcity ruled the day and it ruled art, especially architecture.

There was one interesting difference between the two eras. After World War I, despite the truly radical break with the past, it did not seem as though the "zero hour" had struck, even though the major European empires had crumbled, even though Germany had left its monarchic past behind, forcing the emperor into exile and launching its "adventure in democracy." One reason was that artists had long since begun, as early as the turn of the century, to shake off the historicism of the nineteenth century and to try something new, fresh, that would free them from the decorative residues of eclecticism. The popular names for this new architecture were de Stijl in the Netherlands and Bauhaus in Germany. After World War II and its much more horrific atrocities, however, people did talk about the zero hour—not because it had actually come but because they had wanted it to, had wanted to begin again after the cruel campaigns of conquest, after the horrible devastation throughout Europe, after the propagandistic tirades that had ruined an entire people, after the murder of millions. Ruins covered the country. Large parts of Hamburg, Cologne, Berlin, and many other cities were devastated. Yet, the reality proved very different. There was not a completely new beginning, where the threads of 1920s modernism might simply have been knotted together at the point where they had been cut off by the Third Reich. Instead, embarrassingly, things continued just as before.

It is clear today that there was never a true stylistic break from the democratic 1920s to the dictatorial 1930s, or even after Hitler, as the defeated Germany was reborn in the west as a democratic state. Continuity was retained throughout. The architects of the Nazi era (very few had needed to emigrate) were now the architects of reconstruction. The principle of the times was to build sparingly, simply, modestly. It was not an aesthetic principle but a realistic one of which aesthetic advantage was taken, especially in architecture. What was built was not incisive or innovative, as high modernism with its expressionistic cascades of fantasy had been; after World War II and its devastation, no one could afford that luxury. There were no visionaries, only pragmatists.

And as a result, there were no revolutionary architectural or planning ideas. Designers simply continued in the style of the war years, although they did cast long and curious looks abroad. To this extent, architects did not establish a link to the 1920s but to what the 1920s had become, especially in the United States, Scandinavia, Finland, and Great Britain, to what may be called a second modernism. Exemplars were the newly American Ludwig Mies van der Rohe and Skidmore, Owings & Merrill (Germans erroneously thought it would be easy to imitate their architecture) as well as Alvar Aalto and Arne Jacobsen, as opposed to Bruno Taut, Hugo Häring, Walter Gropius, and Erich Mendelsohn.

It must be said that the two decades that followed, the 1960s and 1970s, brought a deluge of unspeakably bad architecture. In Germany this architecture came to be known as *Bauwirtschafts-Funktionalismus* ("developer's functionalism" or "finance functionalism"). It reflected the hysteria brought about by postwar housing shortages: every apartment seemed beautiful simply because it was needed, even if it was unattractive and structurally damaged. The sudden flowering of sociology, which focused only on society and its supposed needs, and rejected both building as an art and the aesthetic ambitions of architects, fostered this attitude. These decades did see, however, some very good architects and exquisite buildings; some of these designers are featured in this book.

The German Architect

In Germany, the desire to hold competitions among architects has always been enormous. In fact, they are required for all publicly financed buildings as well as for private buildings of public significance, like those which affect a city's skyline. German architectural magazines prove the point: there are pages of reports on competition results in cities and villages, pages of announcements

13. James Stirling, Neue Staatsgalerie, Stuttgart, 1977–84

about new competitions. Topics include urban planning, buildings, gardens, and landscapes.

In addition, any self-respecting city or real estate developer invites foreign architects to participate; if possible, the entire international elite from New York to Tokyo. This is the reason why Germany has more international architecture being built than any other country. For instance, Richard Meier's buildings can be found in Frankfurt am Main, Munich, and Ulm; Charles Moore's in Berlin; and Frank Gehry's in Weil am Rhein, a small industrial city near Basel. Jean Nouvel has built in Cologne and Berlin; Philip Johnson designed the art museum in Bielefeld; Berlin, Bremen, Mönchengladbach, Frankfurt, and Bonn are the sites of buildings by Austrians Roland Rainer, Wilhelm Holzbauer, Hans Hollein, Gustav Peichl, and others. Alvar Aalto built a cultural center in the Volkswagen city of Wolfsburg and a residential high-rise in Bremen; Arne Jacobsen, a school and an administrative building in Hamburg; the Copenhagen natives Dissing and Weitling, a museum in Düsseldorf. Berlin is indebted to Le Corbusier.

Also in this vein are Berlin's IBA of 1957, the Interbau, in which at least two dozen foreign architects were invited to build, and the IBA of 1987. This last enterprise alone, so quintessentially of Berlin, is immensely signifi-

14. Weissenhofsiedlung, Stuttgart, 1929

15. Bill and Gugelot, School of Design, Ulm, 1960

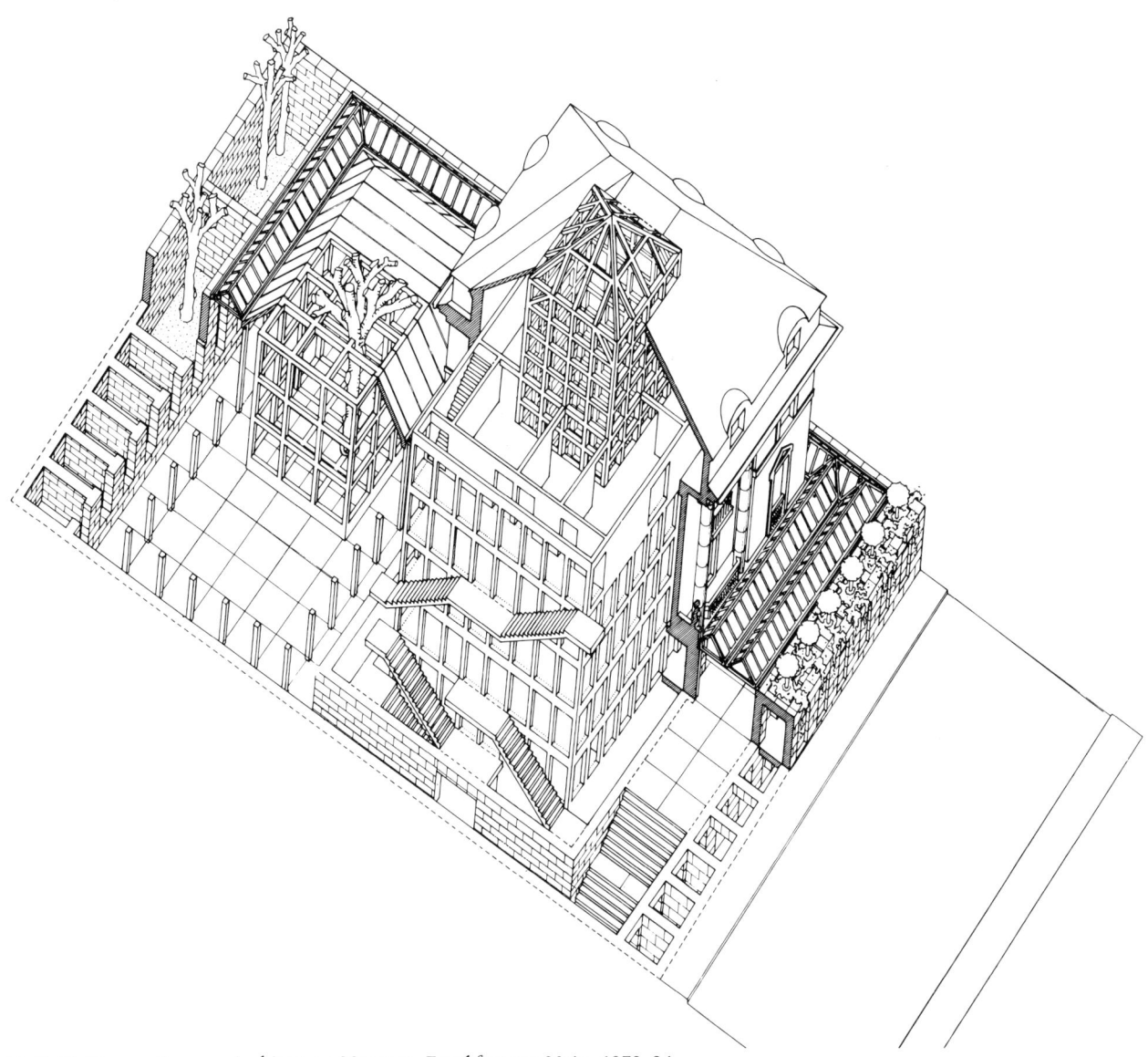

16. O. M. Ungers, German Architecture Museum, Frankfurt am Main, 1979–84

17. Olympic Stadium, Berlin, 1936

18. Günter Behnisch, Olympic Stadium, Munich, 1972

cant if for no other reason than that it was an "exhibition in progress," still not completely finished in 1992. It had three aims: to make the inner city livable once again; to critically reconstruct the city's historical layout; to revitalize those areas of cities that had fallen apart, like Kreuzberg in Berlin, as had the South Bronx or Lower East Side in New York.

One of the foreign architects to gain great fame in Germany was the Scot James Stirling. He built two spectacular structures, creating a furor with both: the science center in Berlin, directly behind Mies van der Rohe's National Gallery, a conglomerate of classical structures including a Greek stoa, a Roman amphitheater, a Christian basilica, a Norman castle, and a campanile; and the Neue Staatsgalerie in Stuttgart (13), a monumental mix of buildings overflowing with allusions to architects from classicist Friedrich Weinbrenner to Le Corbusier to postmodernist Charles Jencks, and now the most popular art museum in the country.

Once, in the mid-1970s, I asked Philip Johnson whom he thought was the most interesting architect in Germany. His answer, after just a moment's thought, was James Stirling. Johnson, playing the flirt, knew what effect his answer would have. But not many German names were obvious: Oswald Mathias Ungers, who for years taught at Cornell University and later became a great master of four-square planning; Gottfried Böhm, whose expressive architecture defies easy classification (he received the Pritzker Architecture Prize, as Stirling had); or Josef Paul Kleihues. It was not surprising that Johnson would not pick a German architect, especially because neither Germans nor those outside the country have made significant attempts to publicize German architecture for a wide audience.

Another uniquely German trait is the committed involvement of the mayors of Germany's cities and towns. While democracy may be expressed in terms of majority votes, it is individuals, not parties or even committees, who show initiative when it comes to good architecture. The city of Dessau is a case in point. Without Lord Mayor Fritz Hesse and his political and artistic sensitivity and courage, the Bauhaus would have perished in conservative Weimar, instead of flourishing in socially liberal Dessau. Without Mayor Daniel Sigloch in Stuttgart, the world-famous Weissenhofsiedlung (14) would never have been built in 1929. (It was, in fact, he who monitored the sometimes careless architects, headed by Mies van der Rohe, Gropius, and Le Corbusier, who had never set foot in Stuttgart.) The city of Ulm would probably never have built its renowned School of Design (15), which was to carry on the tradition of the Bauhaus, were it not for the support of Lord Mayor Pfizer; and without his successor Ludwig, the city would have never been able to realize a long-delayed project to revitalize the Münsterplatz, or to award its design contract to Richard Meier.

Another good example is Frankfurt am Main, Germany's "American" city, the only real high-rise city in the country, which for years has been called "Mainhatten," or crueler yet, "Bankfurt" (in reference to its role as the nation's banking center) by its detractors. Lord Mayor Wallmann was inspired by the Marburg art historian Heinrich Klotz to build the German Architecture Museum, designed by O. M. Ungers (16), and since then has been a major proponent of good architecture. He realized the single way to change the atmosphere within the city was to make it more beautiful. Only then would he be able to motivate the residents to take pride in their city. He made better architecture an issue in local politics and transformed Frankfurt into the most architecturally interesting city in Germany. Architects of the greatest stature have built there, especially along the Main River and its "museum bank"; among them, Hollein, Peichl, Meier, Kleihues, and Ungers, not to mention a large number of younger talents. Frankfurt even managed to make the design of preschools a subject of serious debate in municipal politics. Frankfurt also became the site of Germany's tallest skyscraper, a rocket of sorts, designed by the German-American Helmut Jahn, who enjoys almost alarming popularity among real estate developers.

A third German characteristic is to respect the historical context. This is rooted in the ambition to restore the architectural legacy which had survived World War II knowledgeably, but without replicating every last detail, so as not to commit a historical "lie." Aside from some looming half-timbered buildings from the Middle Ages (such as the Knochenhauseramtshaus in Hildesheim), incomparable architectural masterpieces (like Dresden's impressive Frauenkirche, which should definitely be rebuilt), and a few frivolous reconstructions, the motive is different: to restore the old with care but to express what is new in the architectural language of the present. That had been, in fact, the rule followed until around the turn of the century, and it was consistently demonstrated that even the most opposite styles can be compatible as long as both are of the highest quality. The undisputed master of these efforts is Karljosef Schattner, for thirty years the master builder for the bishop of the Bavarian city Eichstätt; another is Gottfried Böhm in Cologne.

A final typically German trait is a deep mistrust of all kinds of monumentality and pompous displays of power, thanks to their abuse in Adolf Hitler's Third Reich. This explains the praise lavished on Behnisch's Olympic architecture in Munich as a perfect example of clarity and lightness. When Munich was selected for the 1972 Olympic Games, it was impossible not to think of the 1936 Berlin Olympics, the propaganda event staged by the Nazis (17). In Munich, however, there was none of that heaviness or grim seriousness (18). Sports were intended to be high-spirited play, not bitter combat, and the focus was on competition among athletes, not sports war among nations. Behnisch and Partner, with the help of technical designer Frei Otto and engineer Fritz Leonhardt, created a cheerful, light architecture whose dominant feature was transparent tent-like roofing.

19. Fehling and Gogel, European Southern Observatory, main administrative building, Munich-Garching, 1976–80

20. Fehling and Gogel, Max Planck Institute for Astrophysics, Munich-Garching, 1980

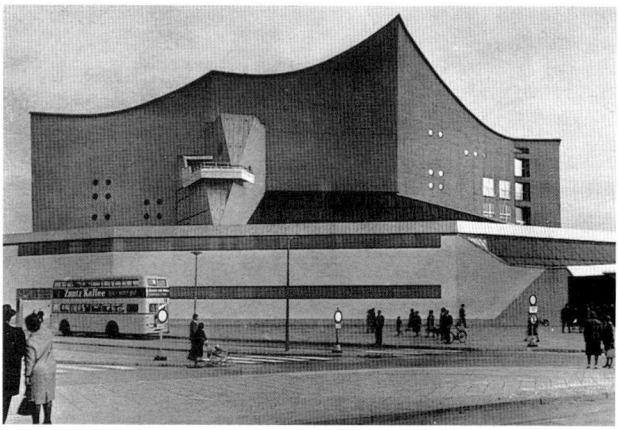

21. Hans Scharoun, Berlin Philharmonic, 1963

The aversion to monumentality was all too evident in the hornet's nest that broke out when James Stirling won the competition for Stuttgart's Neue Staatsgalerie in 1977. The adversaries were Stirling, the postmodern monumentalist, and Behnisch, the modern master of clarity. It was a religious war of sorts; its stakes, the definition of an architecture of democracy. Whereas in the United States the stylistic debate was between the late-modernist "Whites" and the postmodernist "Grays," in Germany ideological differences took precedence: Stirling versus Behnisch, power versus democracy. Coincidentally, a book published at about that time, *Totalitäre Architektur*, tried to denounce all buildings with axial and symmetrical layouts that were especially voluminous, heavy, and statuesque as examples of an architecture that glorified power.

Of course this accusation caricatures and oversimplifies the problem. A building which exudes monumentality and self-containment is not a priori a demonstration of power, and a building that has transparent glass walls is not necessarily a democratic building. Are buildings, one is tempted to ask, really more influential than the spirit of the people who live in them? The debate on whether architecture can exert this type of influence is undecided, although architects surely dream about their beautiful buildings somehow making people better. And ideological criteria, in any case, say little or nothing about the quality of architecture, its functionality, its relationship to the environment, its contextuality, or its user-friendliness.

Just as the 1979 exhibit "Transformations in Modern Architecture" at the Museum of Modern Art in New York clearly illustrated—and with these characteristics notwithstanding—Germany has no pervasive, distinct, national, contemporary style; there are only subjective means of communication. There are expressionists and constructivists, rationalists and late modernists, and many others. As a result, alongside postmodern absurdities and deconstructive overexertions is a renewed awareness of the essential, and by no means exhausted, message of classic modernism.

22. Gottfried Böhm, pilgrimage church, Neviges, 1964–83

The Recent Past

The first building of German postwar architecture to make an international splash was the Berlin Philharmonic by Hans Scharoun *(21)*. It is a beautiful, acoustically pleasing concert hall, rich in atmosphere and variety, a circus tent of concrete, a stroke of genius. In its design, Scharoun fulfilled a dream of the early 1920s: a "people's

23. Gottfried Böhm, Züblin Construction Company, main administrative center, Stuttgart, 1984

24. Auer and Weber, Landratsamt, Starnberg, 1985–87

house" for the new, enlightened humanity, which abhorred war and adored art, an expressionist theme. While he never formed a school, he had many kindred spirits, like the Berlin duo Hermann Fehling and Daniel Gogel, who approached their work with an almost medieval attention to detail, executing most drawings themselves. Among their few—for obvious reasons—buildings, two are exemplary: the Max Planck Institute for Astrophysics *(20)* and, directly opposite it, the main administrative building of the European Southern Observatory *(19)* in Munich-Garching, two similarly sweeping, expressive structures.

Gottfried Böhm's architecture is of an altogether different ilk. He never joined a movement, let alone a passing fashion; he did not even subscribe to all of the tenets put forth by the functionalists. He remained what he had been from the outset—a sculptor—and retained a characteristic not common among architects: a playful intelligence in dealing with issues of space. His fame was established with the town hall of Bensberg, a castle restoration and conversion with an added element: a new, angular, very sculptural tower. The same approach is evident in his restoration of and addition to the baroque castle of Saar-

25. Kurt Ackermann, sewage plant, Munich, 1988

brücken. Initially, the Saarland government had wanted to reconstruct the castle completely and authentically as a municipal administration center, but Böhm swayed the government with his suggestion of restoring the castle wings to the state they had evolved into while creating a completely new design for the center pavilion. It became a bold tower housing a bright, spirited hall painted by the architect himself. Böhm's other great love is glass halls. He first revealed it in a town hall design for Cologne and developed it masterfully in the main administrative center of the Züblin Construction Company in Stuttgart *(23)*. His delight in playful spaciousness, in expansiveness, is evident in his Deutsche Bank in Luxembourg. Yet his most impressive work is probably the pilgrimage church in Neviges *(22)*, a small town in Germany's Ruhr region. It is a truly powerful, truly expressive house of God: the roof of folded concrete, a multitude of niches and galleries underneath that veil the structure's size and demonstrate another example of protective monumentality.

A much stricter taskmaster of contextual design is Karljosef Schattner of Eichstätt. His objective is to preserve the old diligently, to renovate it imaginatively, and

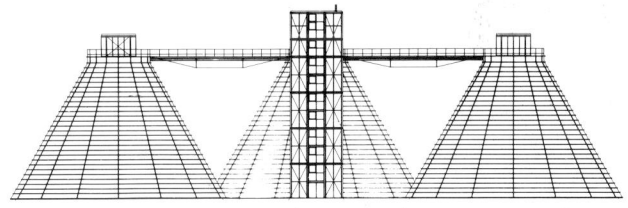

26. Kurt Ackermann, sewage plant, Munich, 1988

to juxtapose to it what is newly built as boldly as possible. His creed: contrast. These contrasts are often extreme, frugal, angular forms that distance rather than embrace the baroque. Until the end of the 1950s, Eichstätt was best known as an enchanting baroque city; since then it has also become Schattner's city. His employer, the conservative bishop, relishes Eichstätt's new architectural renown.

Meanwhile Schattner has also seen to it that other top-ranking architects have built in Eichstätt, among them Günter Behnisch, whose style is entirely different from all those previously mentioned. He is an extremist when it comes to lightness, an improvisor, a lover of surprise. In many of his buildings, elements often collide—different materials, different details, often with no readily

27. Sampo Widmann and Stephan Romero, burial chapel, Eching, 1985–86

apparent sense of context—but the spaces themselves have compelling atmospheric qualities. This is true of such different buildings as his library at the Catholic University in Eichstätt and the wild architecture of the Hysolar Institute in Stuttgart (which bears the unmistakable stamp of this former member of Coop Himmelblau), as the new plenary hall in Bonn (when the German parliament moves to Berlin another use for the building will have to be determined), a masterpiece of modified modernism, and the German Postal Museum in Frankfurt.

Fritz Auer and Karlheinz Weber, former partners of Behnisch, never wanted to abandon this quality, even after they formed their own firm, and have managed to develop their own variation of this light, transparent architecture. Auer and Weber's style, however, reflects greater austerity, more clarity of design, and a finer elegance, with no outbreaks of arbitrariness—though the work is just as courageous. One of their most famous works is the Landratsamt

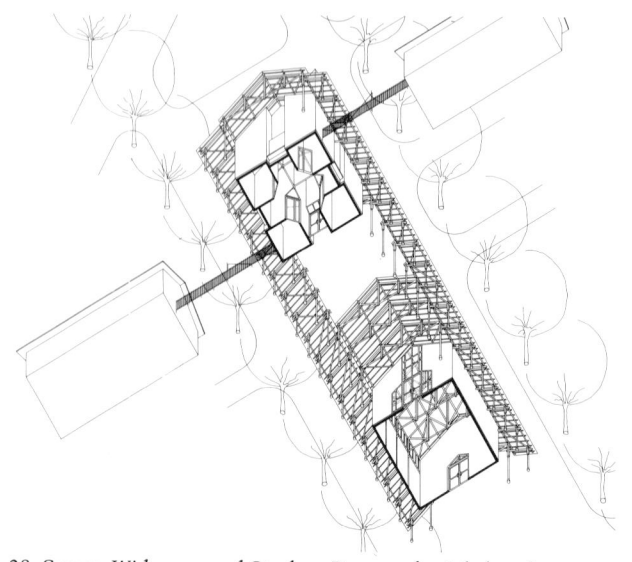

28. Sampo Widmann and Stephan Romero, burial chapel, Eching, 1985–86

29. Peter Seifert, Kap Pool, Albstadt, 1978–80

in Starnberg *(24)*; another is their design for the German pavilion at Expo '92 in Seville, unfortunately rejected for the flimsiest of reasons; a third is the administrative complex for the Munich airport operating company, which appears to float above the earth. The elongated staircase embracing the office wings on both sides reflects an idea also used by Otto Steidle and Uwe Kiessler in their large Gruner & Jahr publishing house in Hamburg: attenuated, exciting corridors, interrupted by long staircases and lighted from the top and the sides, serve not only for movement but for communication as well.

Kiessler, who builds in steel and glass, is stylistically similar to Behnisch, but his designs are more robust. His most intriguing structures are a bakery in a rear courtyard in Munich and the new factory and administrative building in Lüdenscheid for Erco, a lighting company. And comparable to Kiessler is Thomas Herzog, a construction designer who tries to transform scientific insights, like discoveries regarding energy technologies, into architecture in a way that is both imaginative and disciplined. As a result, the guest house he designed for the youth educational center of a Bavarian monastery and the two-family residence he built in Pullach are full of technical and architectural finesse in their treatment of the sun, heat, and light. Two other architects who design structurally inspired buildings are Kurt Ackermann (an ice rink and a sewage plant in Munich *[25, 26]*) and Peter von Seidlein (the Süddeutsche printing house, also in Munich).

There is also in Germany architecture which is not so much technically designed as built: solid, physical architecture with a broad and diverse range. Jochem Jourdan and Bernhard Müller, for instance, whose forms of expression are indebted to the stylistic eclecticism of postmodernism, build like this. Architects like Heinz Hilmer and Christoph Sattler have a fine sensibility toward the classical roots of modernism, as do Andreas Brandt and Rudolph Böttcher, Hans Kollhoff, and Christoph Langhof.

Finally it is important once more to mention Josef Paul Kleihues and O. M. Ungers. Kleihues, who refers to himself as a poetic rationalist, is a master of reconciling function with his own solid preconceptions of form. Ungers is the only architect in the country without an aversion to monumental expression; he strives for it self-confidently. He is also the only designer who has developed—for himself—a strict theory based on the square and has followed it with absolute consistency and, perhaps, some morose pleasure as well. In a way, it is a search for perfection which results in a heavy, nonsensual, somewhat sterile architecture. The architect creates unmistakable symbols—symbols not about architectural prototypes but about himself.

It is important to mention two other singular phenomena that have emerged in Germany. One can be char-

30. Joachim and Margot Schürmann, post office, Cologne, 1984–90

acterized with the catch phrase "art in building." It was originally socially motivated, since usually two percent of total construction costs in all public and publicly financed buildings had to be reserved for art; this was one way to provide regional artists with commissions. Cities such as Bremen and Hannover, however, soon tried to break away from local artists and raise artistic standards by raising a good deal of money and concentrating on the motto "art in public spaces—the city." What began as a desperate attempt to disguise poor-quality architecture and the architectural sins of the postwar period has blossomed into a firm objective to integrate art into the city and, where possible, into architecture and also into the landscape. And Bremen and Hannover were especially successful in these endeavors. They handled with sophistication even the most passionate controversies about contemporary art, and instead of deciding the conflict between the plastic arts and architecture, raised the public's artistic awareness and stepped up the demand for compelling, imaginative architecture.

The other development, completely unexpected, was the rediscovery of the potential of wood as a building material as it had been used in Austria and especially in southern Germany. The resulting structures are not picturesque huts or wild, weird houses, but austerely designed, very modern residences. They are built sparingly, logically, intelligently, and can be planned in a manner that can be altered and expanded and, often, completed by the clients themselves. Among these projects are the two-family house by Thomas Herzog, mentioned earlier, and a large number of single-family houses designed by the Lahr group in Baden-Württemberg and Sampo Widmann in Bavaria *(27, 28)*. There are also architects like Peter Seifert; he has used wood to build half a dozen swimming pools—fun pools—simple, logical wooden structures, marked by almost archaic forms *(29)*. Currently, the use of wood is getting even bolder. In Ulm, on the Danube River, perched on an idyllic, wooded hill, Otto Steidle has designed his Engineering Sciences University II, a 300-meter, linear complex characterized by light green, yellow, orange, and bright blue painted wood, all in many gradations, as conceived by the artist Erich Wiesner.

A Last Word

In such a brief foray into the architecture of an entire country, the desire for generalizations usually arises; there are some particular indications. Now that the banal acrobatics of postmodernism have become tedious, and feigned historical decorum has exhausted itself, architecture is once again becoming robust and ambitious but also relaxed and even matter-of-fact. Postmodernism was a liberating warm-up after the inhibitions of high modernism, but now many young architects are once again returning to modernism, primarily to explore its true message. It seems a long time since architecture has been as simple, clear, solid, high-spirited, and intelligent as it is now.

And it also appears that the users of architecture as well as the wider public have become more critical, open, and to a certain extent, able to demand greater architectural imagination. Fifteen years ago, for instance, the government postal service would never have commissioned an architectural team like Joachim and Margot Schürmann to build a superbly designed post office, as it has in Cologne *(30)*. The excitement and awareness of the public have helped to create new types of buildings, in which people feel comfortable and energy is used efficiently. These beautiful buildings sit comfortably alongside their neighbors, honoring them with their self-confidence.

Were he asked today who the most interesting German architect is, Philip Johnson might not give his cheeky reply of the 1970s: James Stirling. He would probably be aware that any of the many excellent German architects at work today could easily be the best.

FROM CITY PLANNING TO URBAN DESIGN

Rebuilding Germany 1945–1992

Casey C. M. Mathewson

O<small>N MAY</small> 8, 1945, the war in Europe ended and a traumatic and painful time of readjustment began. World War II left Germany, and much of the rest of Europe, in ruins both physically and mentally *(31, 32)*. All the major urban centers, institutions, and industrial complexes were decimated; many ancient cities were firebombed; more than five million housing units were destroyed. Millions of refugees fleeing the Red Army increased the already crippled population of West Germany, and the new East German regime continued, in a new guise, the repression of Hitler's Third Reich.

Architecture and urban design were left in a similar state, having to deal with not only the physical destruction of the war but also the repercussions of dogmatic Nazi thought that had for years strangled innovation and compelled the best architects and planners to leave the country. Those who remained behind either served the system or barely managed to survive by working on industrial buildings that were less subject to the strict control of the Nazi party apparatus. Not only the cities, but also the architectural profession had to be rebuilt from the ground up.

Although the pressing problems facing architects and planners in Soviet East Germany and in the West German states were similar, a devastating division began to separate architectural as well as political thought, a division which was to deepen throughout the 1950s and ultimately take on macabre dimensions in the form of the Berlin Wall and the Iron Curtain. The Berlin blockade of 1948 and the resulting Allied airlift, the currency reform of 1948 in the western German states, and the subsequent founding of the Federal Republic of Germany and the German Democratic Republic in 1949 mark the beginnings of the political cold war which was to continue even into the 1990s and which would find physical expression in the opposing views on architecture and urban design that would influence the shape of cities in both halves of the country and the continent for over forty years. Even now, after German reunification, the social and architectural divisions between east and west must still be overcome if the problems, perhaps less pressing, but no less difficult, of the new Germany are to be solved.

31. Dresden, 1945

The Earliest Efforts

In West Germany after the war, several schools of architectural thought were able to emerge and develop freely, with a constructive dialogue. The immediate postwar years were marked by an architectural scene devastated by war and emigration, but fertile in creating various ways to reconstruct ruined cities and heal a society traumatized by war. The first postwar models for architecture and urban design had their origins in the important architectural schools of the 1920s; the handful of ideologies which emerged after 1945 continues to influence architecture and urban design to this day.

For instance, although the architecture of the traditional German school associated with Stuttgart architects Paul Bonatz and Paul Schmitthenner had been misused by the Nazis, it influenced the reconstruction of such cities as Freiburg, Freudenstadt *(33, 34)*, Munich, Nuremberg, Lübeck, and Münster *(35, 36)*, which all chose to rebuild their urban fabric much as it had been before the war. As far back as 1930 this group, inspired by Heinrich Tessenow, had defined the essential features of a national architecture. They based it on regionalism or on a tenuous classicism; the style sought repose and harmony without surprise or violent contrast. The Bauhaus masters and their followers, another school of the 1920s, had left or been forced to leave Germany by the early 1930s. The few who remained were scattered, and among them there was no Gropius or Mies capable of rallying the stragglers. A third school consisted of architects who had studied with or worked for Hans Poelzig in Berlin in the 1920s, such as Bernhard Hermkes, Egon Eiermann, and Paul Baumgarten, all architects who were instrumental in defining postwar German architecture, both through their built work and as teachers at the technical universities in Berlin and Karlsruhe.

In East Germany, former Bauhaus student Hermann Henselmann formed an architectural collective that would gain influence as the division in thought between east and west deepened. At first, Henselmann and his colleagues worked with Hans Scharoun, Berlin's first postwar city architect. But soon the East German political machine began to exert control over all facets of society, including architecture and urban design. At that point, Henselmann and his team developed an urban design based as much on the relentless monumentality of Albert Speer as on the Stalinist city propagated by Moscow.

In 1946 Hans Scharoun, in his capacity as Berlin city architect, along with a loosely banded architectural collective conceived the first "Bandstadt" reconstruction plan for the city called "the New Berlin." This urban scheme, if it had been realized, would have meant the end of many of the buildings in the center of Berlin that had survived the war intact. Scharoun's vision called for a total razing of the city center and the replacement of traditional blocks with buildings loosely sited in the landscape. This plan might well have provided inhabitants with ample light and air, but would have deprived them of the urbanism even rudimentarily preserved in Berlin, and it was symptomatic of the desire for a complete negation of the city's urban tradition. Hitler's romantic nostalgia and brutal monumentalism were to be replaced by their opposites.

In the 1950s, the nation sought to discard every vestige of the Nazi era, and many cities explored a new vision of urbanism that broke with cultural tradition and subscribed to modernism's faith in a technologically oriented future. Architects replaced the conventional relationship of the building and the street with the Corbusian ideal of the city in the park. The same dogmatic urge to reinvent the city which shaped Germany so greatly in the first period of reconstruction continues to find supporters even today as the same problems recur in rebuilding the cities of the former East Germany. But in spite of the lively architectural debate of the time, built results were for the most

32. Berlin, 1945

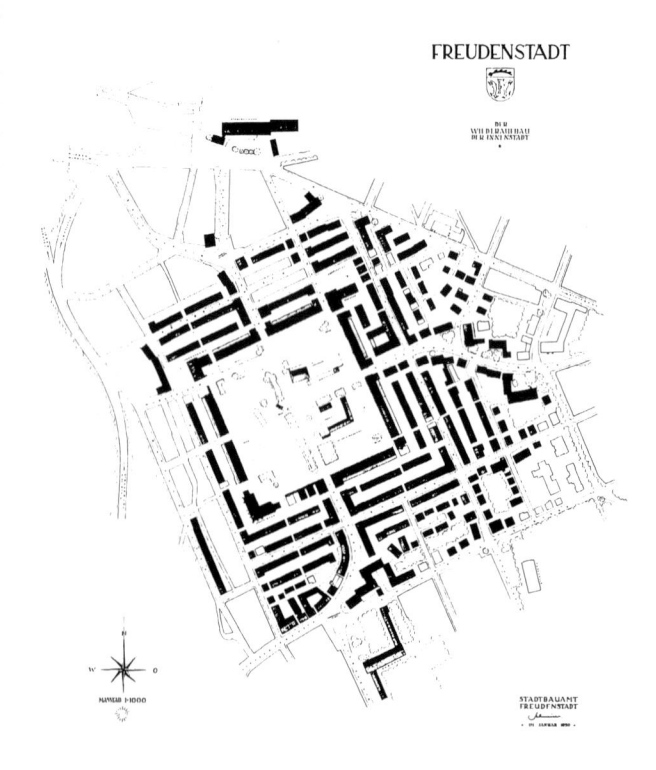

33. Ludwig Schweizer, Freudenstadt reconstruction plan, 1950

part disappointing. The severe problems of the destroyed culture and the ruined built environment simply hindered substantial work. Max Frisch, Swiss author and architect, characterized a difficult time: "We were afraid to have ideas, and because we had no ideas, we were afraid."[1]

Reconstruction Phase I: 1949–61

In the 1950s, with an unprecedented building boom in West Germany, the often dogmatic ideas of the early postwar years became built reality, often with disastrous results. Simultaneously, as the division between east and west steadily deepened, architecture and urban design were increasingly used as tools to demonstrate their opposing ideologies.

In East Germany the first urban reconstruction efforts demonstrate the growing influence of communist ideology on city planning. East German leader Walter Ulbricht defined an urban planning strategy that was to transform East German cities from 1950 to 1955: "During the Weimar Republic [1918–33] many buildings were built in our cities which did not reflect the wishes of the inhabitants, nor did they respect our national traditions. These buildings reflected rather the formalistic thought of a number of architects who sought to impose the primitive quality of industrial architecture on housing. This 'barracks style' was further developed during Hitler's reign. Now many architects, especially those working for the city architect [Scharoun], plan to rebuild portions of the inner city with an architecture more fitting for the suburban realm. The mistake of these architects is their failure to respect the form and architecture of Berlin, they believe rather that we should build houses which would fit just as well in the South African landscape."[2] Ulbricht's propagandistic attack on the architecture of the Bauhaus and the modern movement is typical of the East German regime's ability to distort information—and to misinform purposely—under the guise of socialism and equality. Ulbricht's was far from the only attack: "The Bauhaus style is nothing more than a genuine child of American cosmopolitanism—this style must be transcended if we are to achieve a new national architecture."[3]

While architects and planners in West Germany were attempting to define a new architecture based on modernism, the propaganda machine in East Germany criticized it as a "brutal break with national tradition" and labeled its architects "supporters of the war politics of Anglo-American imperialism." Although the reconstruction of Germany's destroyed cities had just started, increasingly the international tensions of the early cold war years began to determine the architectural programs which were to shape the new cities in both halves of the country.

On July 27, 1950, the East German government issued a proclamation defining the "sixteen rules of socialistic urban planning." These parameters were a conscious effort to counter the "Anglo-American–influenced" CIAM city planning defined in the 1933 Charter of Athens. A

34. Freudenstadt, post-reconstruction

35. Münster, pre–World War II

36. Münster, post-reconstruction

central aspect of the sixteen rules was the creation of monumental urban spaces, a simplistic urban planning strategy long practiced not only in Nazi Germany but also in Joseph Stalin's Soviet Union. Edmund Collein, vice president of East Berlin's architecture school, described the plans for the Stalin Allee in 1951: "This quarter, destroyed by Anglo-American bombers, demands a new urban and architectural form which transcends the mistakes of the past. The traditional capitalist city of inhumane dense blocks must be surpassed. A grand urban vision will transform the face of East Berlin."[4]

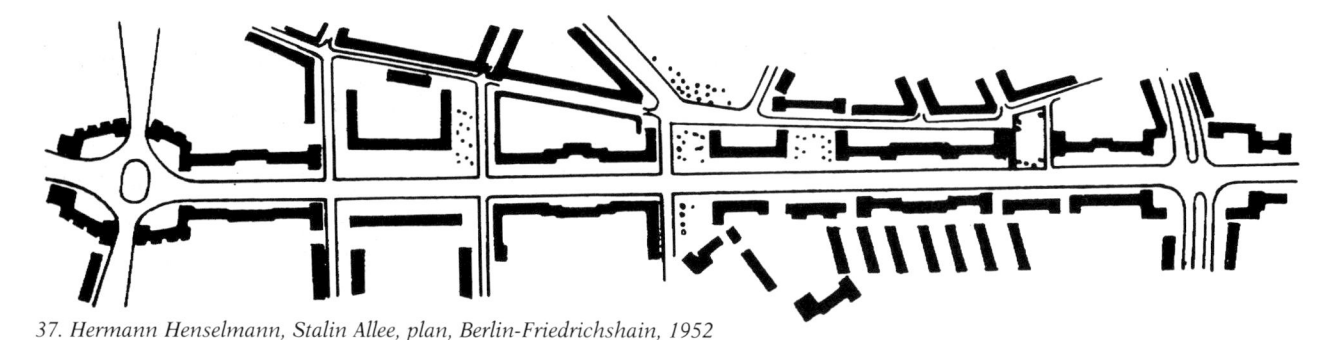

37. Hermann Henselmann, Stalin Allee, plan, Berlin-Friedrichshain, 1952

The Stalin Allee (later Karl Marx Allee, today Frankfurterallee) in Berlin-Friedrichshain (1952–58) is the best example of the first phase of reconstruction in East Germany *(37, 38, 39)*. In contrast to the abstract modernism of early West German projects, an architecture was developed that sought to accommodate the sense of beauty and national consciousness of the citizens by incorporating clear ordering principles and historical forms into urban planning. The Stalin Allee today has lost none of its relentless monumentality. Although Aldo Rossi describes the overblown axis as "Europe's last grand avenue,"[5] the ultimate failure of the first stage of communist urban planning in East Germany lies in its lack of diverse urbanism and neglect of personal scale. The single-function blocks and monotonous monumentality of the bland Stalin Allee express the communist tendency to dwarf the individual and negate self-expression. As is often the case, formalistic urban planning failed to accommodate real human needs.

In other major East German cities, similar monumental areas were erected; for the most part they were adapted to local building traditions. Langestrasse in Rostock (1953–59), Wilhelm-Pieck-Allee in Magdeburg (1953–64), the Rossplatz in Leipzig (1953–58), and the Marktplatz in Dresden (1953–57) offer vivid examples of this Stalinist phase of urban reconstruction. The era ended abruptly with the rise of Nikita Khrushchev in the mid-1950s and with the advent of industrialized building processes that replaced both traditional construction and the self-proclaimed national style of the early 1950s with a technocratic urban blight that would soon pervade from East Berlin to Vladivostok.

In West Germany, a wider spectrum of solutions to the problems of urban reconstruction was developed in a time of lively experimentation. The centrally planned society of East Germany was countered by a set of pluralistic urban strategies to which individual cities and states successfully adapted their unique situations. In small cities, on the other hand, West Germany pursued a more conservative urban vision that was closely linked to tradition and regionalism. Although Freiburg, Freudenstadt, and Münster, for example, were completely destroyed, they chose to rebuild with traditional architectural forms. Freudenstadt, designed as an "ideal city" in 1599 and in which 670 houses bordering the city's distinctive central quadrangle were destroyed in the final days of the war, of-

38. Stalin Allee, phase I, Berlin-Friedrichshain, 1952–58

39. Stalin Allee, phases I and II, Berlin-Friedrichshain, 1952–65

40. Hansa Quarter, West Berlin, in 1985

41. Spengelin, Eggeling, and Pempelfort, Hauptstadt Berlin competition entry, model photograph, 1957

fers perhaps the best example of conservative reconstruction. Rather than superimposing a new order on the city, residents worked with a succession of city architects including Paul Schmitthenner to rebuild on the same building parcels. The variety in use and scale of the old city was successfully retained and reinterpreted, and today Freudenstadt is a lively city where the scars of destruction have all but disappeared.

Other tactics of urban design were developed in the 1957 West Berlin–sponsored IBA (International Building Exhibition), known as the Interbau, which produced the Hansa Quarter *(40)*, a district of apartment towers that vividly illustrates the goals and shortcomings of postwar modernism. The site, adjacent to the Tiergarten park and once densely settled with traditional urban blocks, offered an ideal setting for the prototypical postwar city in the park. The Tiergarten was essentially extended and the buildings composed as objects in the landscape. Walking through the area, one senses the energy and vision of Aalto, Gropius, and Bakema. In the spirit of CIAM, they believed that by maximizing the exposure to nature and the functional utility of each unit, they would produce the ideal urban dwelling.

In spite of the well-meant idealism exhibited in the Hansa Quarter, the diversity of old cities, which depended on a variety of uses and well-scaled urban spaces, is ultimately missing. Traditional city houses form a contiguous enclosure of street and square, setting the stage for urban life. The buildings in the Hansa Quarter retreat into the landscape as independent, individual units, signifying the emergence of the detached individual and the dissipation of collectivity. While the Hansa Quarter remains the best of the first postwar developments, countless clones were to follow, and few of them worked. Zoned to death by a lack of varied and appropriate uses, these dreary "anticities" document the failure of the dogmas which dominated early postwar planning.

Hauptstadt Berlin (West): 1957–58
Hauptstadt Berlin (East): 1958–60

The first phase of postwar urban design culminated in two major competitions for the center of Berlin; their results also demonstrate the opposing attitudes toward planning that had crystallized in East and West Germany by the end of the 1950s. The same divergent trends would continue to divide architectural thought for years to come.

Although the West Berlin city government and the government of the Federal Republic in Bonn had no juris-

42. Berlin Wall

diction over the old urban center in East Berlin, in 1957 they sponsored a provocative international design competition to obtain designs for the city. A pervasive negation of the city structure characterizes the competition entries—even the course of the Spree River north of the Reichstag parliament building was to be diverted to accommodate a freeway interchange. The vision of the city as *Stadtlandschaft* (urban landscape), composed of buildings sited informally in the landscape, was the opposite of the perceived formalism of Nazi city planning and the ensuing communist monumentality, and the paradigm prevailed in West Germany for decades. Unfortunately, this vision was simply another brand of formalism which in the end would prove just as disastrous for the city. As Germany and Berlin were to remain divided for another thirty-five years, the visionary designs remained unbuilt. Fortunately, parts of the center of Berlin were spared from the tradition-negating formalism of the immediate postwar era, and remained available for other types of development.

The winning entry by Friedrich Spengelin, Fritz Eggeling, and Gerd Pempelfort *(41)* shows a relatively high degree of respect for the basic city structure, although vast areas would have been unnecessarily razed to make way for a new business center. The jury comments clearly show the issues of the time: "Some . . . complained that it was a project without passion, without a grand idea, but for many this was its virtue. It was the very model of bourgeois respectability in modern dress."[6] The governmental center near the Reichstag was envisioned as a raised plateau on the banks of the Spree where the parliament buildings were placed as sculptural objects, a type of planning executed convincingly in the neighboring Kongresshalle by American architect Hugh Stubbins in 1957.

The second-place entry by Hans Scharoun proposes a total transformation of the city. Scharoun's "new order" was based on his belief that the new society must find expression in new forms. Although the goals and manifestoes sound convincing, a rigorous analysis of Scharoun's proposal reveals a surprising lack of attention to appropriately scaled urban structures, bordering on a new monumentality. Two gestures were conceived to connect the disparate halves of the city: a huge building complex dubbed "the house of business" which was to stretch well over two miles across the southern part of Friedrichstadt, violating the urban fabric, and the extension of the Tiergarten into East Berlin as a green belt across the city. "The memory of Hitler's obsession with a dominant order would be deliberately replaced by its antithesis—an order of fragmentization and decentralization. . . . The disorder of reality, the inevitability of fragmentation, and the collapse of the imposed and coherent external worlds is the price of freedom."[7] Although Scharoun's grand utopian vision for Berlin was ultimately unbuildable, ten years later he was commissioned to design West Berlin's Kulturforum where he was at least partially able to realize his vision of a new urban order.

In the late 1950s the East German authorities held several limited competitions open only to participants from the Eastern bloc. The structure and the results of the competitions show the increasing irreconcilability of the East and West German ideologies. In 1960, a scheme for a five-year building plan for 1960–65 was presented by an East German collective led by Peter Schweitzer. It ignored the adjacent districts in West Berlin, thereby accepting the increasing division of the city and demonstrating the iron will of the East German regime, which would culminate in the coming year with the Berlin Wall. As it had since World War II, communist city planning focused on monumental urban spaces and colossal building complexes and thus perverted the vision of socialism.

Reconstruction Phase II: 1961–80

At midnight on August 12, 1961, the East German government ordered construction of the Berlin Wall *(42)*. Berlin's urban core became a no man's land separating opposing social systems. Exemplifying the defeat of Nazi Germany, the rigidity of communist dictatorship, and the political paralysis of Berlin, Germany, and Europe, this "sword slashing through a city" epitomized the futility of the cold war. Over the years the wall assumed an absurd normality. The traditional squares and streets in

43. Märkisches Quarter, West Berlin, 1968–74

its path were soon only a vague memory. Although a mere twelve feet in height, the wall's massive social and spatial impact drained the life from the center of Berlin. Politically, economically, culturally, and architecturally, the city was crippled.

Although their division was more pervasive than ever, in the 1960s similar urban planning strategies were pursued in both East and West Germany. The need for housing continued to be an explosive political issue. In addition to rebuilding the housing units destroyed in the war and accommodating the increasing population, hundreds of thousands of housing units were necessary to house the refugees streaming in from eastern Europe. Rather than dealing with the difficult sites in the center of the city, the new housing districts were planned far from the urban centers. The advent of suburban culture and the neglect of the city that characterizes postwar American development found its counterpart in the satellite cities built in western Europe until the late 1970s and in the Eastern bloc until the 1990s. Marzahn in East Berlin and the Märkisches Quarter in West Berlin are characteristic of dozens of other "new towns" throughout Germany.

The Märkisches Quarter *(43)* was the most controversial new town built in the 1960s. Even before building was started, critics declared the venture a total failure. This type of criticism served as a central point of departure for postmodern urban thought in the mid-1980s. Ultimately, the Märkisches Quarter is a bloated version of the Hansa Quarter. The same idea of the city in the park was exploited here: What was projected as a lush park between massive housing blocks became a sea of parking lots. Mammoth concrete apartment bunkers, up to twenty stories high, were placed too far from each other and failed to define usable urban spaces. Dull repetition of industrialized building elements coupled with poor siting made the Märkisches Quarter a dreary anti-city far removed from the dense vitality of the city. Nonetheless, in spite of the failure proclaimed by its critics, the Märkisches Quarter has emerged in recent years as a surprisingly livable neighborhood, at least according a recent survey of its inhabitants.

44. Marzahn, East Berlin, in 1992

The new town of Marzahn *(44)*, East Berlin's answer to the Märkisches Quarter, suffers from similar problems. Unfortunately, the same type of harsh criticism that was leveled at the Märkisches Quarter was repressed in East Berlin until 1990. While the builders of the Märkisches Quarter were forced to plant more trees, remodel entrance foyers, build a shopping center, and complete the park during the 1980s, the citizens of Marzahn were never able to implement the measures necessary to animate their city. One of the major new challenges facing architects and urban designers in the 1990s is the transformation of Marzahn and the dozens of similar settlements in East Germany.

This type of satellite city forced the neglect of housing within cities until the 1980s, at which point a new set of urban renewal strategies, again expressing the divergent goals of East and West Germany, were implemented. Once more, examples in Berlin exemplify the trends which shaped urban cores across Germany in the 1960s and 1970s.

In East Berlin, many elements of the 1960 Schweitzer plan were realized up until the late 1980s, and stand today as the physical expression of communist ideology. The Leipzigerstrasse, for instance, was developed with a mixture of twelve- to twenty-five-story housing blocks. The Altes Schloss, residence of the Prussian monarchy and symbolic center of the city, was razed to make way for the dreary East German parliament building. The Alexanderplatz, once the most densely settled core of the city, was tripled in size and stripped of its vital qualities. The strip between Schinkel's Altes Museum and the Alexanderplatz is still characterized by vast urban spaces that were used only for elaborate parades staged by the regime. Today major governmental buildings, once conceived as monuments to the new order, stand empty: eerie torsos surrounded by the failed city of socialist realism.

In West Berlin, Hans Scharoun was commissioned to design the Kulturforum, a complex of buildings including the Philharmonic Hall and State Library. Here Scharoun was able, at least partially, and with mixed results, to realize his vision of the city as an amorphous *Stadtlandschaft*. The buildings themselves were conceived as cities; they failed to address their surroundings by neglecting the urban fabric. While virtuoso interior spaces abound, the Kulturforum outside remains wind-swept and desolate to this day.

By the early 1970s both East and West Germany had recovered from the worst losses of the war and a new phase of prosperity began. While the industrialized anti-city architecture of the 1960s was further developed in East Germany, new trends surfaced as the failure of much postwar planning was recognized in West Germany. In Munich, a new area of housing and sports facilities, built

45. Heinle and Wischer, Olympic Village housing, Munich, 1972

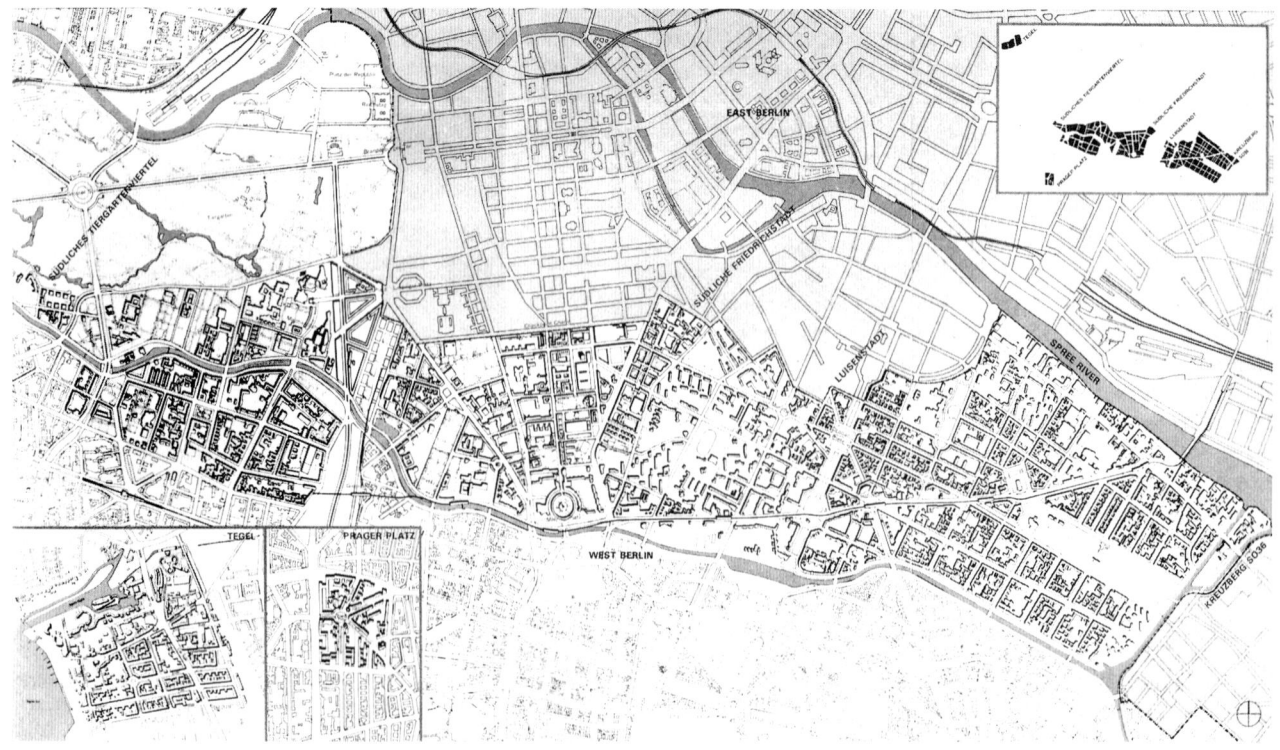

46. International Building Exhibition, Neubau and Altbau sites, plan, Berlin, 1984

47. O. M. Ungers, Berlin proposal, 1990

The 1980s: Tradition Rehabilitated

By the 1980s the failure of much postwar city planning was clear. Nonetheless, it was difficult to effect change in the dogmatic East German society. The lessons of the 1960s and 1970s were left unlearned, and the pursuit of the ideal built expression for the waning communist ideology continued. In East Berlin, the largest European new town of the era—in fact, of the whole postwar period—was built in Hellersdorf, and similar projects were realized on the outskirts of virtually every East German city. In West Germany, on the contrary, a new generation of architects and urban designers began to experiment with solutions to the difficult problems presented by aging and decaying cities that had been neglected for more than twenty years.

In West Germany, the rediscovery of the city centers began in many places simultaneously. Karljosef Schattner carefully and respectfully transformed traditionally Bavarian Eichstätt city blocks with a contrasting, finely detailed style. Ancient Regensburg's center was restored and enriched with new buildings. Frankfurt revitalized its troubled core with new museums along the riverfront, reconstruction in the old urban center, and a new international convention center near the financial district. Hamburg transformed its decaying city center with a lively mix of shopping, offices, and housing. In West Berlin, the lessons from the 1960s—the first experiments in user-participation, the critique of the Märkisches Quarter—developed into the IBA, the most influential architectural laboratory of the 1980s.

IBA sites *(46)* are spread throughout the city in areas that were severely damaged in the war and allowed to decay until the 1980s. In the poor, yet energetic urban neighborhood of Kreuzberg SO36, the Altbau IBA, under the direction of Hardt Walther Hämer, was primarily concerned with revitalizing the urban fabric, fostering some of the most significant, if less photogenic, IBA projects. Empty ruins reminiscent of the decay in many American cities were resettled with urban homesteading programs that provided low-interest loans and professional assistance, and encouraged user-participation. The resulting increase in neighborhood identification proves that the mixture of uses inherent in any city ensures urban vitality. The 1981 "Blauplan" prepared by Hämer and his team carefully documented each building and proposed corrective steps for the individual sites which included both large-scale renovation and the construction of new infill projects.

The Neubau IBA and its director Josef Paul Kleihues experimented with the reconstruction of the urban block structure in southern Friedrichstadt, Tiergarten, and Tegel. Architects from around the world were given the opportunity to realize their sometimes utopian visions; they met with varying degrees of success. The 1984 plan prepared by Kleihues is singularly different from the urban visions of the 1957 Hauptstadt Berlin competition and demonstrates the rediscovery of the city as a spatial and

for the 1972 Olympics, was to become one of postwar Europe's most successful new urban developments.

In 1968 a competition was held for the Olympic facilities on a Munich site where the rubble had been heaped in the first postwar years. The competition winners, Stuttgart architect Günter Behnisch, with a team including Joachim Joedicke, Frei Otto, and others, proposed an informal grouping of tent-like structures embedded into the hilly terrain. This scheme was the antithesis of the rigid monumentality of the 1936 Olympics held in Hitler's Berlin, and represented a new democratic architecture which convincingly documented West Germany's social, political, and architectural revitalization.

Another of the prize-winning firms, the Stuttgart office of Erwin Heinle and Robert Wischer, was asked to design the adjacent Olympic Village *(45)*. Like the Märkisches Quarter, the village received at its inception massive criticism; today it is highly praised by ninety percent of its three thousand inhabitants, primarily because the failures of most other large housing projects were avoided, despite the extensive program and short construction schedule. Several fundamental design decisions were to assure the extraordinary success of the Olympic Village: The south-facing buildings were terraced and had views onto the landscape; inhabitants turned the concrete building forms into virtual hanging gardens. Automobiles were accommodated in an elaborate system of underground streets and parking facilities so that public spaces were free of traffic; lush landscaped parks and playgrounds were thereby created. Two-story buildings were combined with the higher blocks to form well-scaled streets and create urban density. An appropriate mixture of uses—housing, shopping, hotels, schools, churches, offices—was provided. A blend of privately owned and rental apartments attracted various social groups, while the high percentage of individually owned apartments promoted the residents' pride in their neighborhood. Seen in retrospect, the Olympic Village, which seems unlikely as a contemporary housing solution, remains the most convincing example of its era.

philosophical continuum. The 1984 plan envisioned recreating the block structure with medium-density projects in southern Friedrichstadt and Tiergarten. Inner courtyards were designed to allow light and air in and keep traffic noise out. The new blocks formed new street spaces. Parks were planned to replace deserted railyards and to act as recreation areas for the densely populated surrounding areas. Well-proportioned urban squares were conducive to a variety of uses. To ensure diversity no singular architectural style was proposed; instead, a wide spectrum of possible solutions was explored in the laboratory of the city. Today, a strong sense of plurality and freedom of expression remains the convincing achievement of the IBA.

In East Berlin and other East German cities new city center areas were developed, although most new construction remained in the distant new towns. The urban sites in East Germany present a dramatic counterpoint to the revitalization projects in West Germany. East Berlin's Nikolai Quarter sought to rebuild one of the oldest parts of the city with buildings constructed of prefabricated concrete panels. Along the Friedrichstrasse, new hotels and shopping complexes were built. Monotonous housing blocks were constructed along the Wilhelmstrasse where diplomatic institutions and government ministries once stood. With these projects, the East German government continued to force its ideological agenda on the city, inflicting wounds that will take decades to heal.

The 1990s: Between Deconstruction and Reconstruction

On November 9, 1989, the East German authorities succumbed to increasing discontent and opened the borders to West Germany and thus western Europe. The end of the Berlin Wall—the end of the division of Germany and Europe—was in sight. Scarcely a year later, on December 3, 1990, East and West Germany formally united. These events inaugurated a new era in architecture and urban design. While the prevalent West German design themes of the 1980s had been explored and applied to projects in East Germany, new tendencies began to surface that gradually changed the scope of urban design. The East German government left behind devastated cities that had either never been rebuilt or had fallen into disrepair after the war. Architects and urban designers in the new Germany were faced with problems not unlike those of the immediate postwar period, over forty-five years earlier.

In November 1990, the German Architecture Museum and the *Frankfurter Allgemeine* newspaper asked seventeen architects to make proposals for the heart of Berlin. Although the theoretical designs were criticized for their utopian nature when the times demanded more pragmatic solutions, the visionary ideas effectively demonstrate the euphoria of 1990 and address the fundamental urban design issues which were to emerge in the following years.

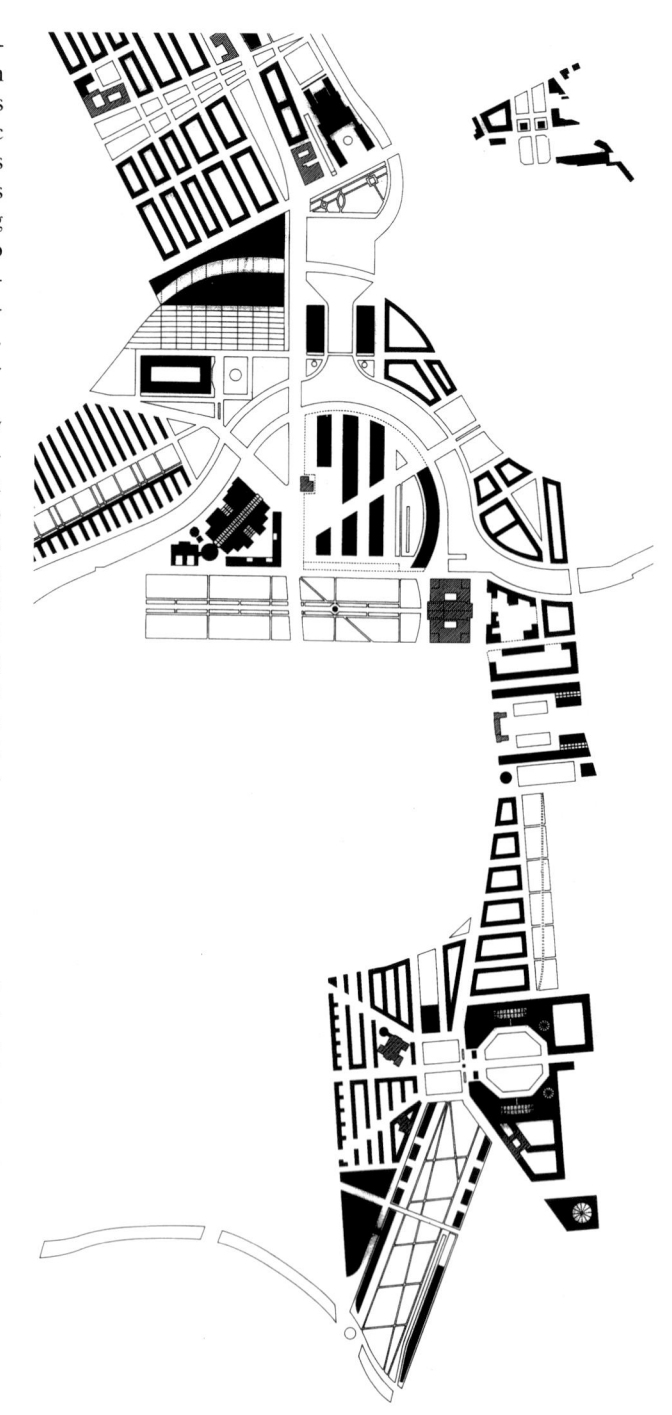

48. Josef Paul Kleihues, Berlin proposal, 1990

Oswald Mathias Ungers proposed constructing "icons of the modern movement" along the Spree River as urban fragments throughout the historic center *(47)*. He developed an "urban archipelago" or "city in the city" in which the district is understood as a collection of fragments. Rather than attempting urban repairs to reduce the disjointed nature of the city, Ungers accepted the chaos of Berlin and tried to preserve and increase it. He recommended that the city first study individual districts to determine their unique quali-

49. Hilmer and Sattler, Potsdamer Platz competition entry, Berlin, 1991

ties; these qualities would then be preserved and intensified so that the entire city would become a collage of fragments. Ungers argued that the sole continuous element uniting Berlin's urban fragments was the dialectic process in which thesis is disproved by antithesis. Thus rather than reconstructing the city center in its historic form, he proposed an architectural and stylistic stance that recognized the uniqueness of the city's disjointed character. On one hand, Ungers's use of "modern icons" was a metaphor for the fate of the city. At the same time he made several concrete proposals for his own urban fragments. The obsolete East German parliament building would be expanded with a "Volkshaus" that would face Schinkel's Altes Museum across Unter den Linden. An eight-hundred-meter block would span the Spree, serving as a gate to the area of the city behind the parliament. The Friedrichstrasse railway station was to be flanked by three new city blocks, as well as an allegory for Mies van der Rohe's as-yet-unbuilt 1920s design for a nearby crystalline tower.

Hans Kollhoff proposed development around the Potsdamer Platz and the Alexanderplatz, and along the Leipzigerstrasse which connects them. By confining development to these limited areas Kollhoff sought to harness the creative power of the free market with skyscrapers modeled after American ones. He argued that the rural area surrounding Berlin could be preserved by increasing density at specific sites in the city core. Thus medium-density infill buildings were to be constructed in the middle of the city, while seventy-story skyscrapers at Potsdamer Platz and Alexanderplatz would accommodate office complexes. The six skyscrapers proposed for Potsdamer Platz would together contain more floor space than the entire surrounding district. Kollhoff cited New York's classic skyscrapers as the model for his proposal, but at the same time avoided many of New York's problems of ultra-high density by limiting tower development to two carefully defined sites.

Josef Paul Kleihues offered different ideas for the same area, focusing on the strip of city between the Potsdamer Platz and the Spree *(48)*. The Spreebogen—a pronounced bend in the river—near the Reichstag was envisioned as the site for Germany's future governmental center. Medium-rise blocks with a few slender towers placed at focal points were proposed for the area around

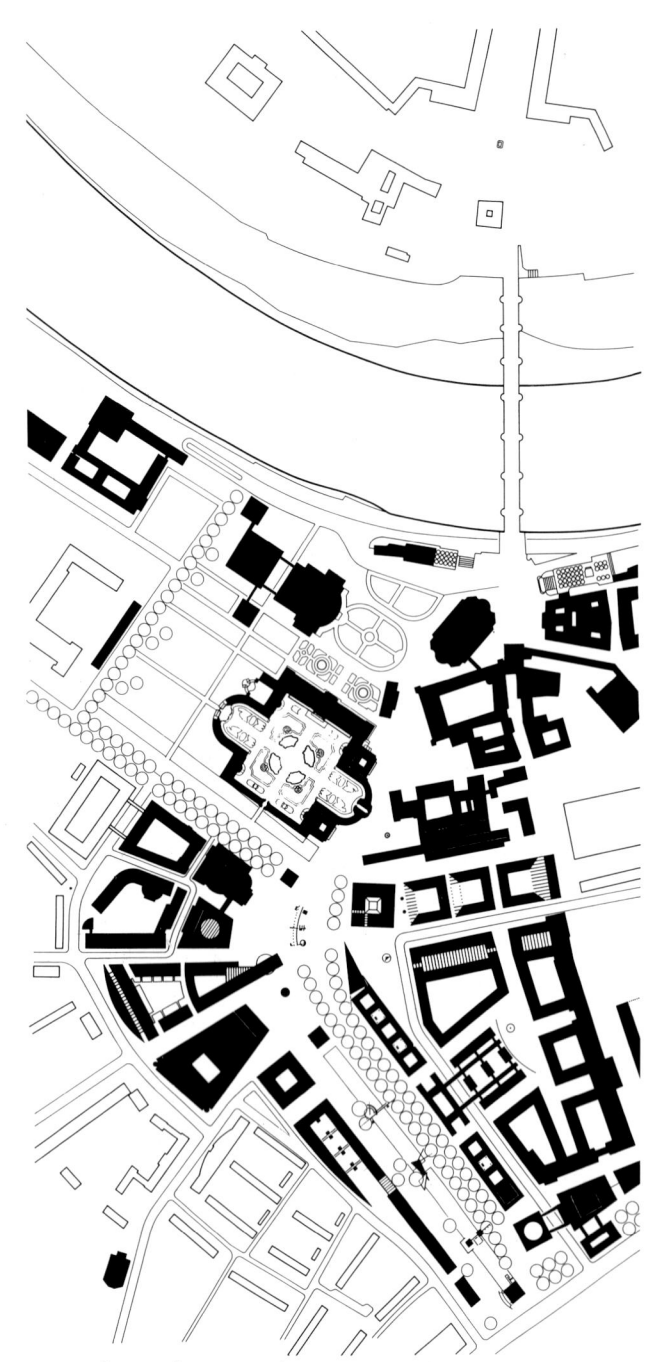

50. Joachim and Margot Schürmann, Dresden Postplatz competition entry, plan, 1992

the Potsdamer Platz. Kleihues resolved the north-south division inherent in Berlin's historic development with a north-south boulevard to connect the city with outlying districts and to serve as a much-needed traffic artery. The few remaining urban fragments between the parliament building and the Potsdamer Platz were integrated into a network of new blocks, thus mending the fractured cityscape.

In 1991 the first official urban design competition for the center of Berlin was held; the problem was the definition of a master plan for the area around the Potsdamer Platz. One of the first sections of the Berlin Wall to be demolished revealed a scorched patch of earth where the Potsdamer Platz, once one of Europe's most lively urban spaces, had existed. The revitalization of this area will be truly challenging. The winners, Munich architects Heinz Hilmer and Christoph Sattler, proposed a stylistically and urbanistically straightforward architecture that sought to perpetuate the city's cultural tradition by complementing and repairing its urban fabric *(49)*. The scheme, a compact zone of ten-story buildings, simply extends the existing block structure. The design is not based on the "globally tried and tested American urban model of skyscraper conglomeration, but rather on the vision of a compact, spatially complex European city." Indeed, the decision to premiate the Hilmer/Sattler scheme signified a clear consensus to experiment with the elements of the humanist city rather than to allow developers to build the aloof skyscrapers proposed by most entrants. By 1992 Hilmer and Sattler revised their proposal to better accommodate the developer's security, traffic, and infrastructural needs; limited competitions were held in the summer of 1992 to select architects for the individual block sites.

As the euphoria following the fall of the Berlin Wall began to fade, the true condition of the cities and new towns in eastern Germany became clear, and new tasks emerged which suddenly shifted the focus of urban design. The historical cities demanded immediate repair; the attention directed at them left the sprawling new towns unfinished and without essential amenities. Most importantly, the necessary mixture of urban uses had been neglected in the drive to build housing. Shopping, cultural, commercial, and governmental facilities were often nonexistent in the immense settlements.

Although the new town of Hellersdorf, not far from East Berlin, was built in the 1980s to house over 200,000 residents, its urban center was never completed. This vast, empty site in the middle of the drab new town offered urban designers their first opportunity to solve the difficult problems presented by the failed new towns throughout the region. Andreas Brandt, Rudolph Böttcher, and Liliana Villanueva's 1991 competition-winning proposal—a densely woven city, in contrast to the usual relentless blocks—defined clear parameters for repairing and completing the unfinished urban fabric. Professing that "every citizen has a right to the urbanism of the city," Brandt composed a tightly knit network of variegated blocks with a mixture of uses as an antithesis to the surrounding anti-city. Five-story buildings would contain commercial, shopping, cultural, governmental, sports, recreation, and office facilities in their lower floors and housing above. Three towers, rising above the surrounding blocks, would serve as urban landmarks visible from nearby neighborhoods. By avoiding the weaknesses of typical modern planning, the team's well-scaled city, with its dense mixture of uses, emerged as one of the first viable solutions to the predicament of the new towns.

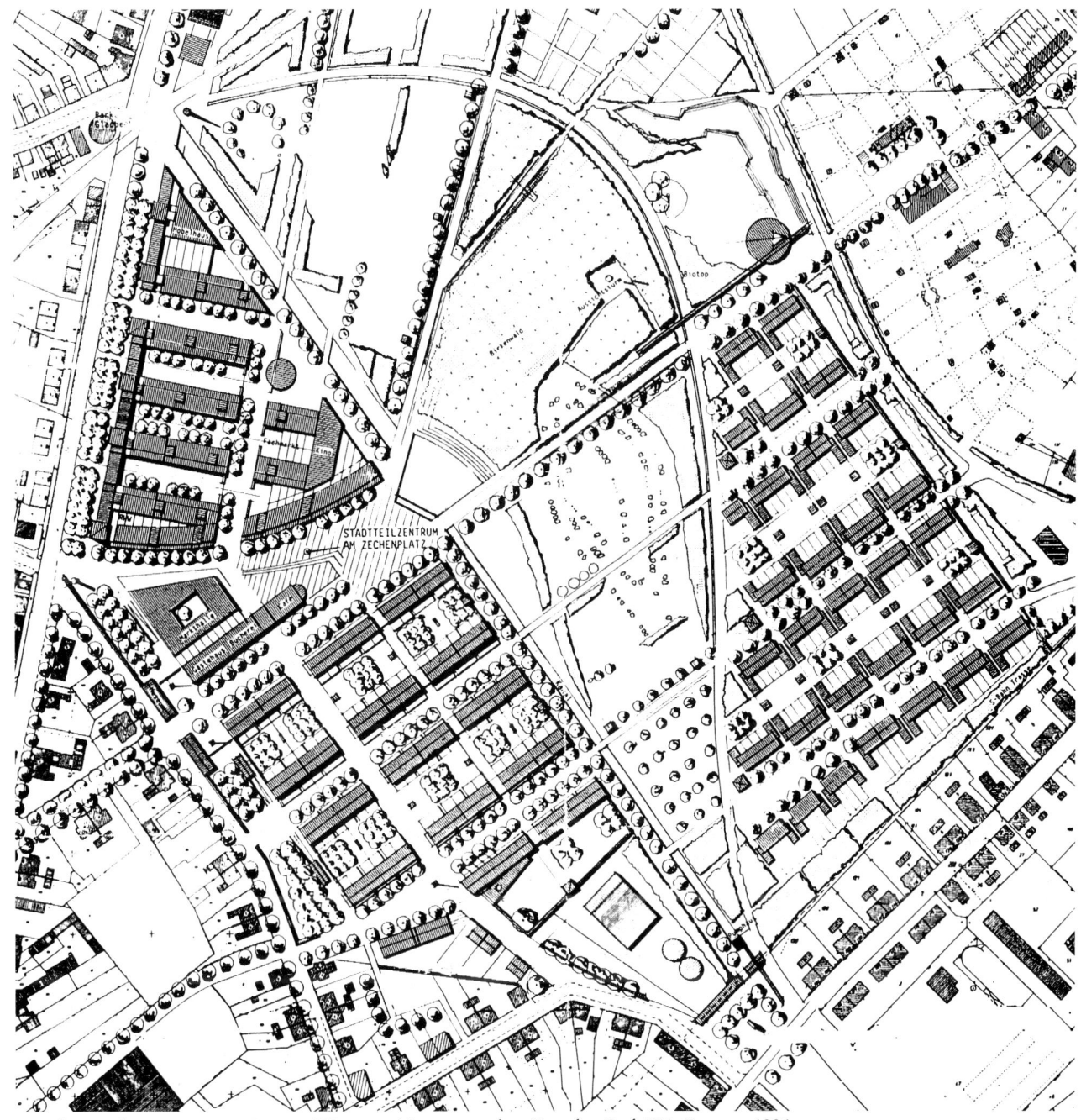

51. Klaus and Verena Trojan, Prosper III competition entry, plan, Emscher Park IBA, Bottrop, 1991

In Dresden, Cologne architects Joachim and Margot Schürmann won the 1992 urban design competition for the Postplatz, focusing specifically on the problems of the monumental city centers in the eastern part of the country *(50)*. By respecting the former path of an ancient city wall and skillfully placing new blocks into the grand urban spaces to create clearly defined streets, squares, and parks, they achieved a new urbanism. By increasing density and at the same time respecting traditional urban development and integrating the nearby baroque "Zwinger" palace, the Schürmanns proposed a diverse, easily identifiable urban zone without resorting to historicist forms.

Along with the new concerns in eastern Germany, other pressing urban design challenges emerged which demanded attention throughout the country and which became the central goals of urban design in the early 1990s. These included an acute housing shortage and the abandonment of many industrial facilities and riverside sites within the cities. Planners attempted to solve the housing shortage without sacrificing the surrounding countryside and to transform deserted locations while respecting the local natural environment.

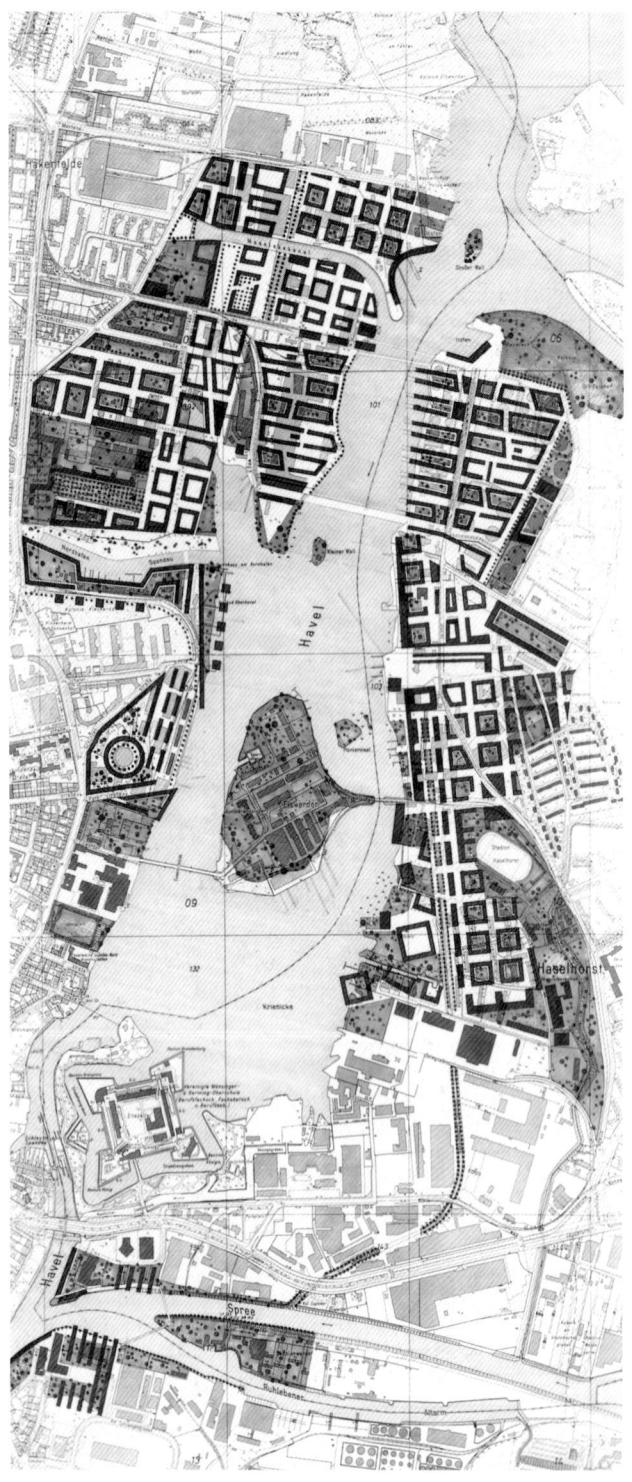

52. Christoph Langhof and Jürgen Nottmeyer, Wasserstadt Spandau planning proposal, Berlin, 1990

The Emscher Park IBA was conceived in the late 1980s to reclaim the formerly heavily industrialized Ruhr region between Duisburg and Dortmund in western Germany. Instead of the careful city repair practiced by the West Berlin IBAs of the 1980s, new, more global solutions were explored which sought to transform a much larger region. Sixteen sites, mostly deserted industrial properties, were set aside for new industries, service companies, and research parks, with the theme "working in the park." Innovative models for joint cooperation between the public and private sectors were explored. Munich architect Uwe Kiessler proposed a research park for the Rheinelbe area of Gelsenkirchen as a new working environment that would succeed the defunct factories. In addition to the development of new industries, more than twenty sites for new housing and urban reconstruction throughout the region were defined in the IBA. At Prosper III, for example, an abandoned factory site in the center of Bottrop, Darmstadt architects Klaus and Verena Trojan won the competition with a new urban quarter containing four hundred housing units and a host of other uses, including shopping, varied types of working environments, service sector industries, movie theaters, a library, and cafés, thus assuring an appropriate degree of urbanism *(51)*. The proposed area is comprised of three neighborhoods, each with a mixture of building types grouped around a central park.

In the early 1990s, the chronic housing shortage which had plagued the country since the war once again emerged as a central theme in urban design, and by 1991, the scale of planned projects had shifted from smaller designs with less than five hundred housing units to new urban extensions with up to ten thousand units and commercial, work, school, and sports facilities. As opposed to the new cities of the postwar era, these projects sought to extend the traditional city without repeating its mistakes. Urban extensions were proposed for Munich-Poing and Freiburg-Rieselfelder that essentially transferred traditional urban patterns to new locales outside the traditional centers. The Freiburg project, by local architects Böwer, Eith, Mürken, and Spieker, seeks to integrate the new districts with clearly defined connecting streets. The design centers on some ten closed blocks with a periphery of more open building forms that delimit a variety of streets and squares. The main square of the new city is clearly defined, enlivened by a mixture of uses, and connected to an adjacent park and recreation area to the north.

In Berlin, four teams of architects developed prototype designs for a new lakeside city for ten thousand inhabitants, the Wasserstadt Spandau. Located on former industrial sites northwest of Spandau's center, the Wasserstadt (waterfront city) is the most ambitious of the new urban extensions currently under development. The site, despite its proximity to the urban center and the Oberhavel Lake, had developed into an industrial center. When the Berlin Wall fell, the opportunity arose to relocate the industries, and simultaneously to develop the valuable properties into attractive new neighborhoods. Several strategies were defined to achieve a dense, yet livable city while avoiding the mistakes of the new towns. In addition to the housing, twenty-five percent of the space was set aside for new, "clean" industries, service sector jobs, shopping, schools, and community buildings. Hans Kollhoff and Helga Timmermann, Christoph Langhof and Jürgen Nottmeyer *(52)*,

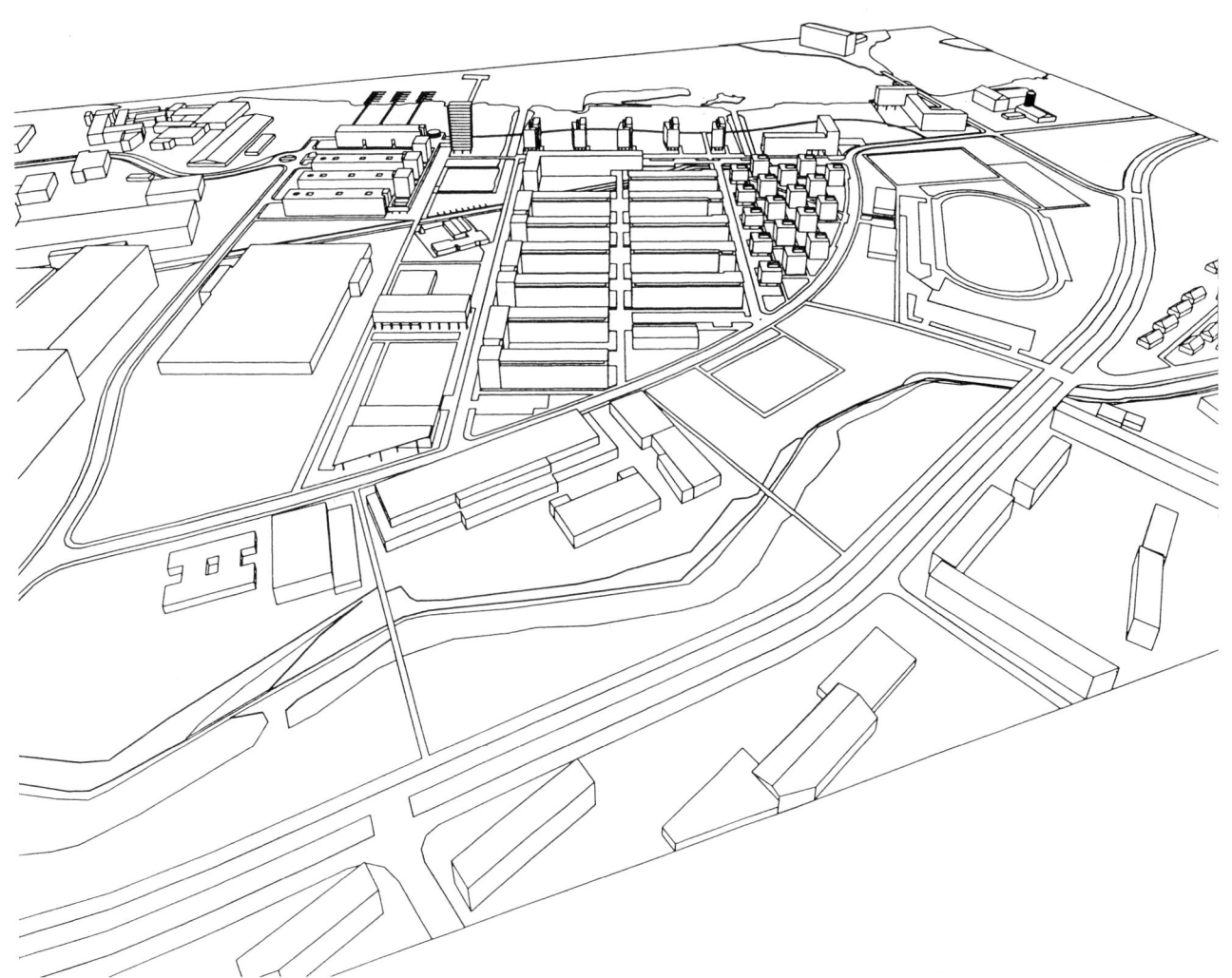

53. Gernot and Johanna Nalbach, Pulvermühle area proposal, perspective, Wasserstadt Spandau, Berlin, 1992

and Claude Zillich were commissioned to prepare proposals during 1990. Each study, while pursuing the same goals, arrived at the creation of an urban edge to the waterfront and different approaches to both the degree of enclosure and the network of parks and natural spaces.

An urban design competition was held in 1992 to obtain designs for the first phase of the Wasserstadt, the Pulvermühle area. Gernot and Johanna Nalbach proposed 1,200 housing units and an accompanying infrastructure of commercial and office space, public buildings, and parks, all oriented around a central green, the site for the kindergarten and school *(53)*. To the south, the factory district was to be expanded with new production and service sector facilities. North of the central green, an area of mixed-use blocks was to be bounded by a curving building that would form the northern edge to an already existing park with sports facilities. The waterfront was kept free of new building to respect the natural setting. Unfortunately, the idea of a coherent urban lake edge proved impossible to realize due to public opposition.

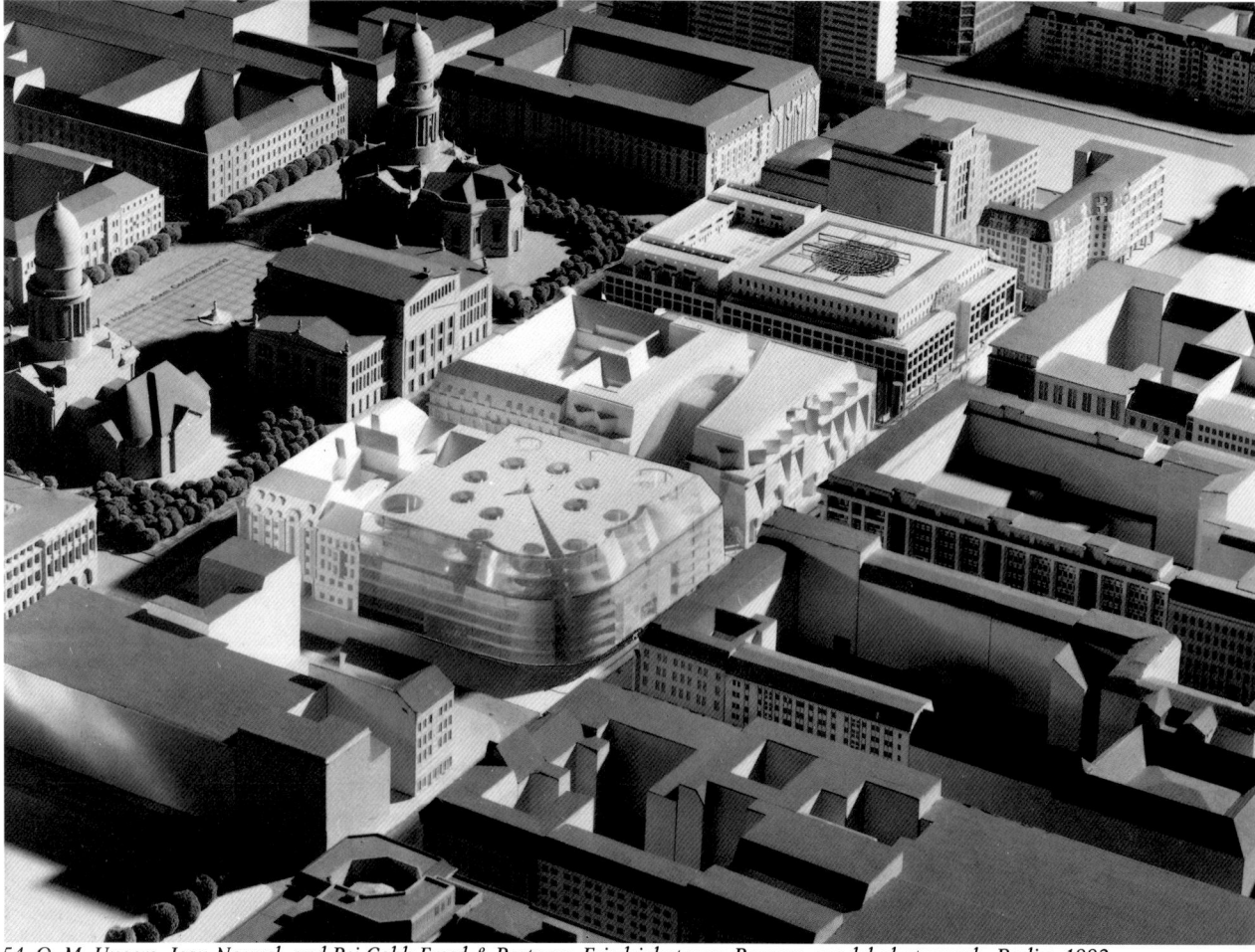

54. O. M. Ungers, Jean Nouvel, and Pei Cobb Freed & Partners, Friedrichstrasse Passage, model photograph, Berlin, 1992

Simultaneously, other parts of the Wasserstadt project were planned. Across Oberhavel Lake, the Nalbachs designed the Nordhafen quarter, a mixed-use neighborhood with five hundred housing units and commercial, school, hotel, light industrial, and office facilities. Rather than delegating the required industry and office space to the edge of the site, the team integrated them into the center of the district. The periphery is reserved for housing, which will have views to the Oberhavel and the surrounding landscape. A triangular village green connects the neighborhood to the amenities along the lakeshore, including other school and community facilities. The Nalbachs, through their skillful integration of old buildings, the planned mixture of uses, and appropriately scaled urban spaces, provided the needed impetus for the fledgling Wasserstadt.

Berlin: The Capital of Unified Germany

In June 1991 the German parliament, at that time still located in Bonn, voted to make Berlin the permanent capital, thus causing an immediate and incredible pressure to develop the city as governmental and financial institutions planned to move there. In an effort to prevent the building boom from unnecessarily damaging the urban infrastructure and fabric, the city government has developed a strategy of "critical reconstruction" as a guideline for building in the city center. The first projects in this vein have already rejected the "developer city" which has transformed so many other cities with bland monofunctionality.

The first critical reconstruction project was developed in the Friedrichstrasse, once the city's main north-south connecting artery. O. M. Ungers, Jean Nouvel, and Pei Cobb Freed & Partners were each selected to design one of the three blocks adjacent to Schinkel's Schauspielhaus theater *(54)*. The commission was divided in this way to ensure in the new projects the variation already inherent in the traditional city; three mutually respecting yet individually expressed architectural languages were envisioned side by side. The new complex was connected to the surrounding neighborhood with passages arising from the extension of the street network. In 1992 the ruins of a shopping center planned for the site in the late 1980s by the then-failing East German government were torn down, and building on the new Friedrichstrasse Passage began.

In 1992 Bernard Strecker and Dieter Hoffmann-Axthelm made the first attempt to define design guidelines for the Pariser Platz, the plaza at the Brandenburg Gate where the British, French, and American embassies and other public institutions once stood. The virtually forgotten parcel structure and the property lines of prewar buildings were reconstructed and used to define a new district on the foundations of the old, further developing the idea of critical reconstruction. But instead of copying the grand prewar buildings, new forms were explored that respected the original scale and the historical significance of the area but did not resort to superficial historicism. In their scheme, the plaza is enclosed with three-story volumes divided into six individual building fronts. The reconstructed square is also defined by seven-story buildings around the block perimeter. The architects derived an appropriate variety of scales and uses without specifically defining the style of the individual buildings.

An urban design competition open to participants from around the world was held in 1992 for an adjacent site on the banks of the Spree River near the Reichstag building; one thousand entries were submitted. The primary challenge was to integrate institutions for the federal government without creating a "forbidden city" of monumental government buildings. The opportunity to define an appropriate urban representation of the principles of democracy and pluralism which today characterize German society—and which was successfully realized in Bonn in the period from 1945 to 1992—offered designers a unique forum for experimentation. Whether the competition will really define the outlines of a new city center or the winning entries will simply remain utopian visions—as did the 1957 Hauptstadt Berlin projects—the vital core of the city, and indeed the country, will certainly be transformed in the coming years.

Outlook

The creation of a new democratic capital in Berlin, revitalization of the dilapidated cities and poorly planned new towns in eastern Germany, critical reconstruction of sensitive city sites, transformation of abandoned industrial areas, and creation of hundreds of thousands of housing units and workplaces in new mixed-use districts all emerged as the central urban design issues of the early 1990s. But in spite of the innovative quality of contemporary designs, one emerging theme has been neglected: the preservation of the limited natural environment outside the cities. Urban development on the periphery of towns and cities often happens without cohesive urban design parameters. Rather than reusing abandoned districts within cities, new buildings—row houses, gas stations, light industry, shopping centers—devour the natural surroundings at an increasing rate. Urban designers must now discover methods to prevent needless destruction of the countryside and preserve what is left of limited natural resources.

In the postwar years, developments in urban design have essentially been determined by the same antagonistic ideologies that emerged in the late 1940s. Now these opposing styles, grounded in either traditionalism or modernism, are losing their relevence in the face of the increasing ecological debacle. While the debate between the irreconcilable urban ideologies will certainly continue, the true test for urban designers in the 1990s will be to transcend the limitations of postwar thought to create more inclusive cities which address the difficult challenges of the present without negating the past: to make cities that will be able to accommodate the human needs of the future.

NOTES
1. As quoted in Ulrich Conrads, *Neue Deutsche Architektur 2* (Stuttgart: Gerd Hatje, 1962), 16.
2. Walter Ulbricht, "Die Großbauten im Fünfjahresplan" (speech at the third Socialist Unity Party conference), July 22, 1950, as quoted in *Neues Deutschland*, July 23, 1950.
3. Wilhelm Girnus, as quoted in Johann F. Geist and Klaus Kürvers, *Das Berliner Mietshaus 1945–1989* (Munich: Prestel, 1989), 272.
4. Edmund Collein, "Das nationale Aufbauprogramm," *Deutsche Architektur* 1952, 16.
5. As quoted in Werner Durth, Volker Martin, and Karl Paechter, "Einzig: die Stalinallee," *Stadtbauwelt,* March 28, 1991, 619.
6. Alan Balfour, *Berlin: The Politics of Order, 1737–1989* (New York: Rizzoli International, 1990), 174.
7. Balfour, *Berlin,* 177.

THE
ARCHITECTS

AUER AND WEBER

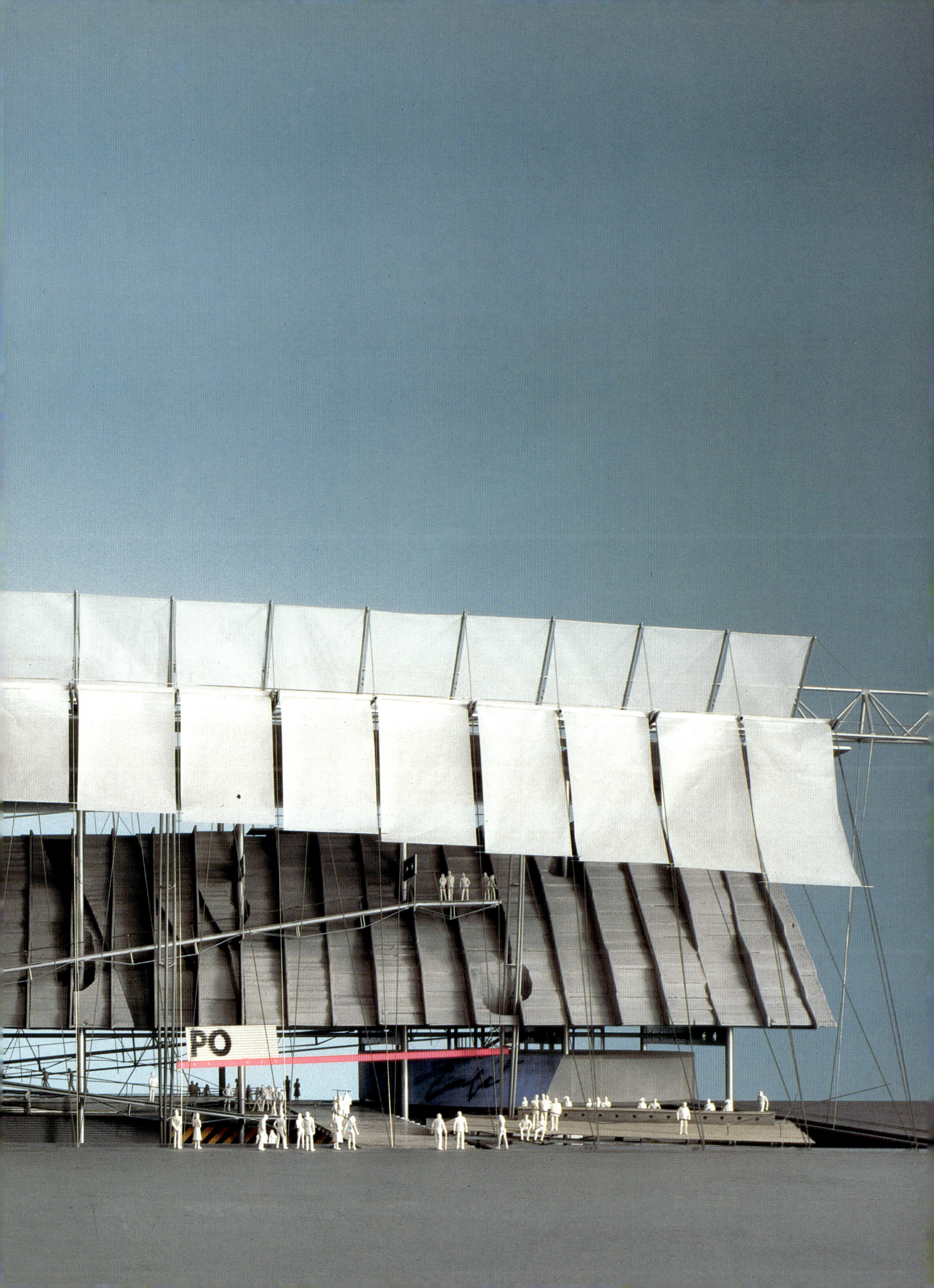
PO

German Exhibition Pavilion • Seville • 1990

The German pavilion for Expo '92 was conceived as "constructional art" or an "artistic construction" and is akin to taking a symbolic, sensual, critical, humorously ironic discovery tour through the newly emerged *Deutschlandschaft* (German-scape). The design was meant not as a final formula but as a concrete strategy for further work. It is before this intermediary backdrop that the still malleable correspondences between various interpretative and presentational stages are to be viewed.

The external appearance of the pavilion represents a field of tension between the structural and the sculptural. The interplay of the architectural structure—both the stage, which circumscribes and conditions the interior exhibition space with primarily functional components, and the umbrella—and the open yet enclosed exhibition space—a freely unfolding shell, sculpturally interpreting the exhibition themes—creates a dialectic tension which renders the pavilion appealing, unique, and memorable without resorting to contrived formalistic drama.

The concept of *Deutschlandschaft* is an equivocal interpretation of German reality: the German word *landschaft*, like its English counterpart landscape, is open to multiple interpretations: natural, industrial, spiritual, political, educational, and artistic. *Landschaft* is also viewed by many outside of Germany as a typically German concept, like *leitmotiv*, *zeitgeist*, *wanderlust*, and *gemütlichkeit*. As a general idea, *landschaft* is dualistic, containing both image and essence, exterior and interior, surface and depth, appearance and reality, space and time, the senses and reason. The signification of this contribution to Expo '92 could very well lie in this concept, conveyed through and within a synthesis of architecture, art, and technology, and expressing German reality, its ties, liberties, obligations, and hopes, in a grand exhibition guided by serene yet critical self-awareness.
Auer and Weber

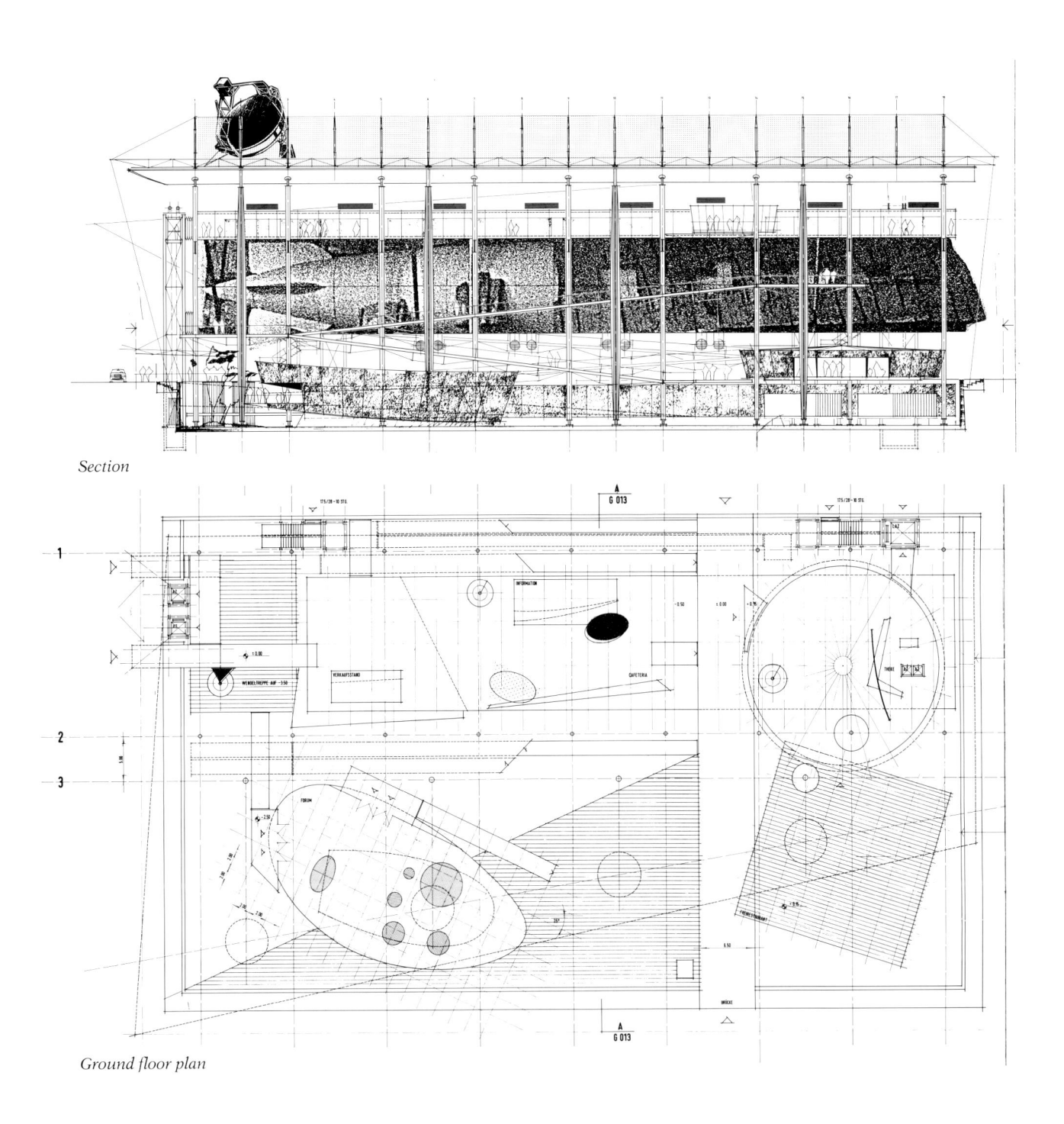

Section

Ground floor plan

Airport Administrative Complex • Munich • 1986–91

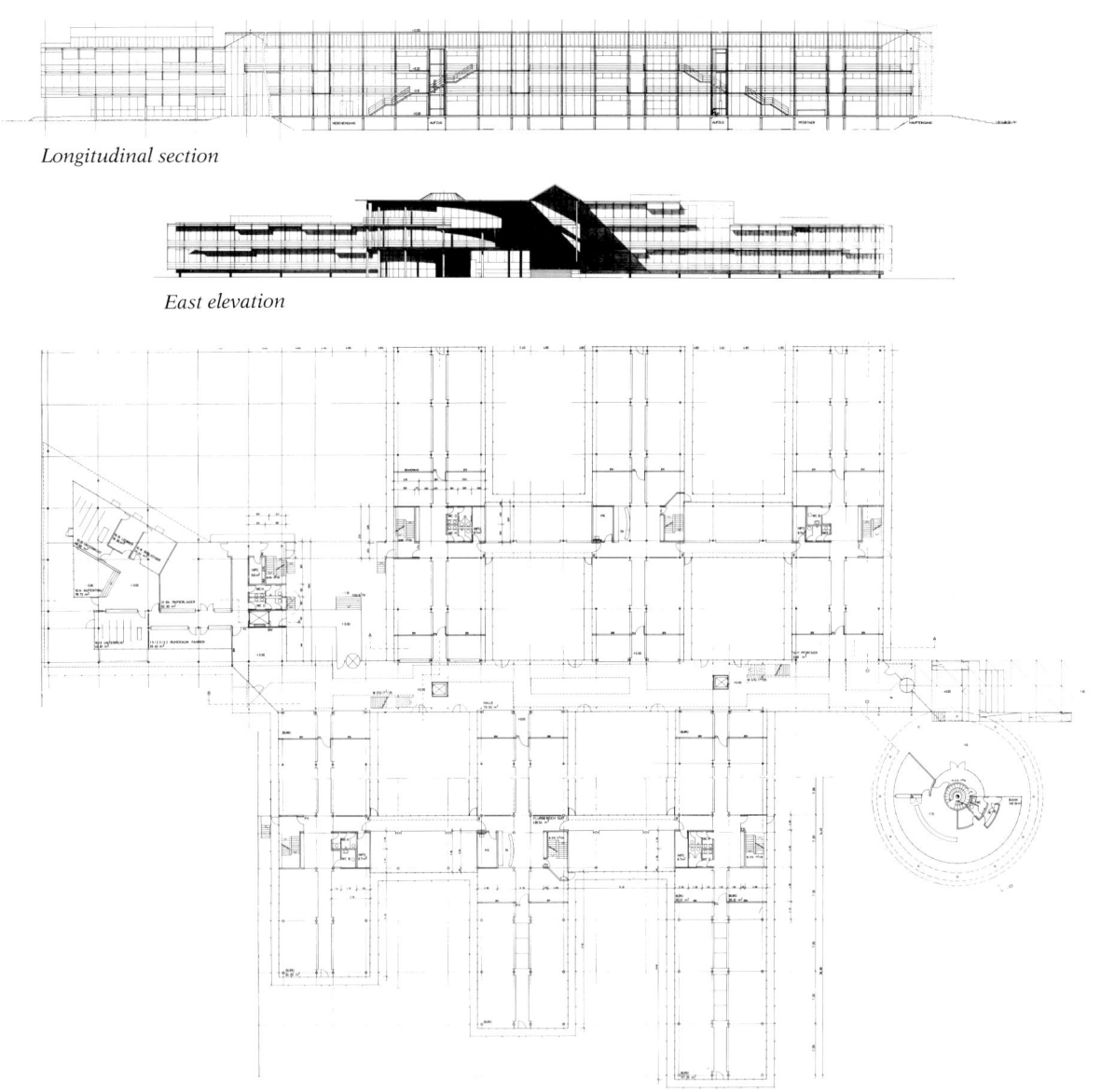

Longitudinal section

East elevation

Typical floor plan

The buildings were designed not as structural volumes but as utilitarian planes. The main floor is above ground, underscoring the dominance of the landscape and the artificiality of the buildings, which appear to float. The office building is planned for maximum interior flexibility and exterior expansibility. The backbone of the administrative complex is a straight hall running its entire length; the administrative departments open off of this axis. In contrast to the light, airy space of the hall, the office areas are characterized by spatial austerity. The hall and office areas are further differentiated by varied ceiling, floor, and facade treatments.

In corridors adjoining the hall, uninterrupted strips of skylighting emphasize the continuity of the ceiling plane, and skylights and glass block panels set into the floor draw powerful natural light into the building's interior. In addition to their structural purposes, the materials are used in keeping with their innate properties to emphasize the distinction between landscape and building. The overall impression is largely shaped by the alternation between rough and finished elements. *Auer and Weber*

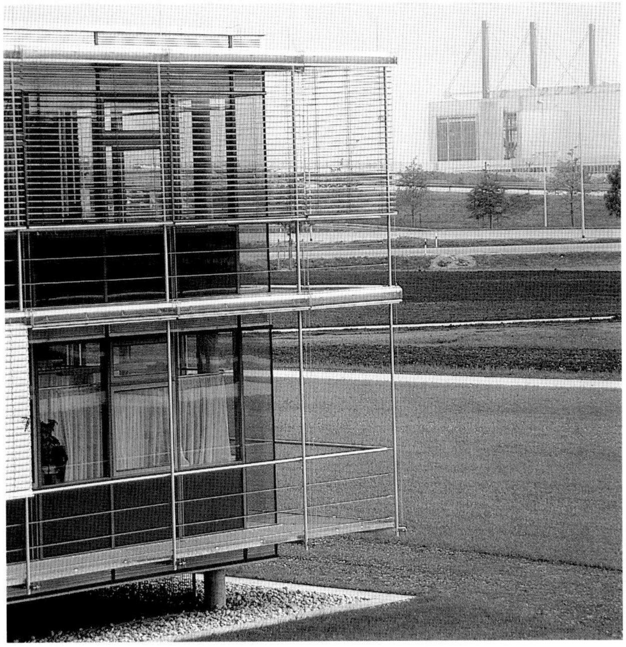

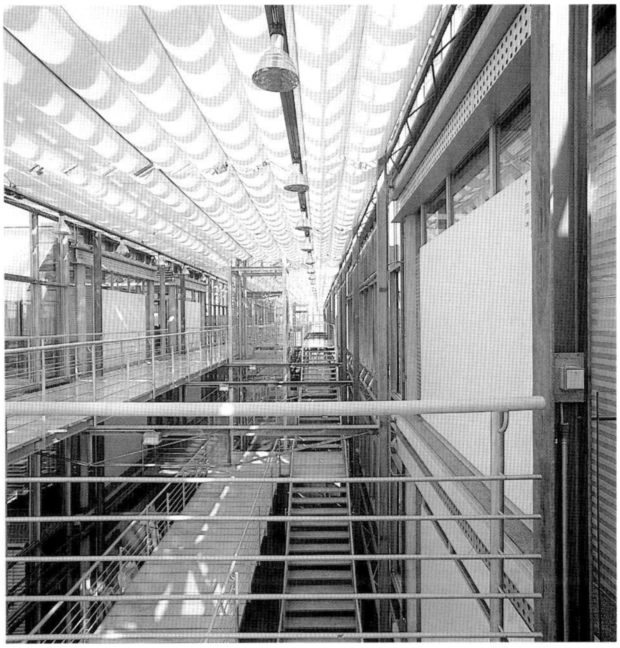

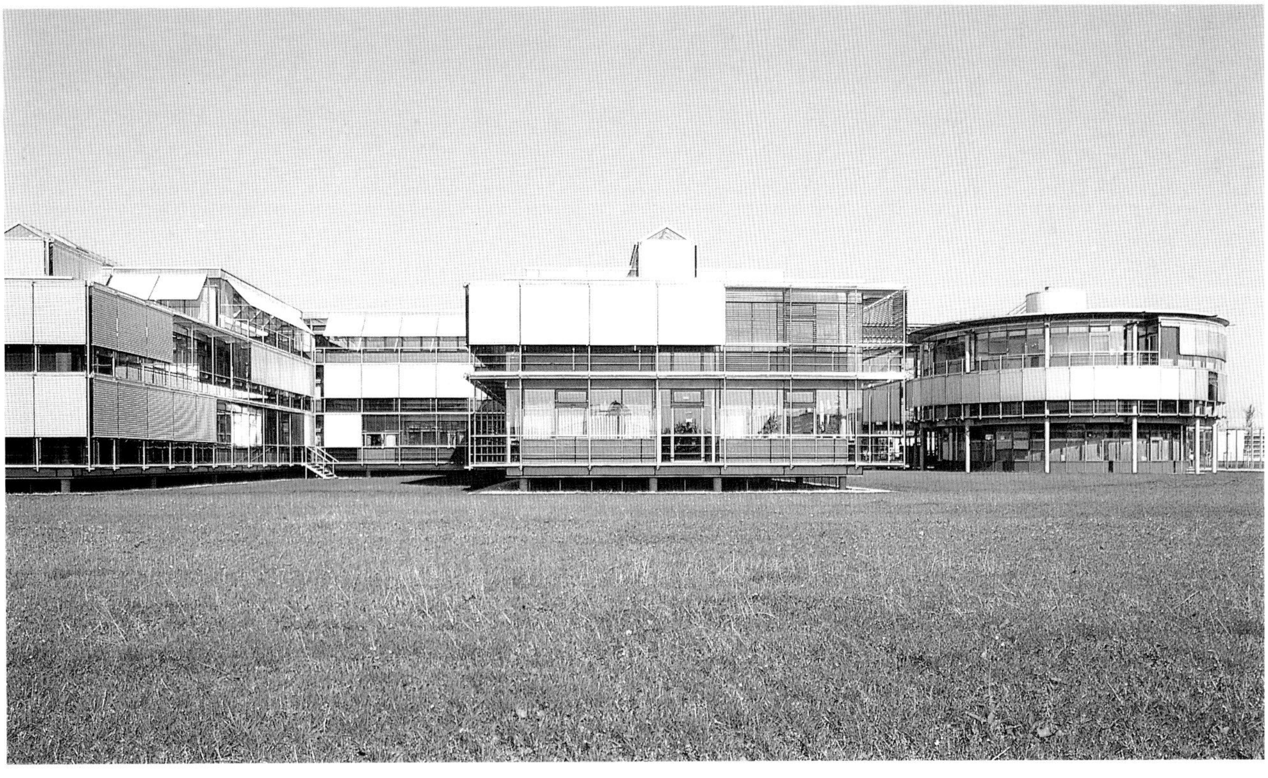

BANGERT AND SCHOLZ
ORIGINATED AS BANGERT JANSEN SCHOLZ SCHULTES

Schirn am Römerberg Gallery • Frankfurt am Main • 1981–85

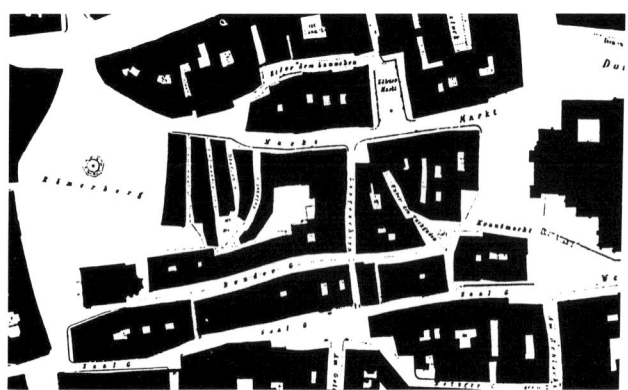

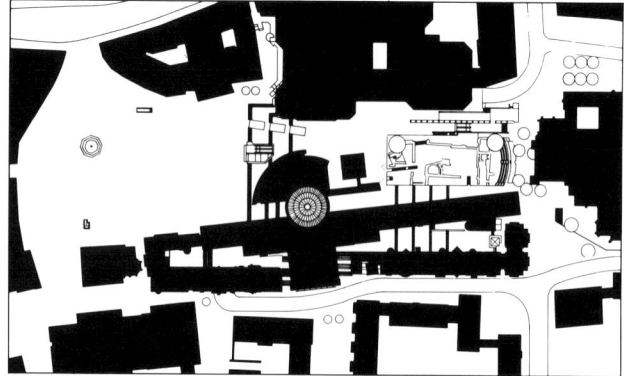

Historic site

Site plan

Schirn, once a term used for butcher shops in the center of the medieval city, is now the name of a public building project devoted to a range of cultural activities. This prior use determines the project's singular character. The commission presented an unusual opportunity to turn a first-class site between Frankfurt's Cathedral and Römer—the historic city hall—into a piece of urban planning that could be experienced as a historical location, not by carefully balancing old and new but by provoking a many-sided, dialectical relationship between the site's historical strata and architectural elements. One significant goal of the project was to use history to discover a new identity for the location, to reveal the history of the city and efforts to come to terms with it, thus preserving it and integrating it into a complex harmony: to use architecture to create a place which people can call their home.

The flight of steps and the expanse between the Cathedral and the Römer are the topographical basis of the project. Correction of and compensation for grade changes while producing a geometrically unified form (excluding the lower-level Historical Garden) was required. The colonnade of the gallery building forms a southern wall to the square and offers a covered passage between the Cathedral and the nearby St. Nicholas Church. The Schirntreff meeting point is an arc in plan with a "table" inside that forms an island within the public circulation area and creates a lane between itself and the gallery building. The Schirntreff interior spreads out toward the square for complimentary cultural activities. The multi-purpose building is a square block with a barrel-vaulted roof; an assembly area emphasizes the cross-shaped plan and has a view toward the Main River. A cylindrical tower with a glazed roof and interior circular galleries both forms the centerpoint of the Schirn, symbolizing its public nature, and provides free passage. Town houses of medieval size on Saalgasse Lane offer a contrast to the public building. These residences complement the contours of the block and recall the site's historical layout. *Dietrich Bangert*

Worm's eye axonometric

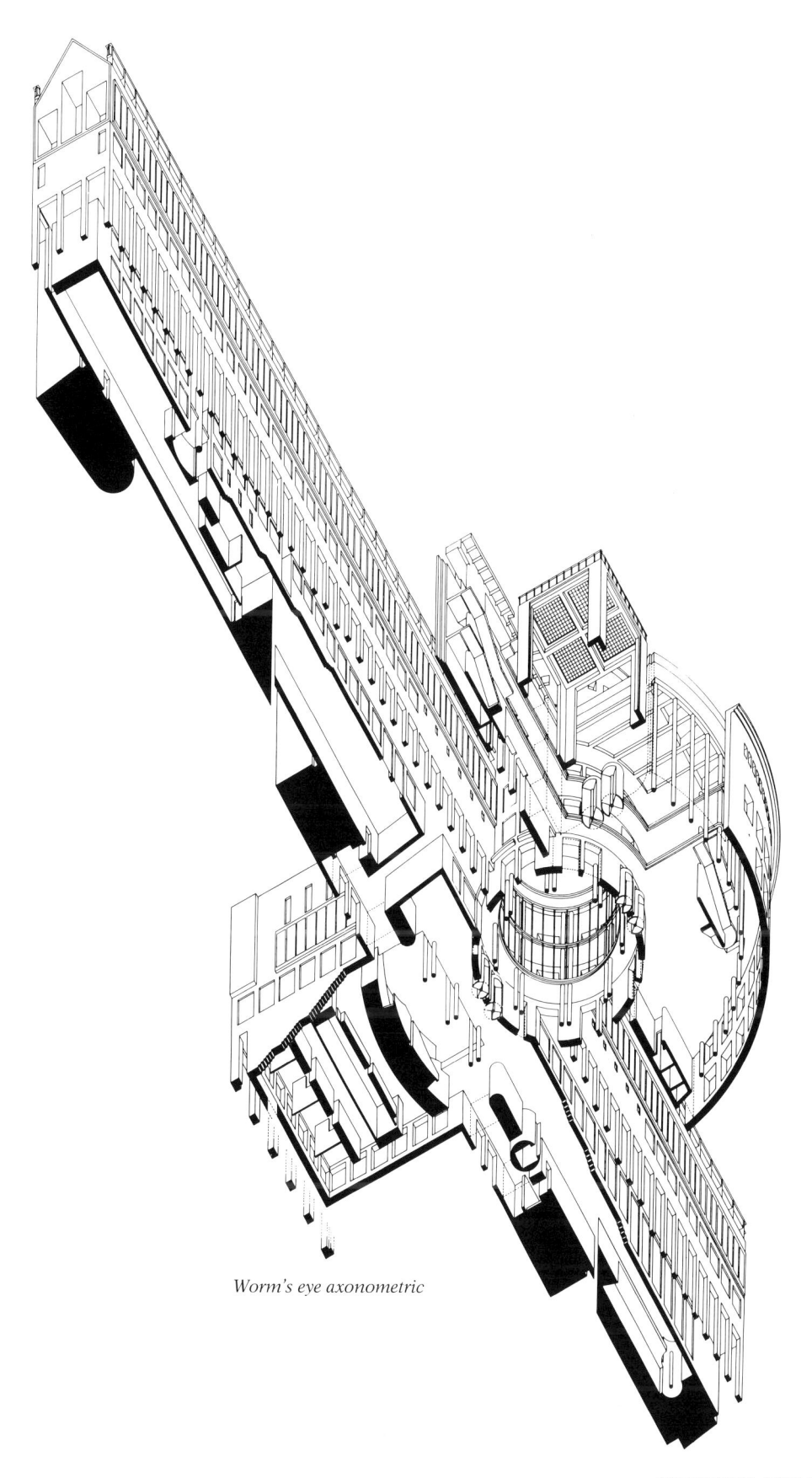

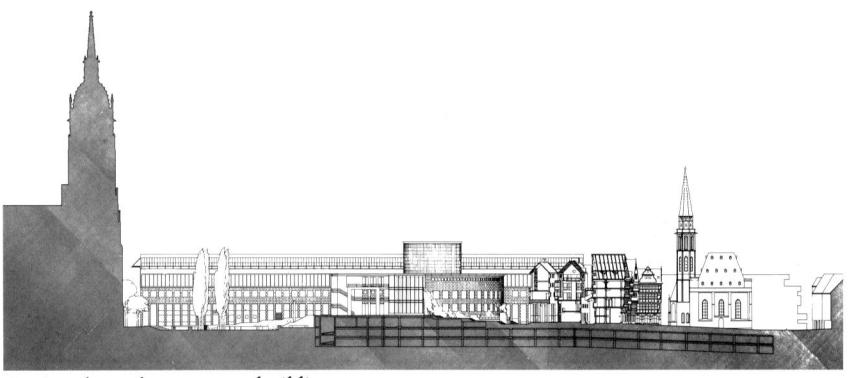

Section through apartment buildings

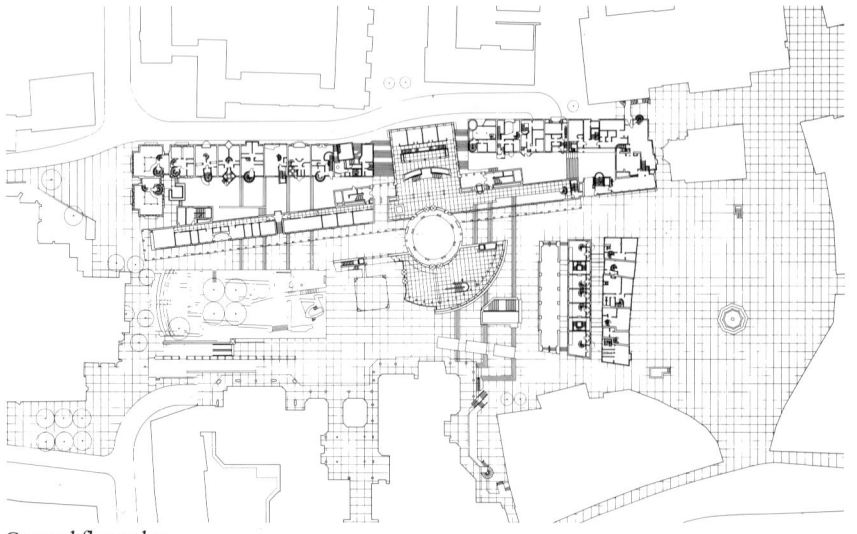

Ground floor plan

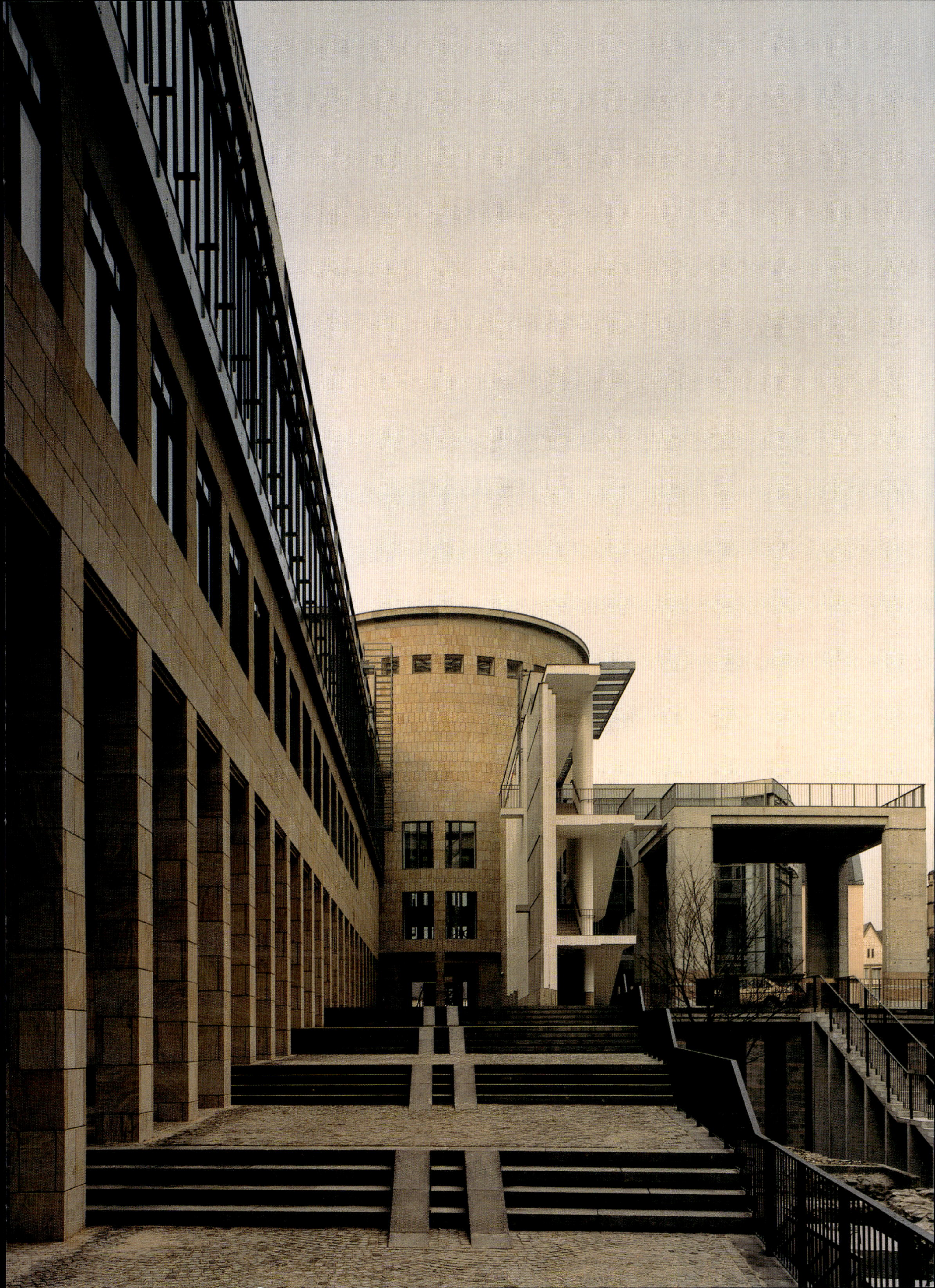

High School Extension • Berlin-Neukölln • 1988–90

The site of the Albert Einstein High School is on the southwestern edge of the Hufeisen housing development in Britz, part of the Neukölln district. The aim in the extension was to imitate the row-house to four-story character of the housing development, which is oriented mainly on an east-west axis. A further purpose was to develop the structure of the extension as a space-defining element and to site it as a fundamental part of the overall project. The extension is a three-story structure with direct connections to all floors of the original high school. As a result of the semi-elliptical, extended structure and the efficient planning, the usefulness of the high school has been considerably improved.
Bangert and Scholz

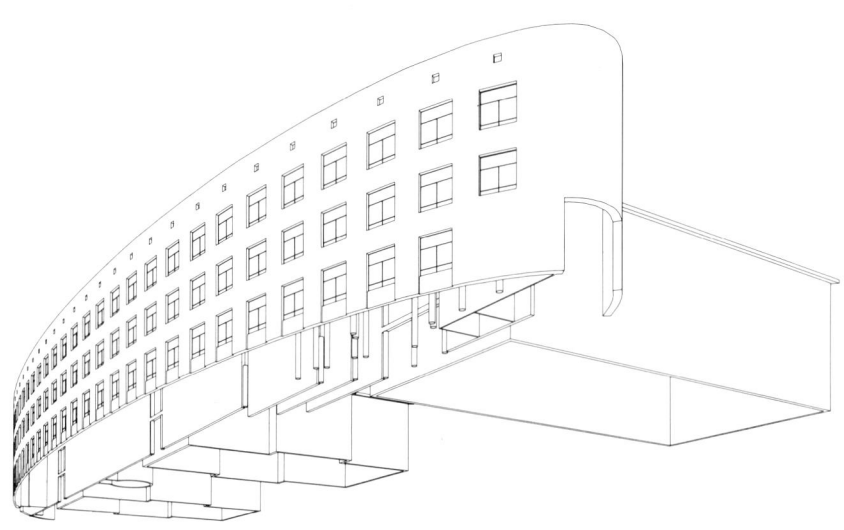

Worm's eye isometric

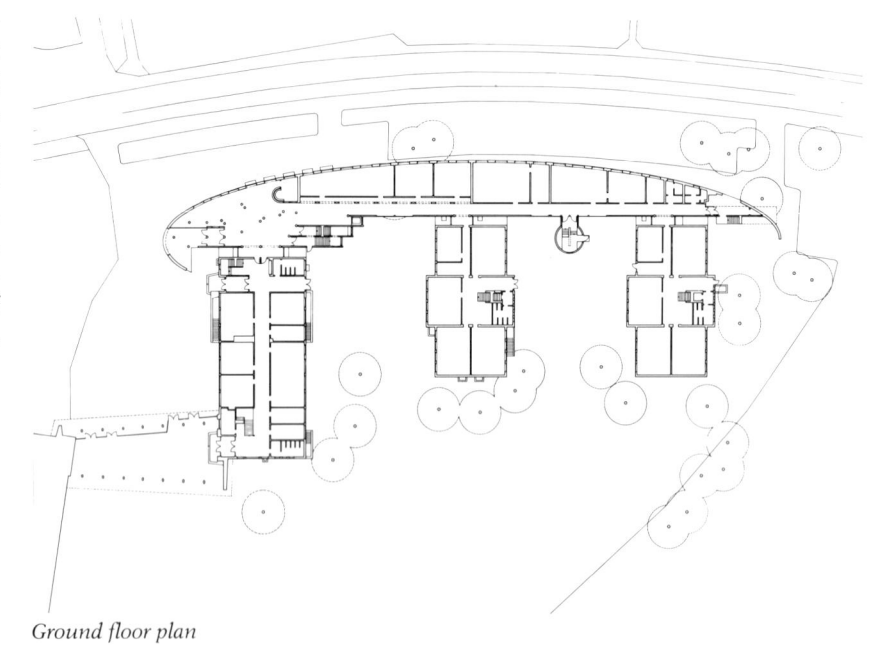

Ground floor plan

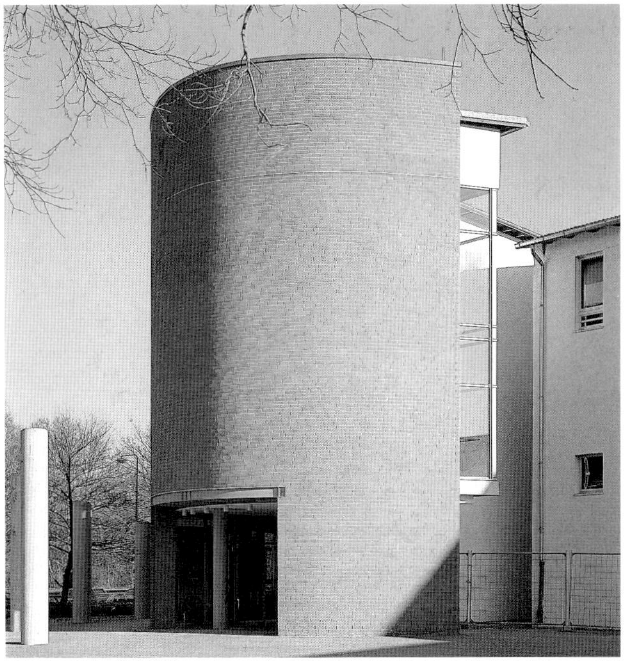

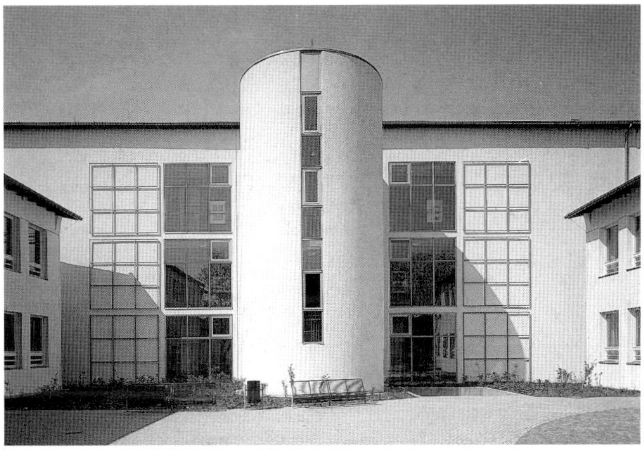

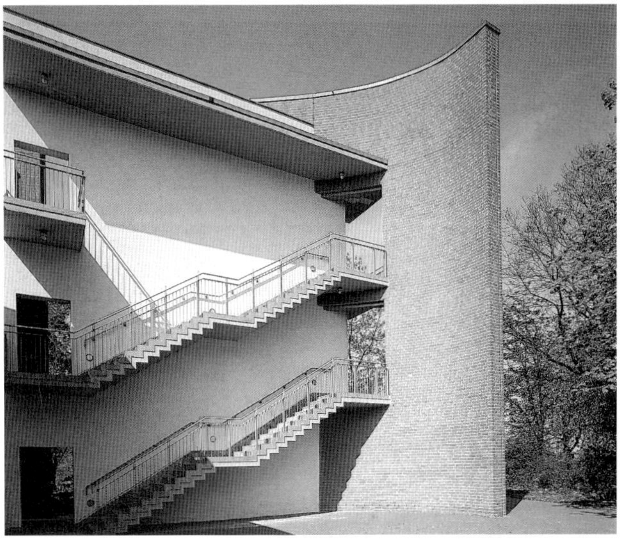

BEHNISCH AND PARTNER
German Postal Museum • Frankfurt am Main • 1984–90

On Schaumainkai, next to the older Staedel Museum, several new museum buildings have been erected, including a film museum, architecture museum, and crafts museum. With these buildings the city of Frankfurt is creating a "museum bank" on the Main River, facing the city center; the Museum of the Federal German Post Office is one of these. The overall site was previously occupied by large villas with gardens, and the city authorities decided that this historical character should be preserved.

Thus, an old villa is now used for the museum's administrative offices. Since this left only a relatively small portion of the site for the extensive museum, major exhibition areas had to be located on two floors beneath the gardens. Above the garden level rises a slender building, containing additional exhibition space and harmonizing with the villa's cubic form. The under- and aboveground sections of the museum are linked by a glass structure. Additionally, the Federal German Post and Telecommunications Office intends to exhibit state-of-the-art communications media in the museum. Therefore, the new building is also intended to project the image of an efficient, technologically innovative organization.
Günter Behnisch

66   BEHNISCH AND PARTNER

BEHNISCH AND PARTNER 67

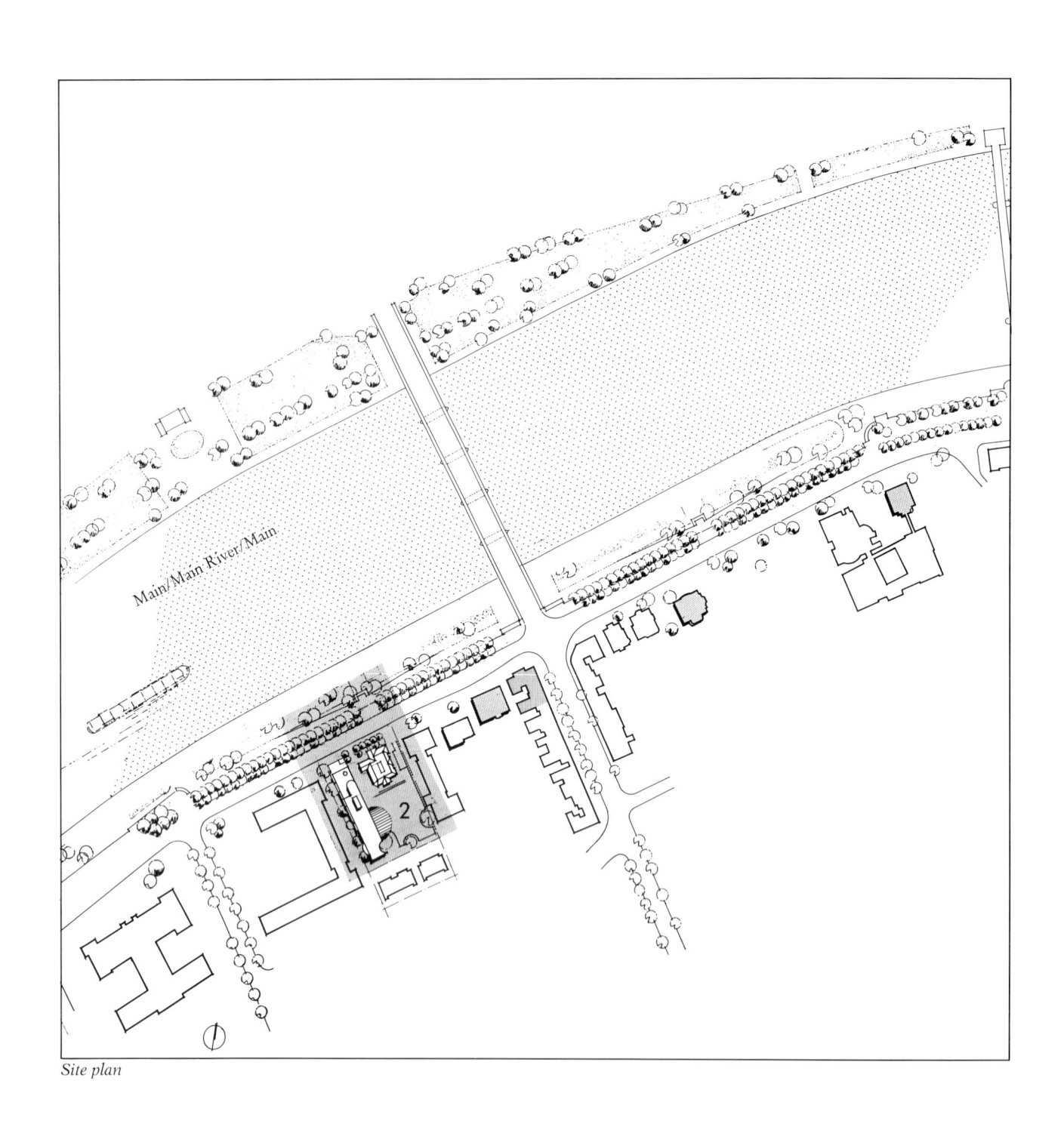

Site plan

68   BEHNISCH AND PARTNER

Second floor plan

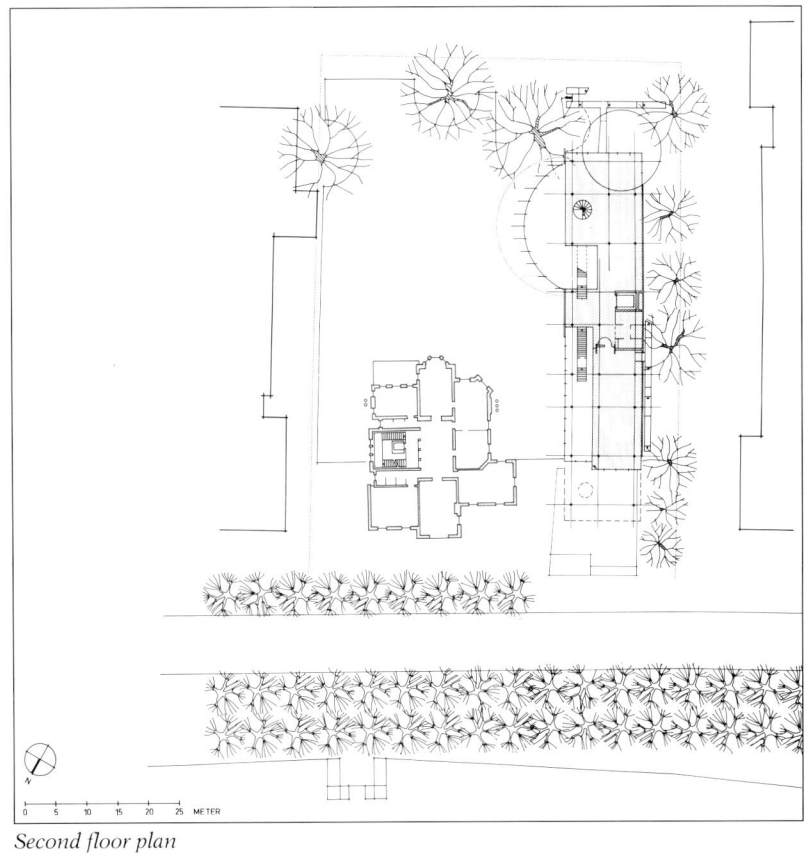

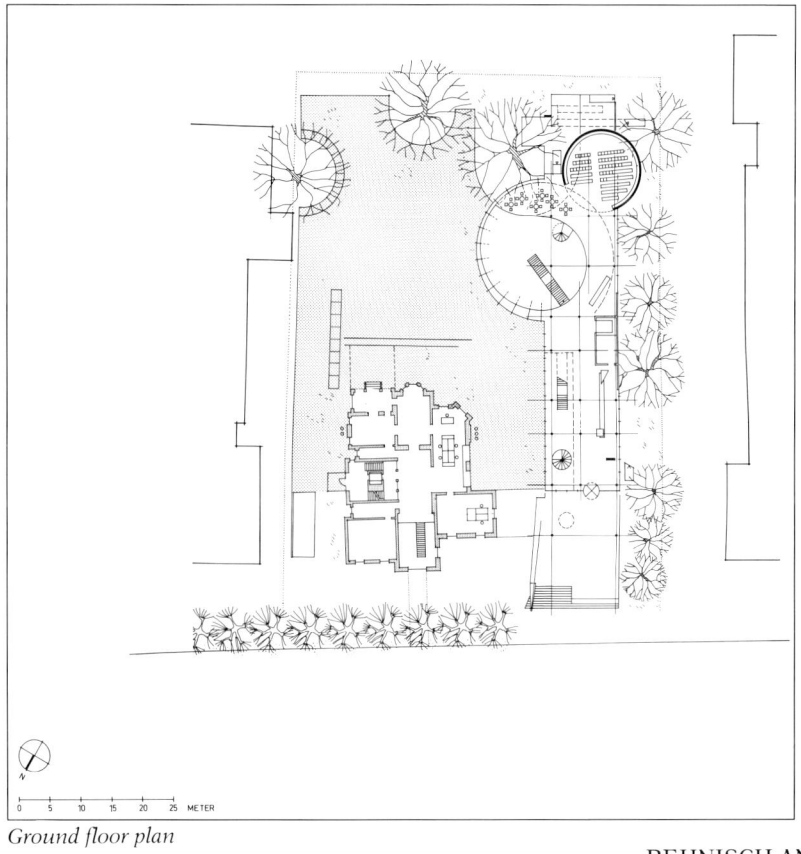

Ground floor plan

BEHNISCH AND PARTNER 69

Bank Expansion • Frankfurt am Main • 1989–92

The existing German Federal Bank lies on the edge of the city, away from the tall, competing buildings of downtown Frankfurt. In addition, its design diminishes any connection with the scale of neighboring residential buildings. The relationship in the area between this building, traffic structures, a communications tower, and the large, open greenspaces will be strengthened by the extension of the Grüneburgpark and the Miquel Gardens (bordering on the southwest) across the site. A large reflecting pool will be built, and the roads will narrow around the trees.

The expansion will feature a large, three-floor ring of offices raised above the ground. This element hovers over the site and should convey the impression that the park continues underneath. Strictly secured areas, such as the data processing department, will be at grade and only one or two stories tall, well below treetop level. The office ring will be bound with the communications tower and the original German Federal Bank building into a memorable ensemble.
Günter Behnisch

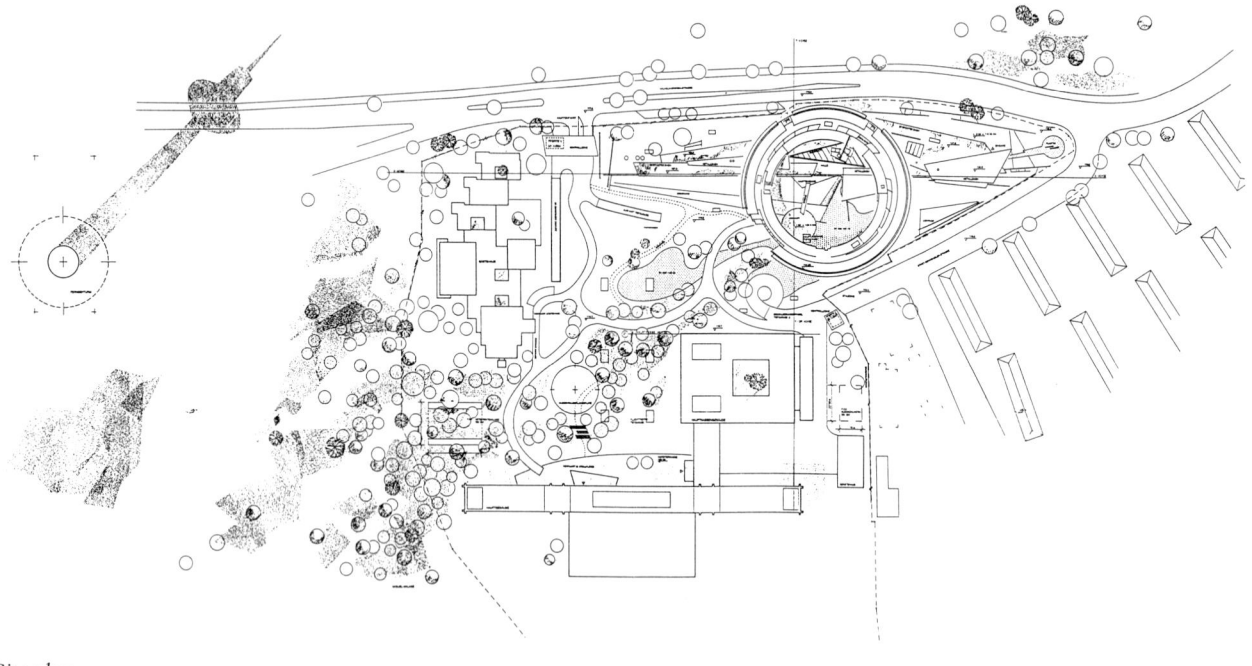

Site plan

BEHNISCH AND PARTNER 71

Catholic University Library • Eichstätt • 1980–87

Eichstätt is the seat of one of the oldest bishoprics in Germany. The small town in the valley of the Altmühl River was destroyed in the Thirty Years War, like many towns in Germany, and reconstructed in the baroque style of the Counter-Reformation. The town survived World War II undamaged, and thus offers a historical townscape with its largest buildings, principally the Catholic church, in the French baroque style.

The town is home to the only Catholic university in Germany. The university needed a building for a central library, not in the town, but on the approach to it, in the meadows on the riverbank. Thus the library took most of its references from nature rather than from the built environment of the town: more openness, formal freedom, and consideration for the surrounding natural shapes, fewer restrictions and obligations, less geometric ordering. The project offered a chance to develop more of a natural order than would a building in the city.

The design frees the building like an island in a sea of greenery; trees in the meadows reach right up to the walls. The relationships of the library to the river, meadow, access paths, landscape, and town were the factors from which the siting of the building was derived. The selection of the materials, structure, and form were similarly derived. Thus, the library is no monolithic, formally harmonized unity; it is rather a patchwork of many distinct shapes.
Günter Behnisch

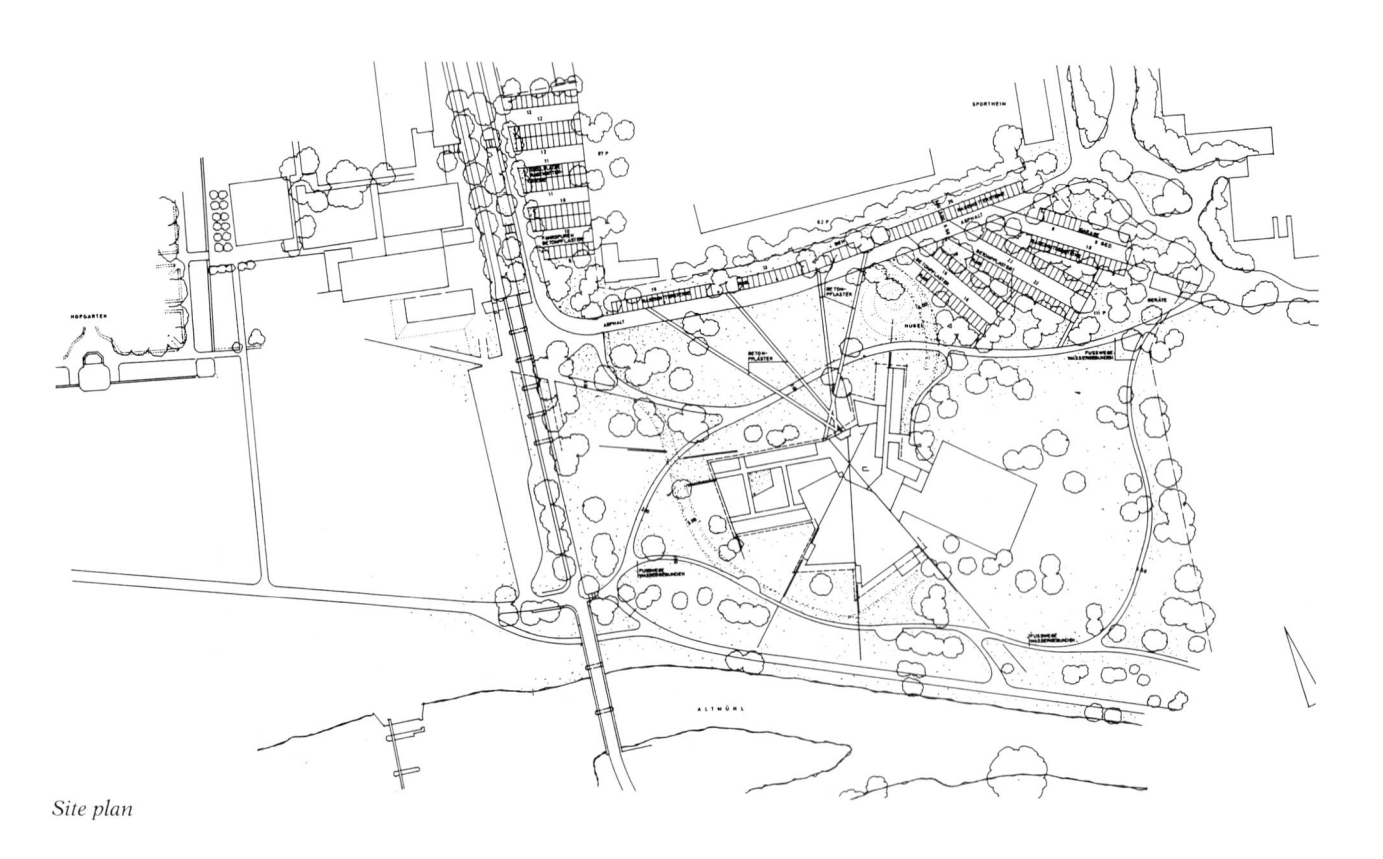

Site plan

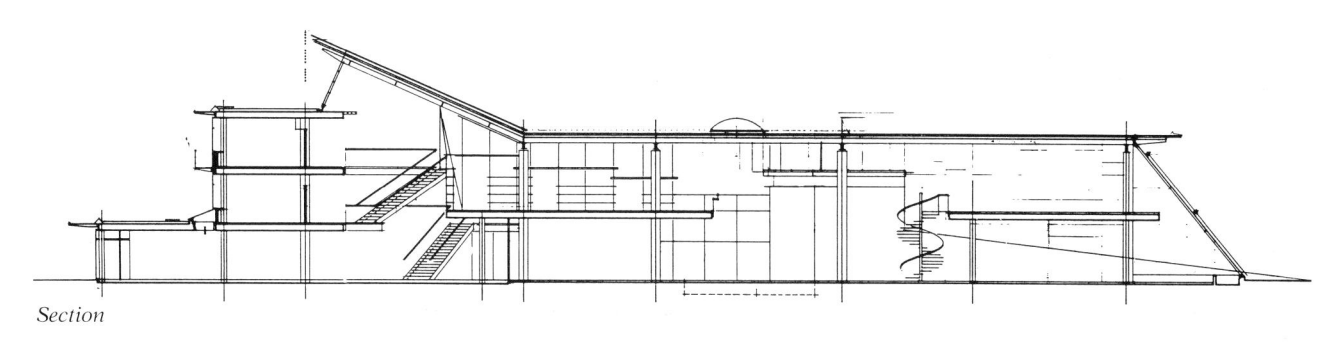

Section

BEHNISCH AND PARTNER 73

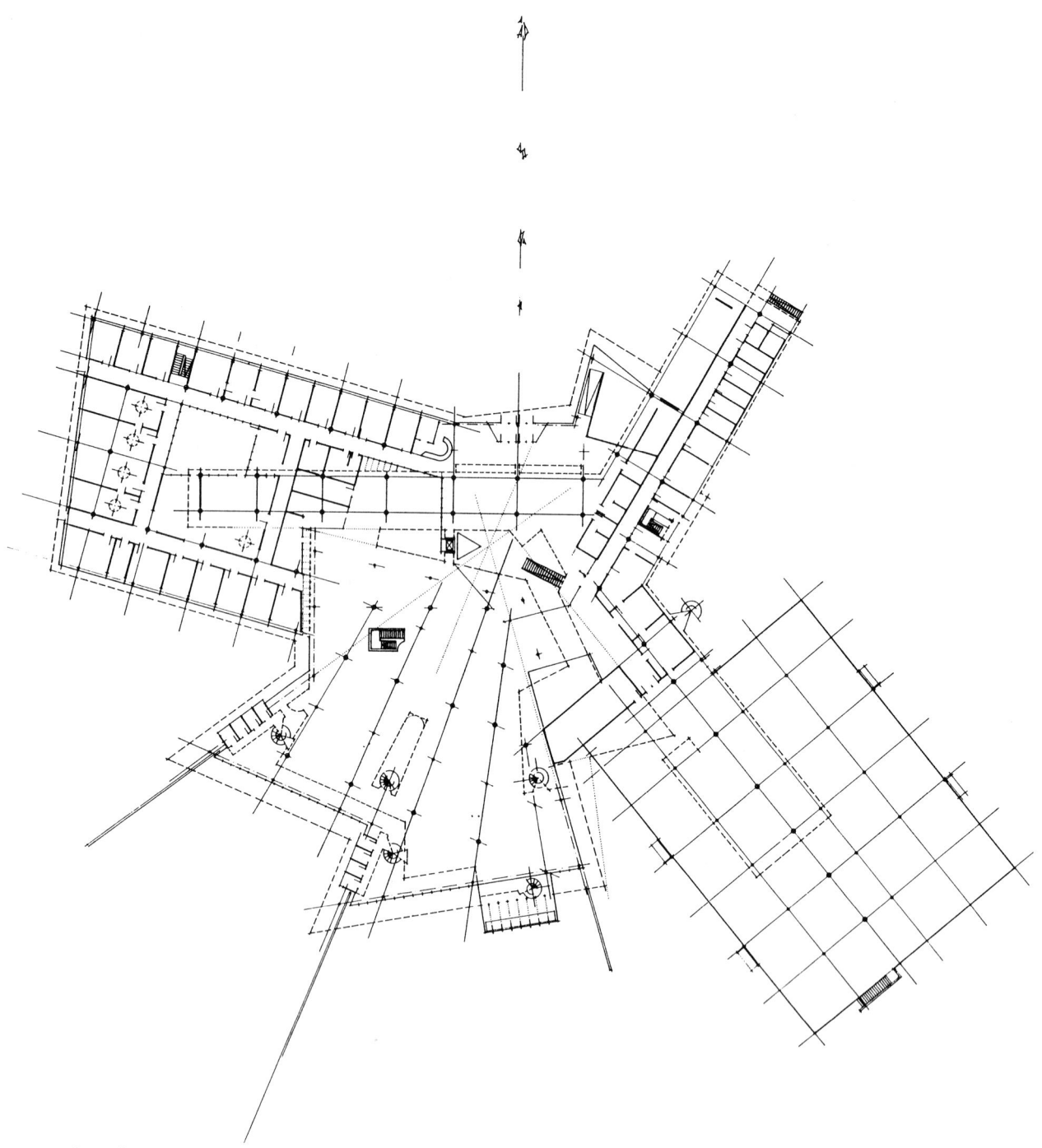

Ground floor plan

74 BEHNISCH AND PARTNER

BEHNISCH AND PARTNER   75

BÖGE AND LINDNER
DG Bank • Hannover • 1986–90

This property had become a forsaken part of the urban fabric in recent years for a number of reasons: because it was behind the train station, because it was cut off from the city center by both an elevated street and the six-lane Berliner Allee, and because the surrounding neighborhood was unattractive and unsafe. To improve and upgrade the area significantly required a building that could shape the locale's character, which explains the distinctly urban bent of the DG Bank. All areas of the site that remain unbuilt are accessible to the public and were designed in conjunction with the open city lots to create a coherent whole.

The main body of the bank not only accepts the discontinuous urban landscape, but makes it the focus of the design. Stretched out along the Berliner Allee, the building forms a street edge. The proportion and scale of the facade reflect the size of Hannover. The curved back of this part of the building creates a setting for the adjoining cube, which picks up the blocky shapes of the surrounding residential neighborhood. The interior spaces are characterized by openness and transparency. Spacious halls with bridges and stairways, natural light coming through glass roofs, and interesting sightlines between various areas are all typical of the interior and create many use and communications options. Interior details are characterized by simplicity and high quality materials. The bank also has spacious public areas for special events, concerts, lectures, and exhibits. *Böge and Lindner*

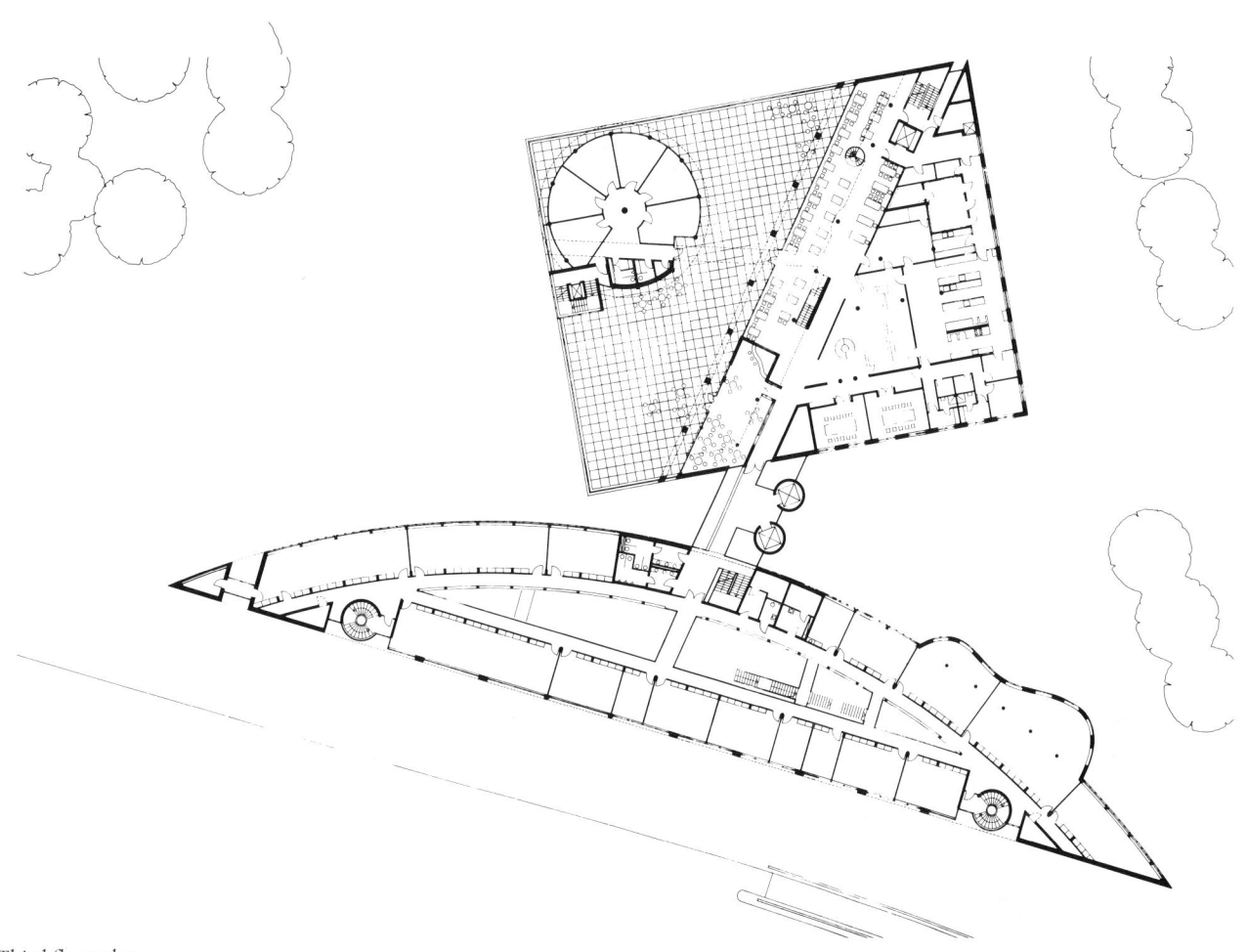

Third floor plan

Section

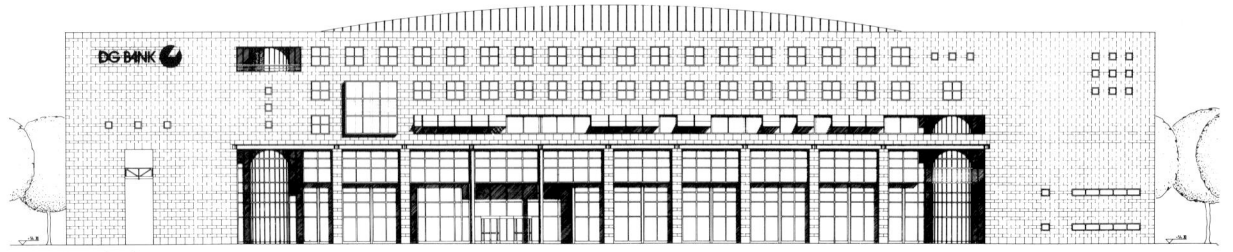

South elevation

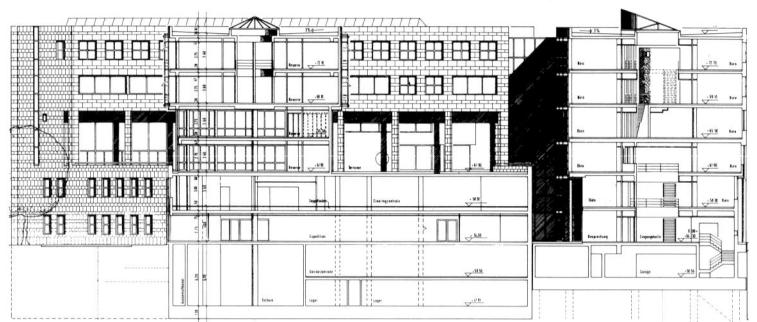

Section

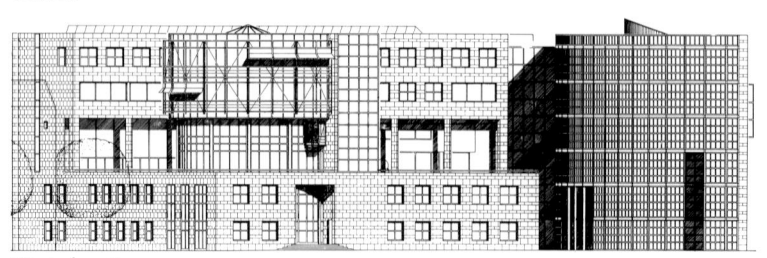

West elevation

78 BÖGE AND LINDNER

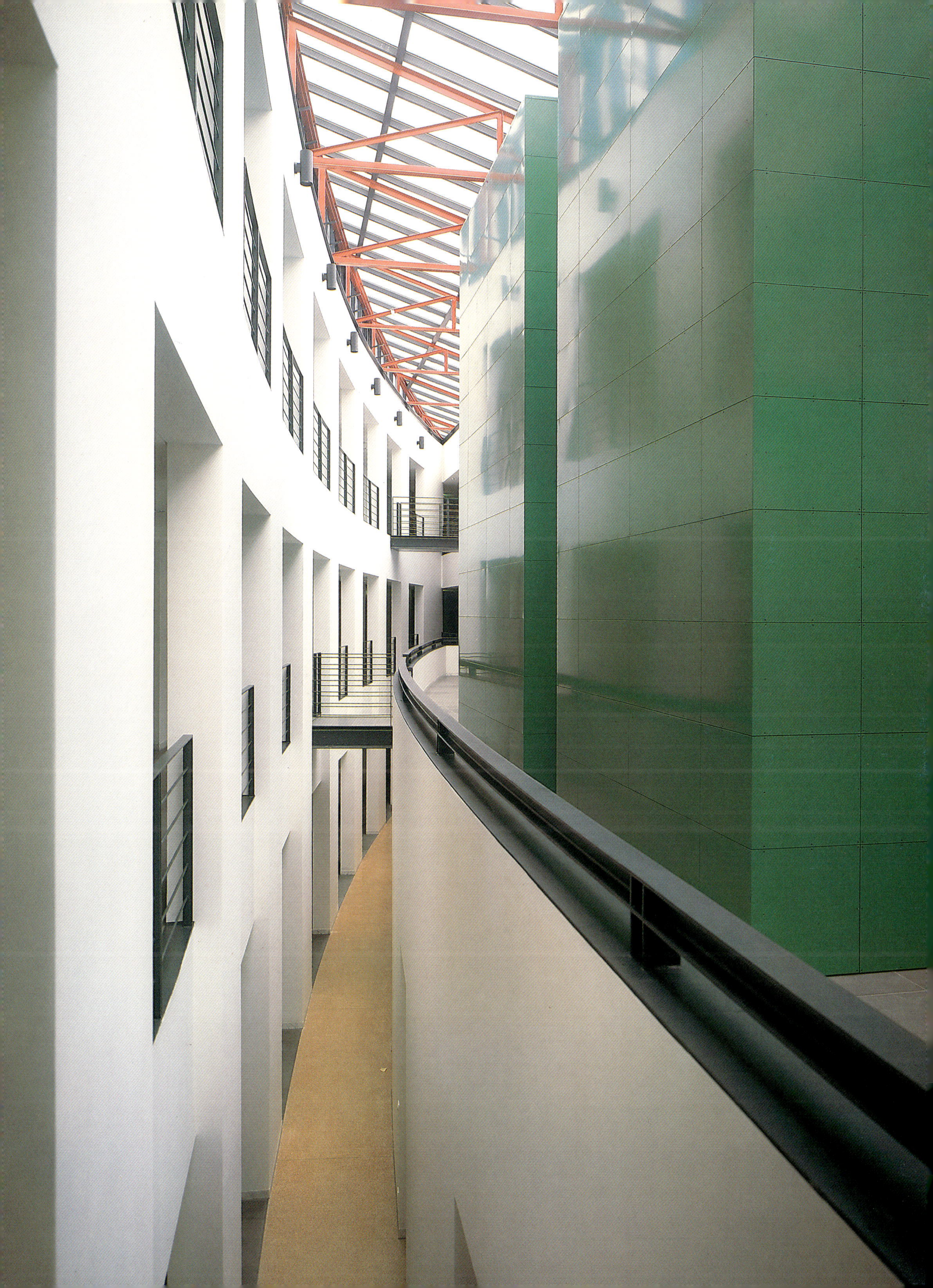

GOTTFRIED BÖHM
Deutsche Bank • Luxembourg • 1987–91

The Deutsche Bank is supposed to convey not only qualities like solidity, security, and trust, but also agility, mirth, and imagination. The cubic building volume, flanked by bold tiers of columns and crowned by a landscape of glazed cones, expresses those qualities without using sculptural or other allegorical representations, as did many older bank structures. Tradition and progress, preservation and development, statics and dynamics are not opposed in this building, but fuse into a harmonious unity.

The bright, cheerful roofscape stands in stark contrast to the compact exterior; it appears that the lively interior has broken through the austere cube both on the roof and at the entryway, giving rise to a mixture of classically ascetic geometry and vital diversity. Inside the main space is a cylindrical great hall, lighted naturally from above. Here, the interpenetration of the solidly grounded cube and the ascending cylinder creates an unusual interplay of static and dynamic forces. Open galleries are reached from upward-spiraling flights of stairs; vertical-horizontal light guides, which can change dramatically in color and mood, take up the interplay, further intensifying the impression of dynamism.
Gottfried Böhm

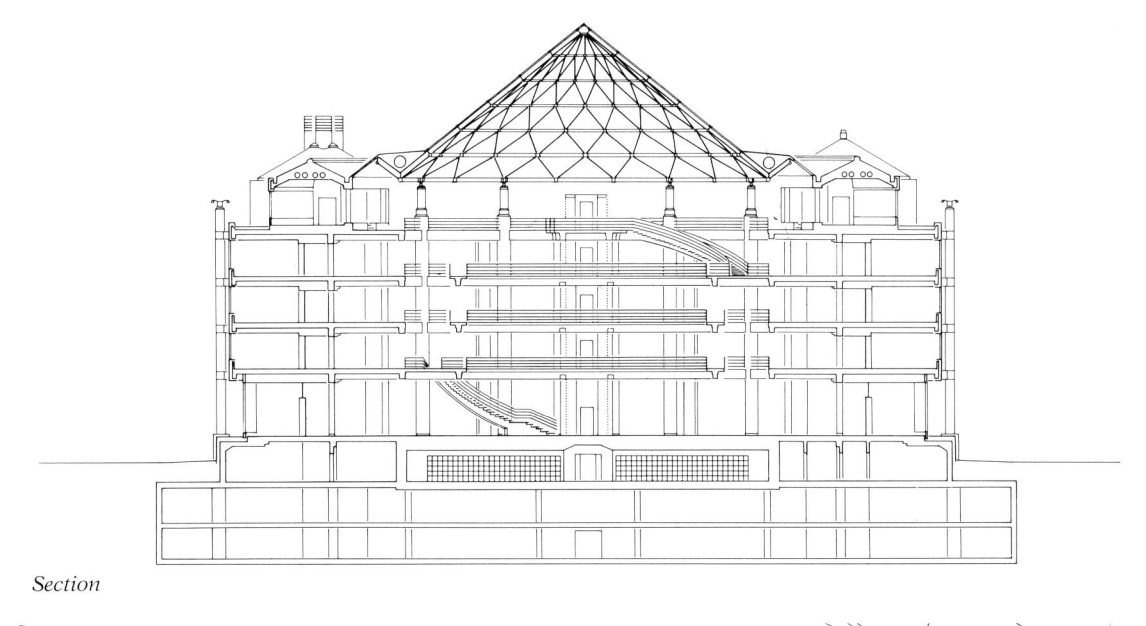

Section

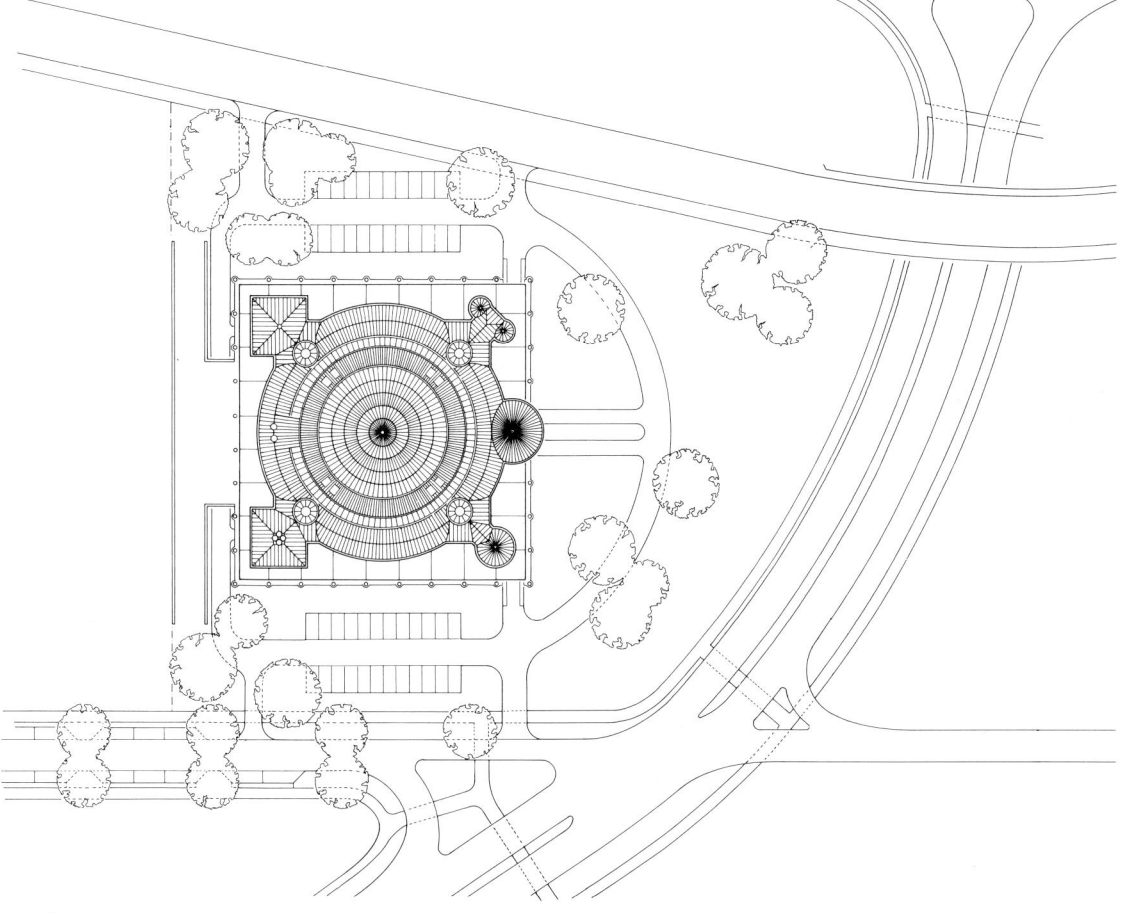

Site plan

GOTTFRIED BÖHM

Second and third floor plans

Fifth floor/roof plan

Ground floor plan

Fourth floor plan

GOTTFRIED BÖHM

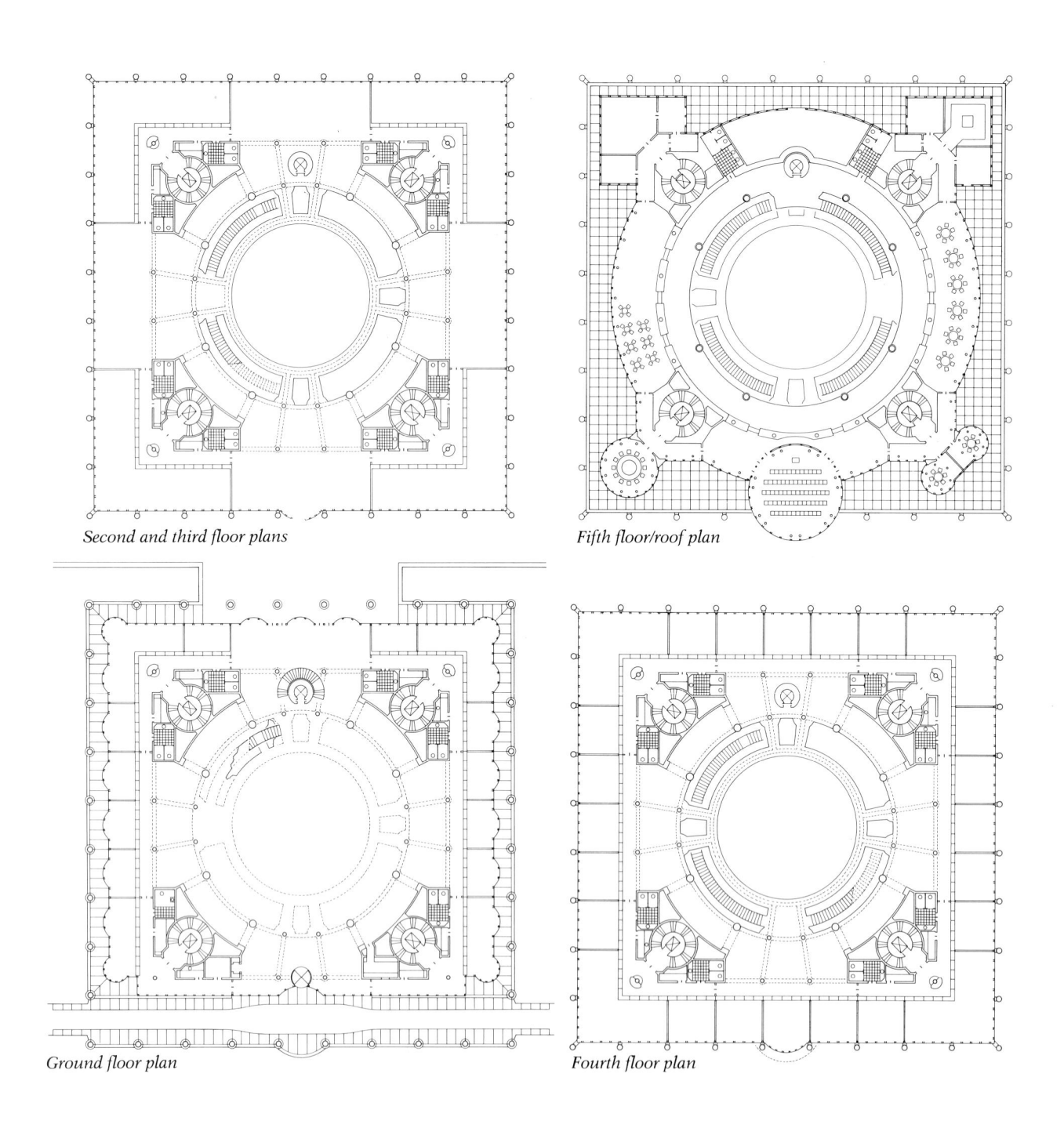

GOTTFRIED BÖHM 83

Saarbrücken Palace Restoration • Saarbrücken • 1981–89

After its construction in the 1740s by master builder Friedrich Joachim Stengel, this baroque palace underwent a long history of change: fire, plunder, remodeling, addition, renovation. Before the present restoration, which included the north and south wings and a new west wing and central pavilion, Hugo Dihm had, in 1872, redone the east side and an earlier, French Renaissance version of the pavilion (demolished for this project, as it was stylistically and proportionally at odds with the original); before that, Johann Adam Knipper had reconstructed the palace in 1810 after it was damaged by fire during the French Revolution. It is therefore interesting to examine the relationship between the restoration and the original.

The most spectacular section is the central pavilion, rebuilt to Stengel's dimensions: its skeletal, articulated, glass-and-metal facade contrasts with the smooth, baroque side wings. The pavilion has as its centerpiece a hall that seemingly floats within its glazed and mirrored walls. At the entrance to the hall, the entire history of the building is visible: on four sides of a paved court are the new west wing, Knipper's reconstruction of Stengel's original north and south wings, and Dihm's restored east side. As a result of the palace's reconstructions and restorations, only a historian can now tell which section is of what age, and what has been added, changed, or incorporated. This is the ensemble's special character, offering a full range of architectural styles. The mixture could never be a homogeneous work of art, but is rather made up of myriad, coexisting parts.
Gottfried Böhm

GOTTFRIED BÖHM 85

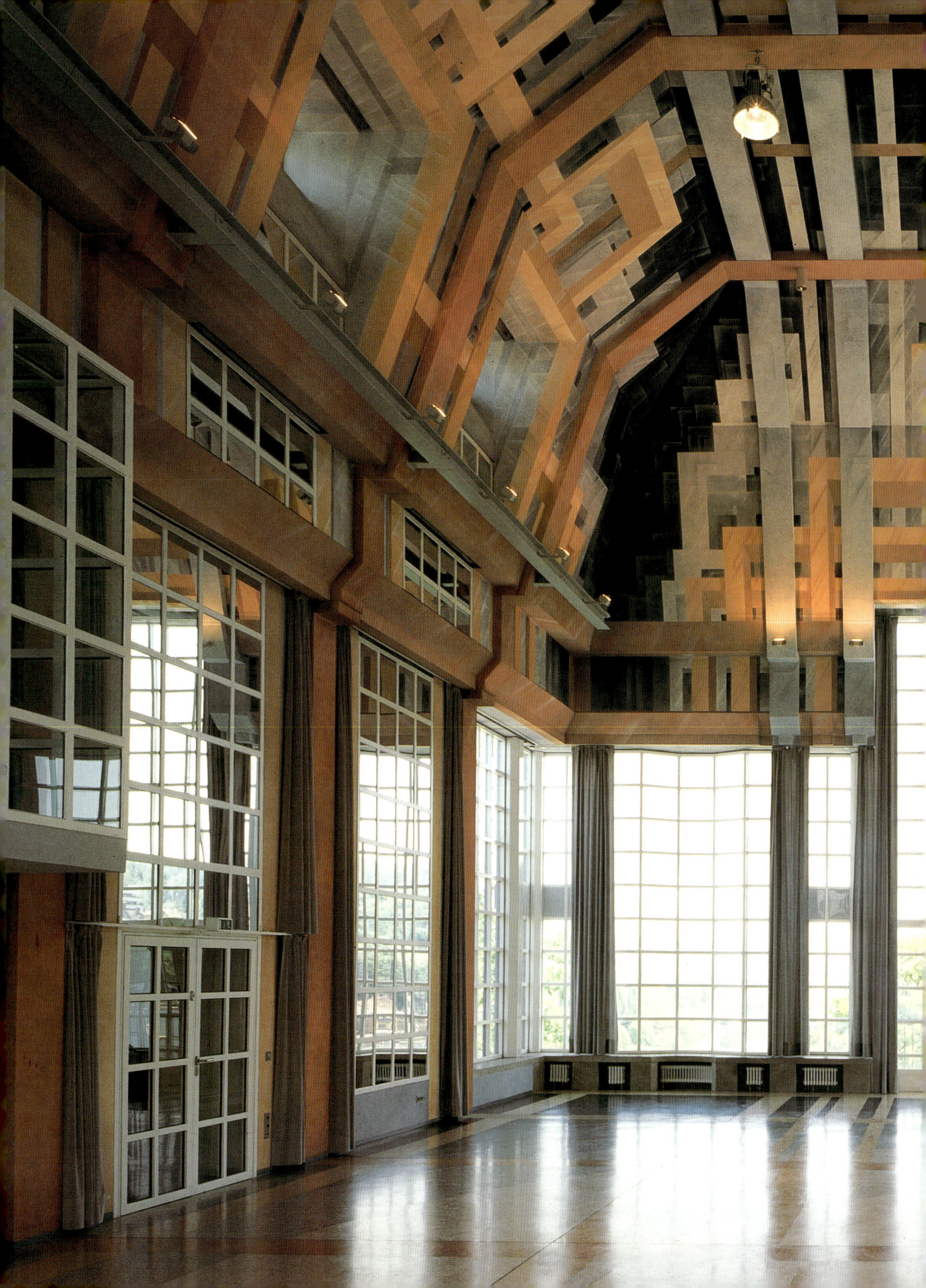

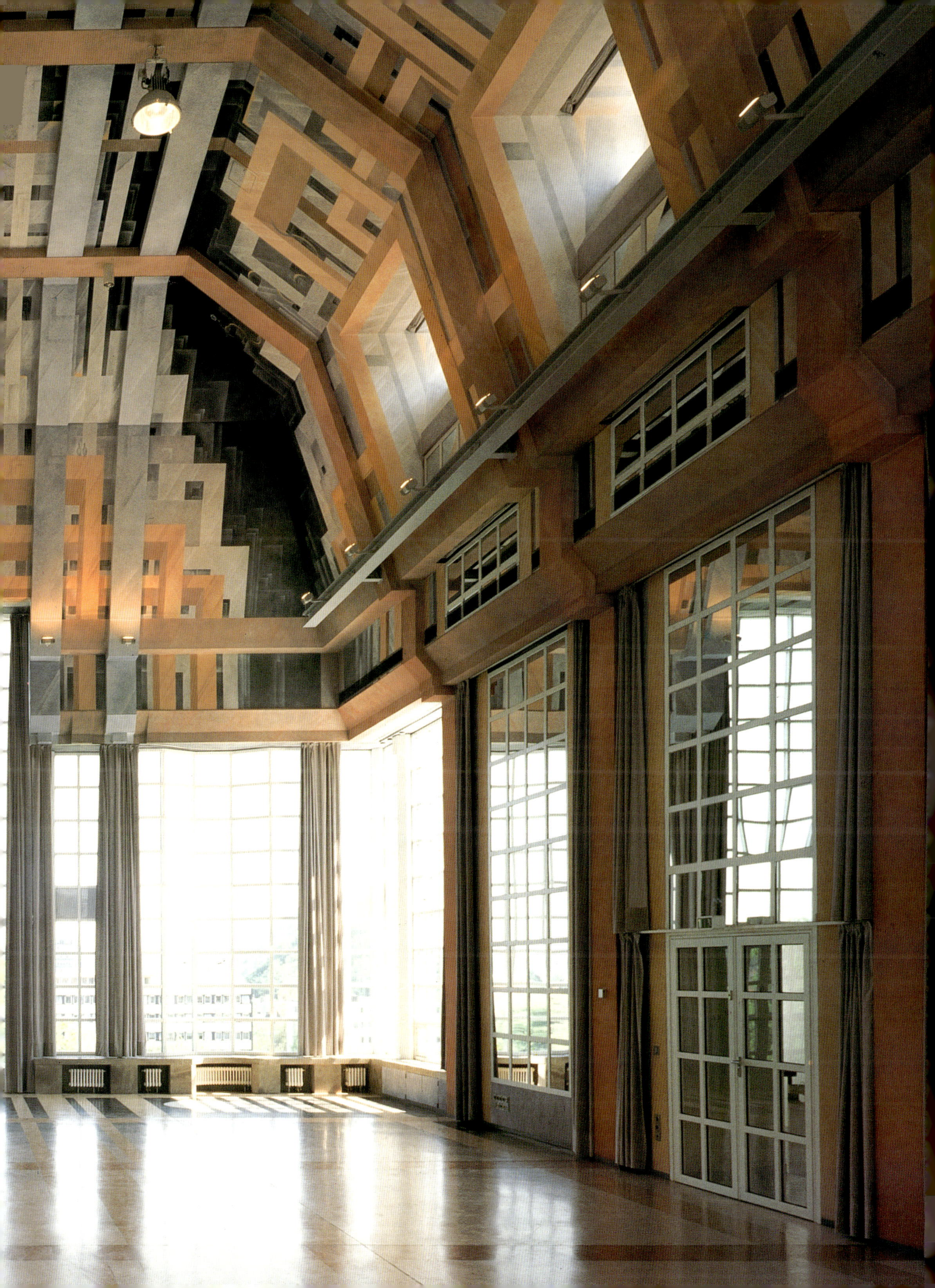

ANDREAS BRANDT AND RUDOLPH BÖTTCHER
Train Station Plaza Roofing • Kassel • 1986–91

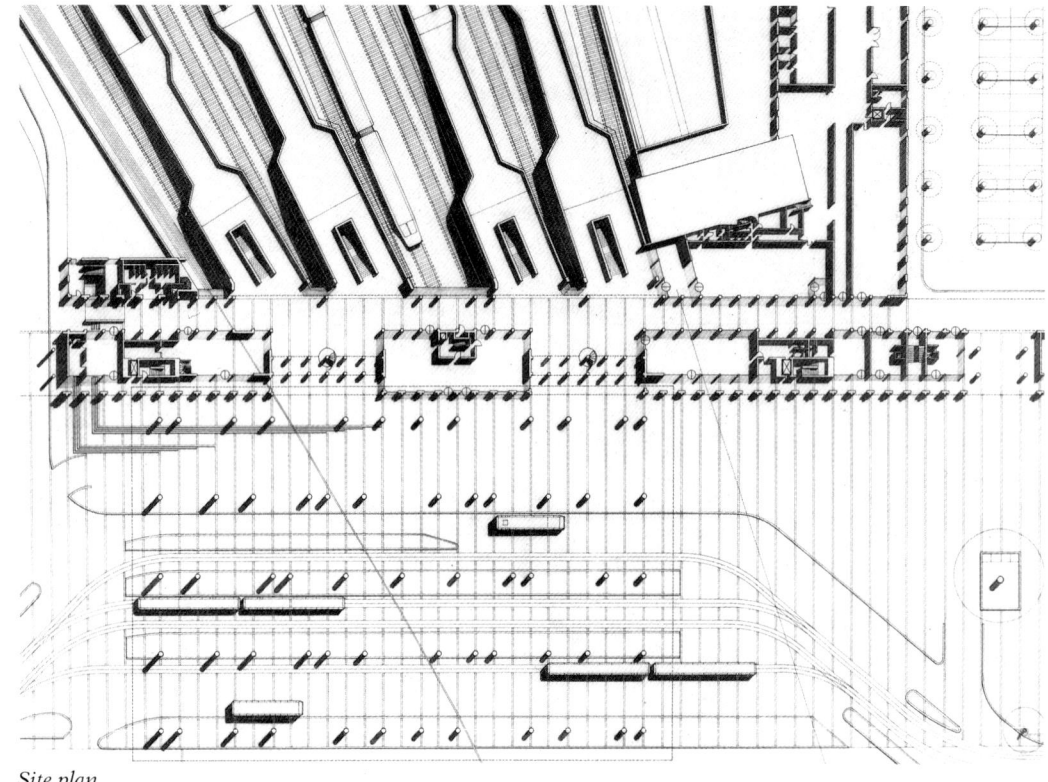

Site plan

The plaza in front of the Kassel train station is in a large niche along the Wilhelmshöher Allee, next to the junction of the street and the rail line. The roof over the plaza is shaped like the inside of a picture frame, a hyperbolic expression of the natural sights that can be seen here.

Fifty-seven columns continuing the pattern of trees planted along the Allee support the roof. The first row of columns relates to the axis along which the Allee trees are planted; the other four rows are positioned to create the impression of looking through a forest. The rows are arrayed at regular 13-meter intervals; within each row, the columns are sited based on an irregular grid of 3.25 meters. (Oak forests planted on the hills around Kassel in the nineteenth century are often so arranged.) The height of the roof was determined by the eaves of the surrounding buildings and by hills to the west of the city.

The plaza roof projects into the Wilhelmshöher Allee. Standing in the square, people who have arrived at the station by train see the silhouette of the western hills. When approached from the local area, the roof marks a spot along the Allee which links Kassel to distant cities. In the winter, when the sun is low in the sky, light penetrates beyond the middle of the roofed area. During the day, light enters through openings above the columns. At night, the columns are lighted from these same openings. The mirror-like, enameled white metal plates turn the roof into an artificial sky. *Andreas Brandt and Rudolph Böttcher*

ANDREAS BRANDT AND RUDOLPH BÖTTCHER

Spanish Square • Hellersdorf • 1991

The project provides a typical urban blend of shopping facilities, commercial and industrial properties, administrative buildings, cultural and leisure facilities, and housing. Altogether the Spanish Square will have a gross area of about 310,000 square meters. The development is a mix of large and small blocks, with squares and a boulevard, alleys and lanes.

The project represents an image of the town in which differing urban cultures intersect. The design repertoire corresponds to the vocabulary which has developed from the history of the European town. Each district is related to an urban typology and thus exerts a particular influence on the shape and atmosphere of the town. The new construction, which will extend beyond the square itself and will be integrated into the existing urban fabric, responds to what is missing today in Hellersdorf to present an autonomous borough within this region of Berlin. *Andreas Brandt and Rudolph Böttcher*

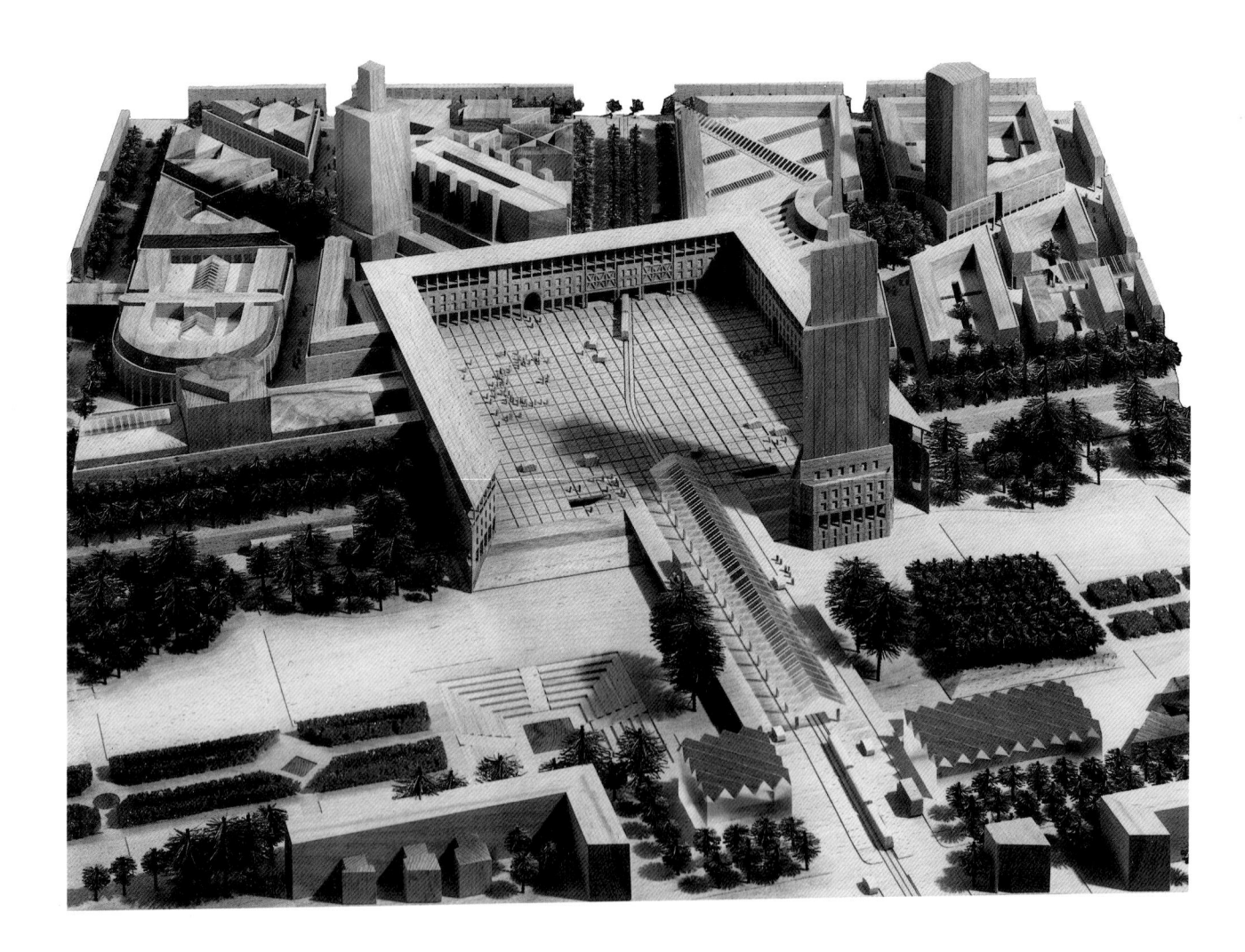

Schematic diagrams

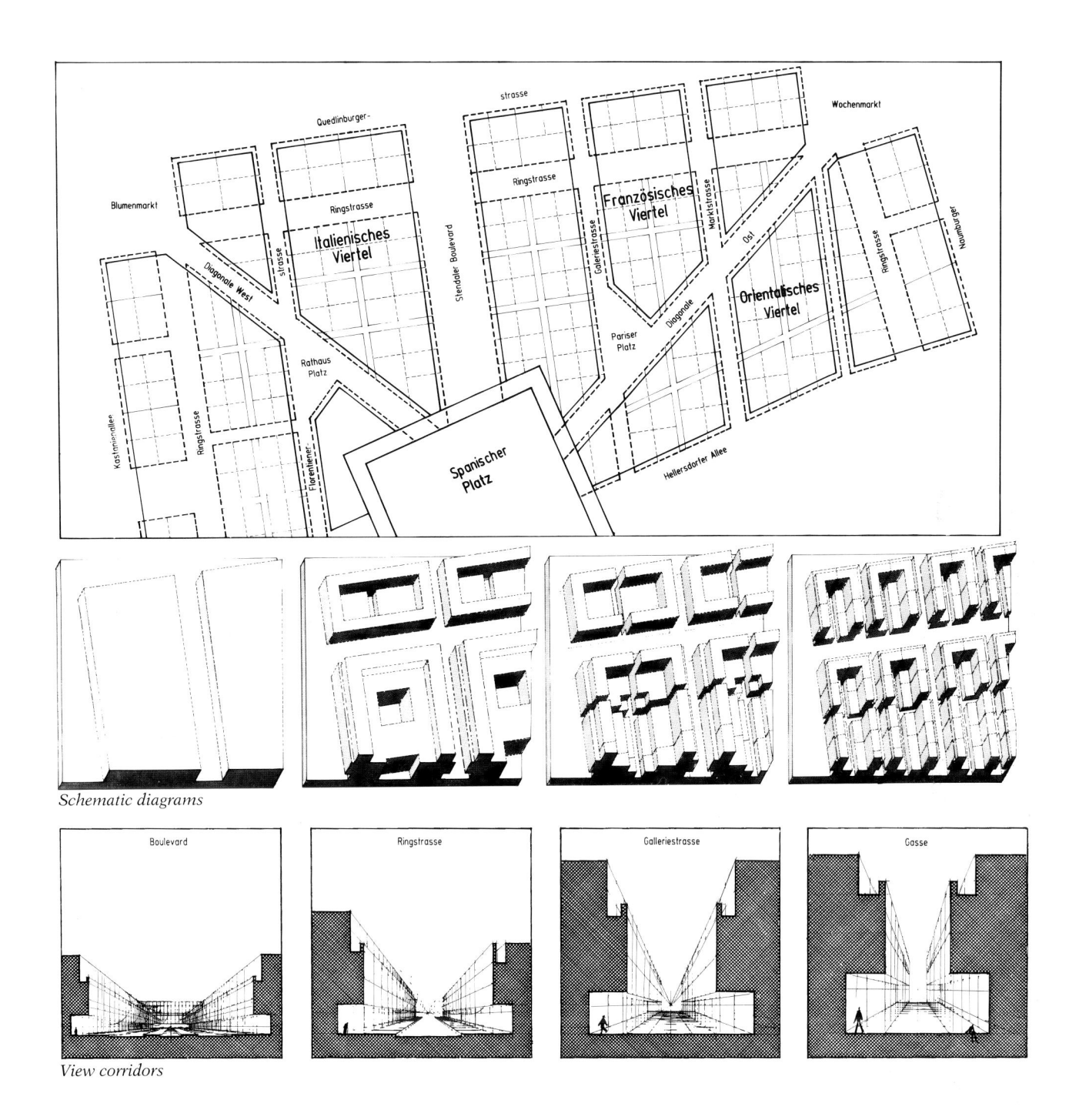

View corridors

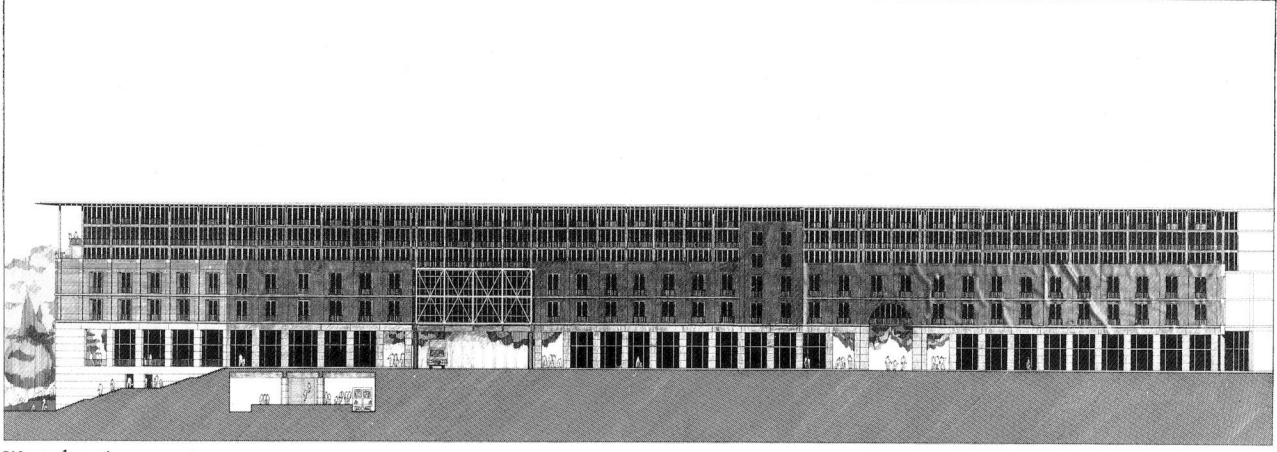

West elevation, court

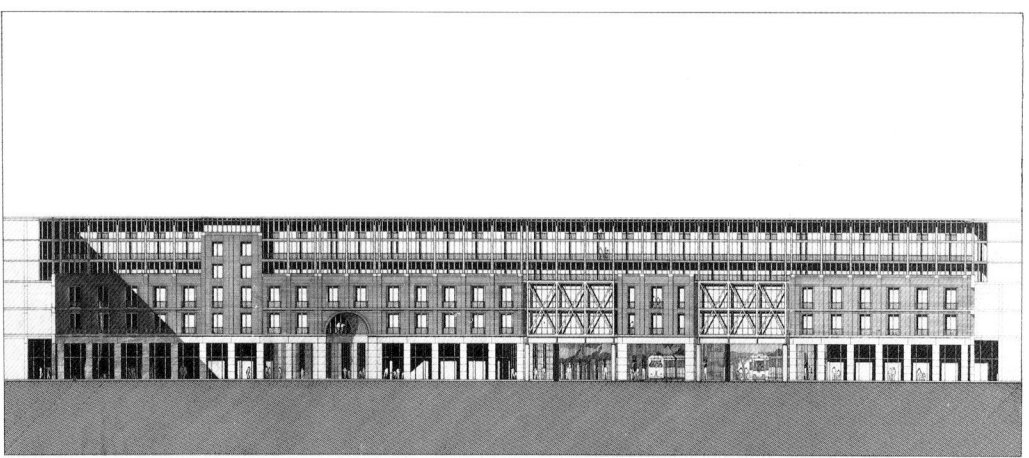

North elevation, court

East elevation, court

92   ANDREAS BRANDT AND RUDOLPH BÖTTCHER

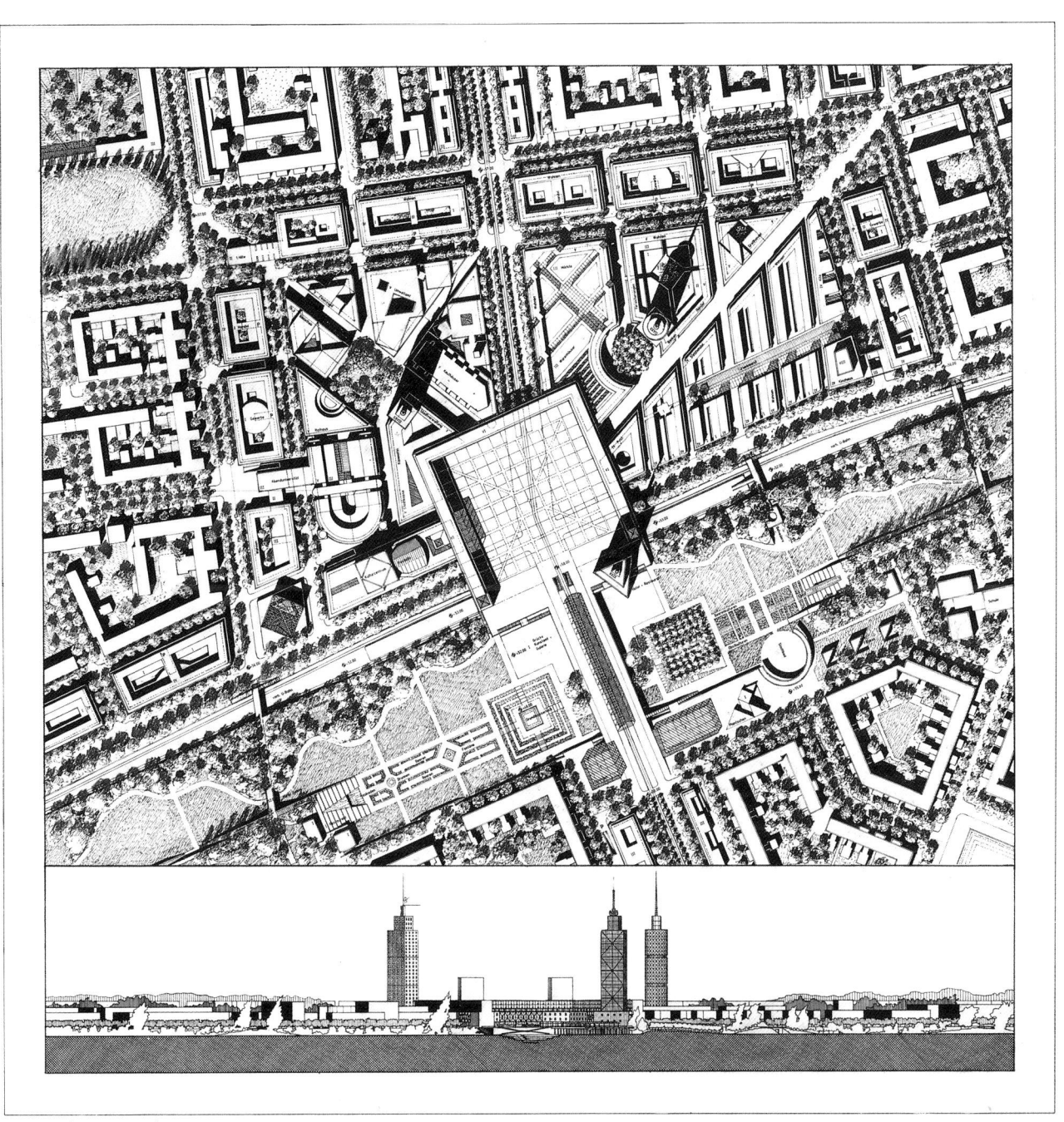

Site rendering/site elevation

EISELE AND FRITZ
Postplatz • Dresden • 1991

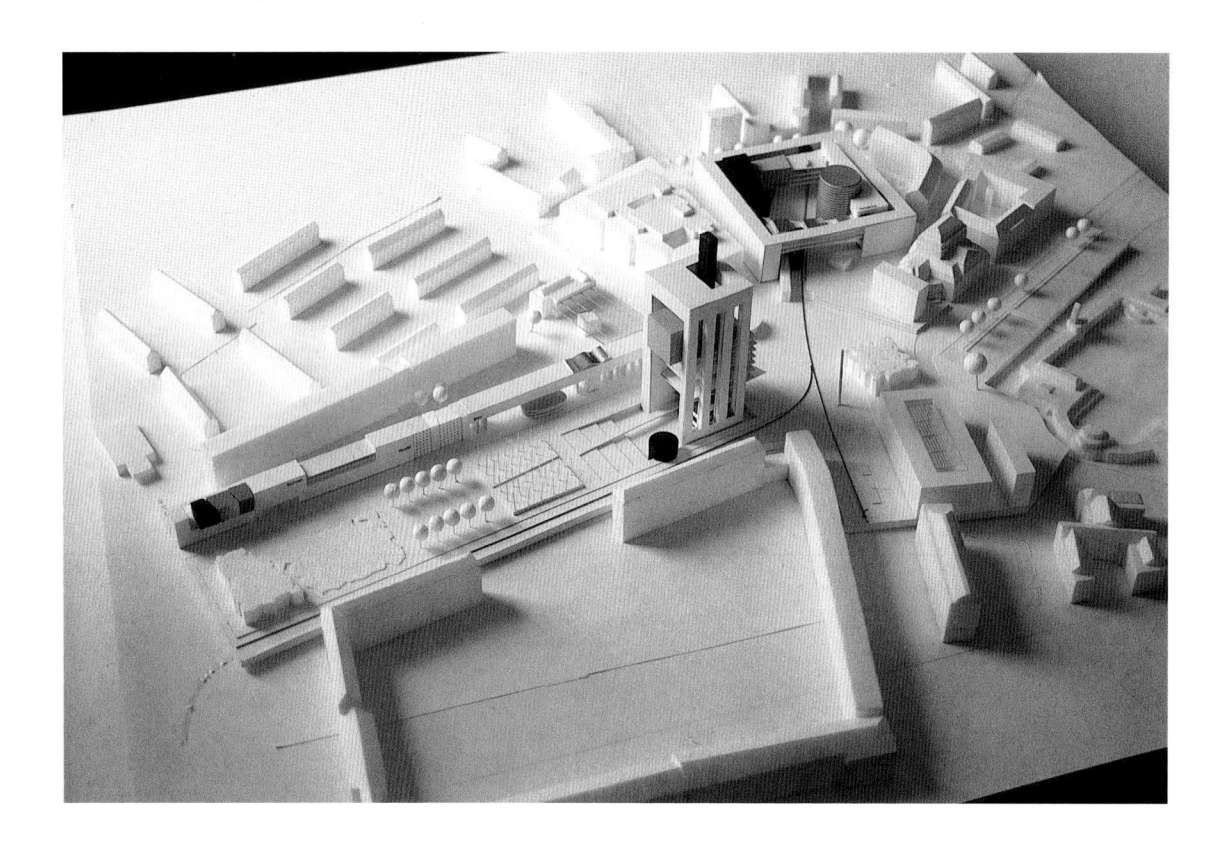

This project was an attempt to plan one part of Dresden. The spatial interventions, additions, and determinations are meant to allow urban life all of its complexity. While the structural break at the city edge cannot be healed, an urban continuity highlighting a usage continuity is possible, and the project was intended to convey that thought.

In cities that have been broken into fragmentary pieces, solitary areas often form limited "cities" that are fully self-sufficient. Their perimeters are clearly circumscribed and identifiable; their interiors play host to varied forms of urban public life. The Postplatz draws fragments together. It is not a square per se, instead dividing into different spaces. It is a place of movement, interaction, and focus for a wide variety of uses. The square's animation, intimacy, and familiarity, the vitality and generosity of the adjoining ensembles and their diverse uses—not simply spatial qualities—represent its value to the nearby areas. *Eisele and Fritz*

Site plan

Site plan study

Apartment House • Frankfurt am Main • 1988–89

The street facade of this building on Saalgasse Lane consists of several different layers; it is comparable to a type case filled with individually wrought parts. The front layer is a projecting, self-supporting, steel construction that acts as a mediator for the neighboring structures while integrating various interior and exterior parts of the building. A semi-public zone—a four-story winter garden—is next, between outside and inside; its function can undergo constant change. The facade is enlivened by that change; it requires no decoration, no formal contrivance. The inside layer is of wood and defines the private living area.

The interior is divided into living spaces and common service areas. The two zones extend from north to south. The readily apparent depth of the rooms and their contact with both facades convey the impression of an extremely spacious interior.

The exterior is constructed primarily of galvanized steel, stainless steel, and aluminum. These cool materials are offset by natural ones: wood, textiles, minerals. The overall composition takes on the features of a spontaneous, collage-like design in the private living areas; they are shaped by emotional motivations and needs, while the public areas are subjected to conscious planning. *Eisele and Fritz*

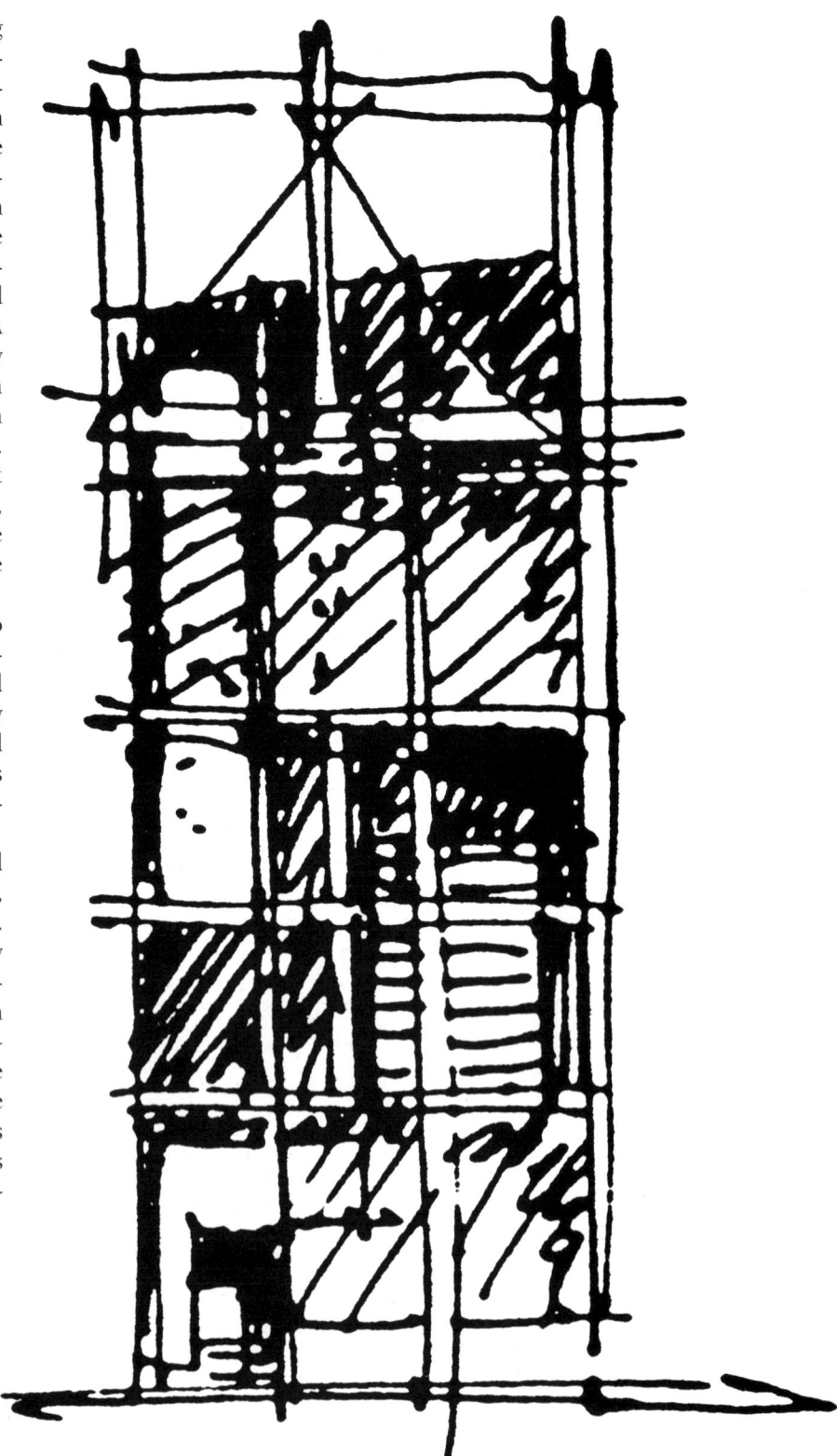

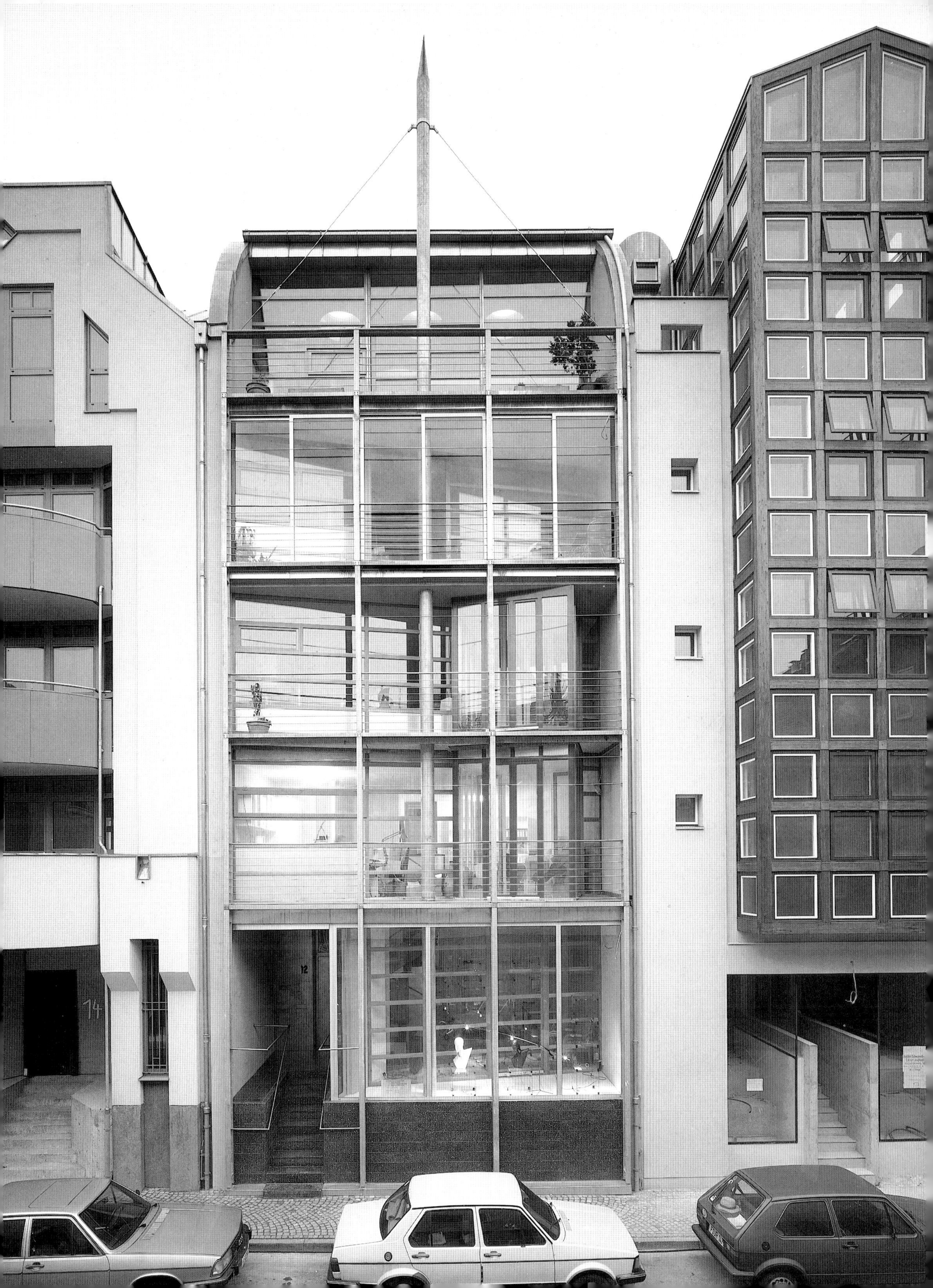

Section

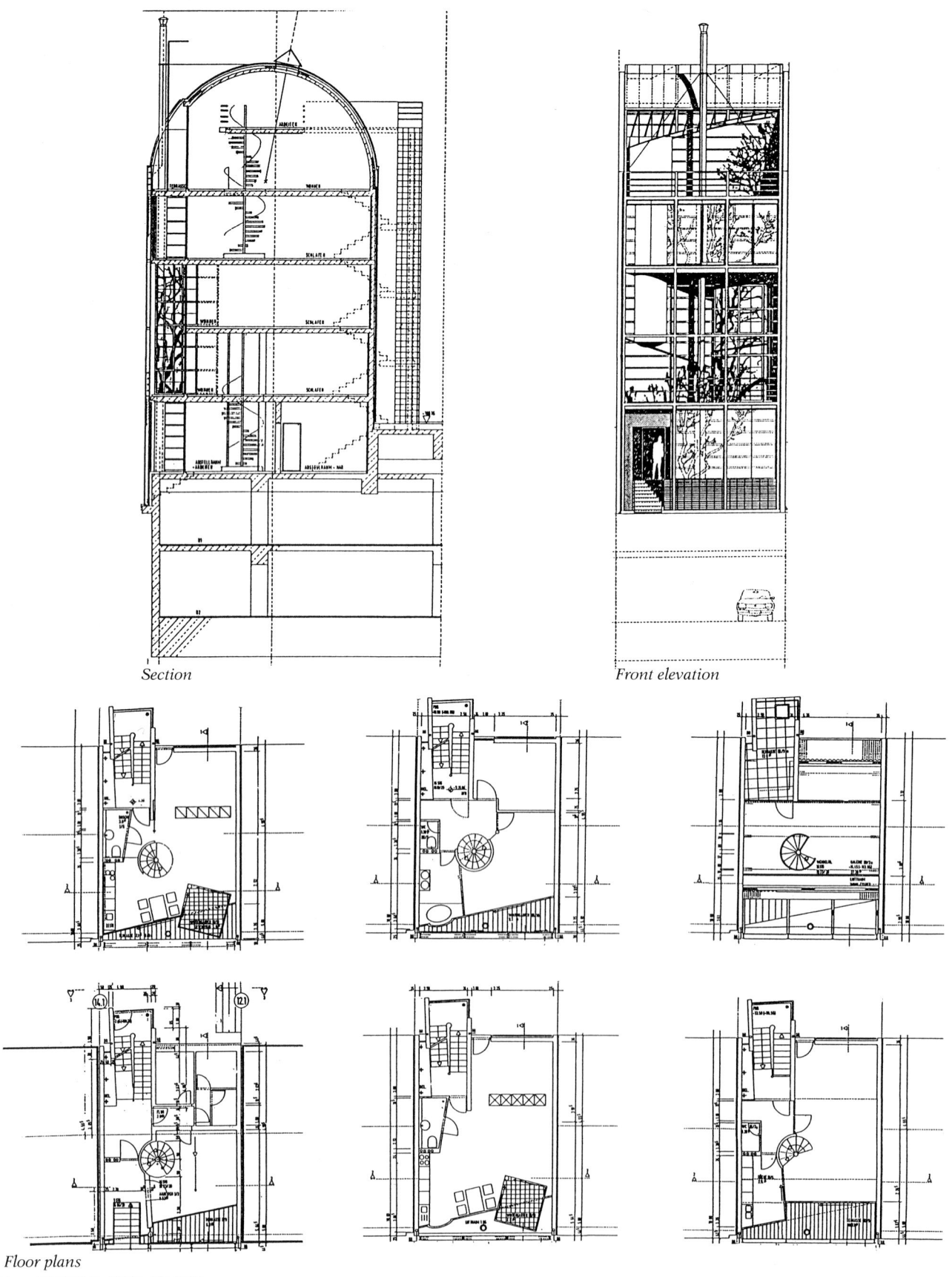

Front elevation

Floor plans

98   EISELE AND FRITZ

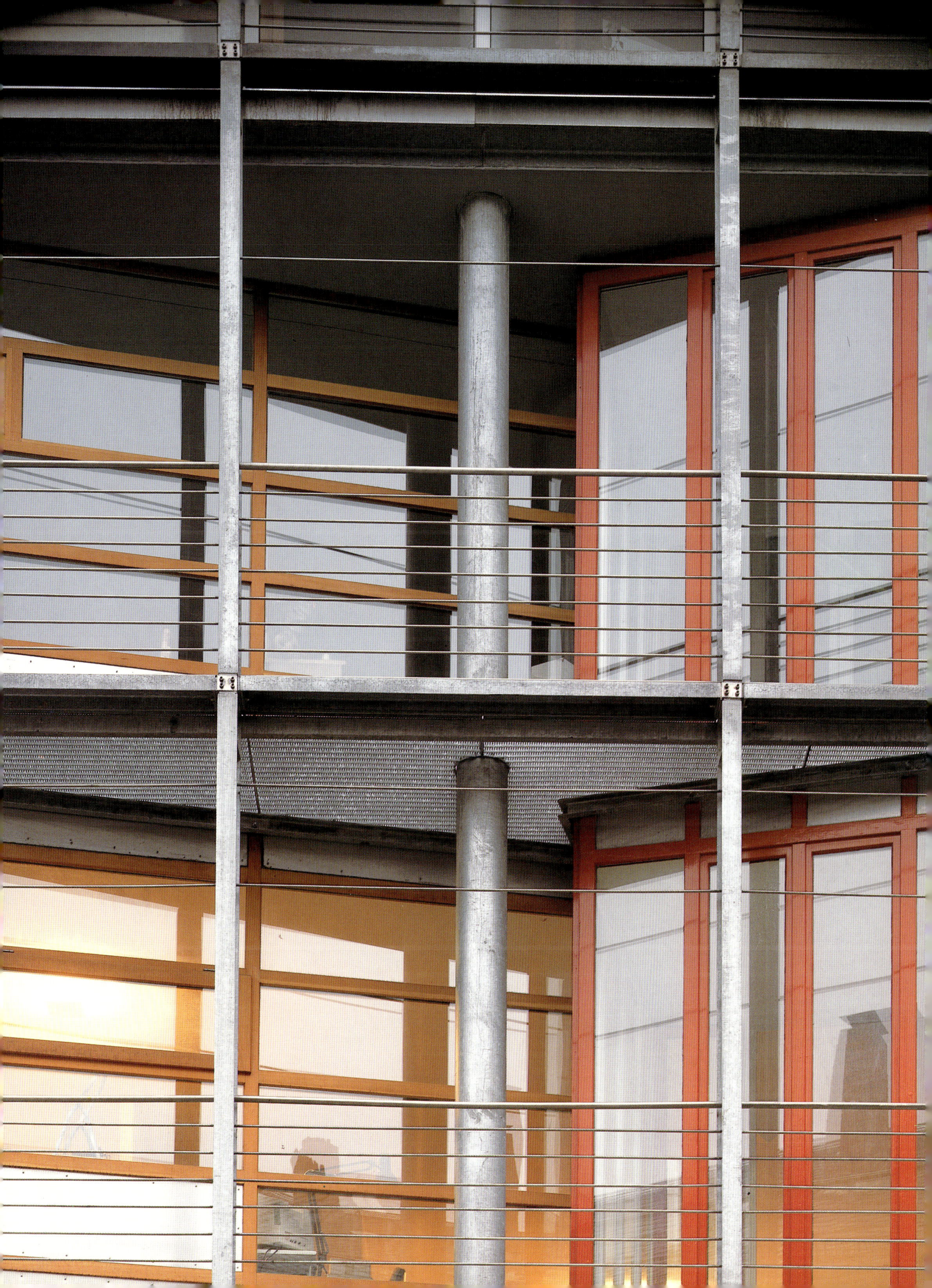

MEINHARD VON GERKAN
Elbschlucht Complex • Hamburg • 1987–90

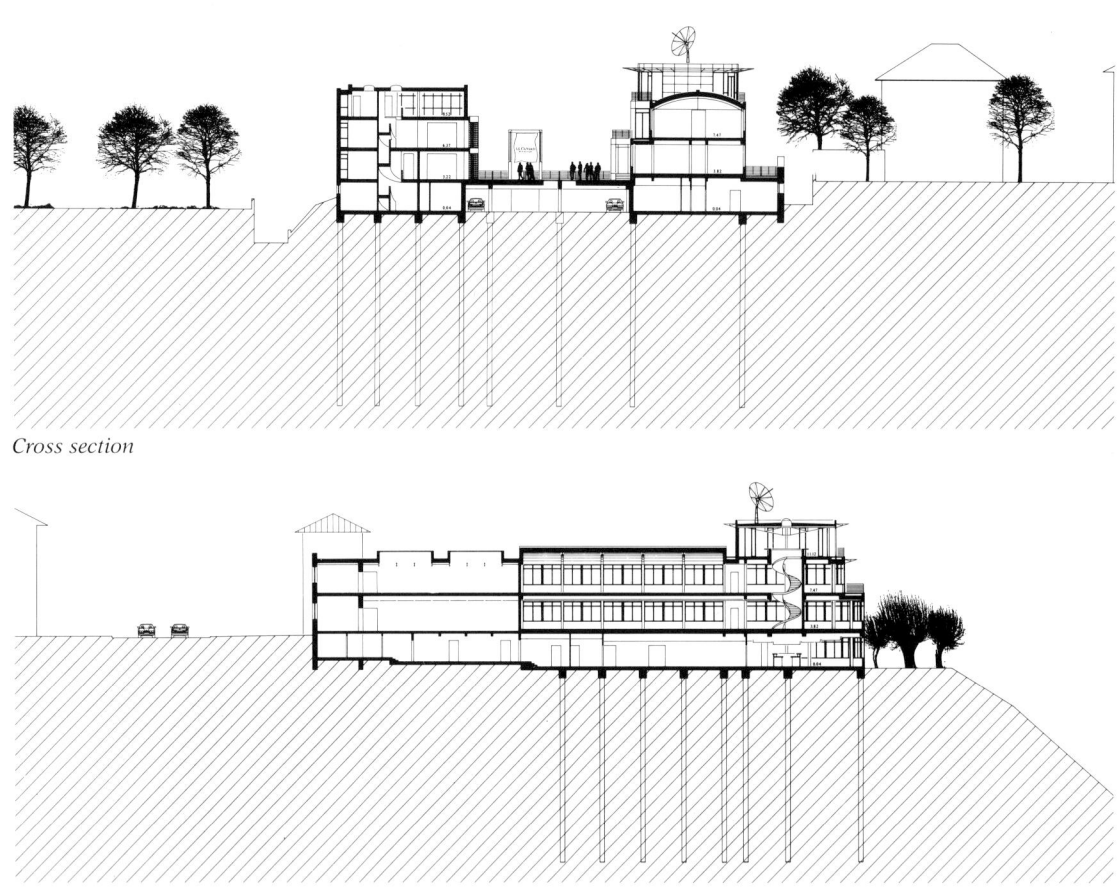

Cross section

Section through west building

To retain the singular spirit of this place, the most typical parts of an original structure on the site near the Elbe River were preserved: the classicist turret, which had lent the property its special identity for decades, and the long wall along the Mühlenberger Path. The silhouette of the complex is bizarre, resembling a 50-meter-long steamer heading toward the river, skirting the length of the long wall and anchored by the turret to the street. Working and living, dining and exhibition are symbiotic here, in a single project.

At the front edge of the trapezoidal entry square, a steel arched gateway frames the harbor view and leads to a ramp supported by the gateway. Projecting over the steep slope, the ramp leads visitors toward the Elbe and then, at the halfway point, turns back toward the building. The west building houses the offices of this architectural firm, with reception and meeting rooms on the first floor, a large studio on the second floor, and a conference room with a panoramic view on the third floor. Complementing the classicist turret, a cylindrical element at the

Site plan

south end of the building resembles the bridge of a ship. A central spiral staircase leads to the third-floor conference room. To the east, at the other corner of the square, is a cubistic villa: the owner's house.

The design language of the new sections avoids drawing any analogies to other typical buildings in the area. The second floor is laid out as a large drafting hall. Window axes are divided according to the workplace design, and a barrel roof with exposed steel construction unifies the room and gives it a workshop-like atmosphere. Open passageways recall a ship's deck. Brises-soleils accent and outline the configuration of the building's parts. Skylights set into the square allow daylight to penetrate into the garage below. In the evening, artificial light emerges from the garage; combined with four slender "light steles" it creates an almost otherworldly effect. The only color accents are red flags that act as signposts, the red light steles, and garage door supports; trees that were preserved on the site provide a green contrast.
Meinhard von Gerkan

Lower floor plan   *Ground floor plan*

102   MEINHARD VON GERKAN

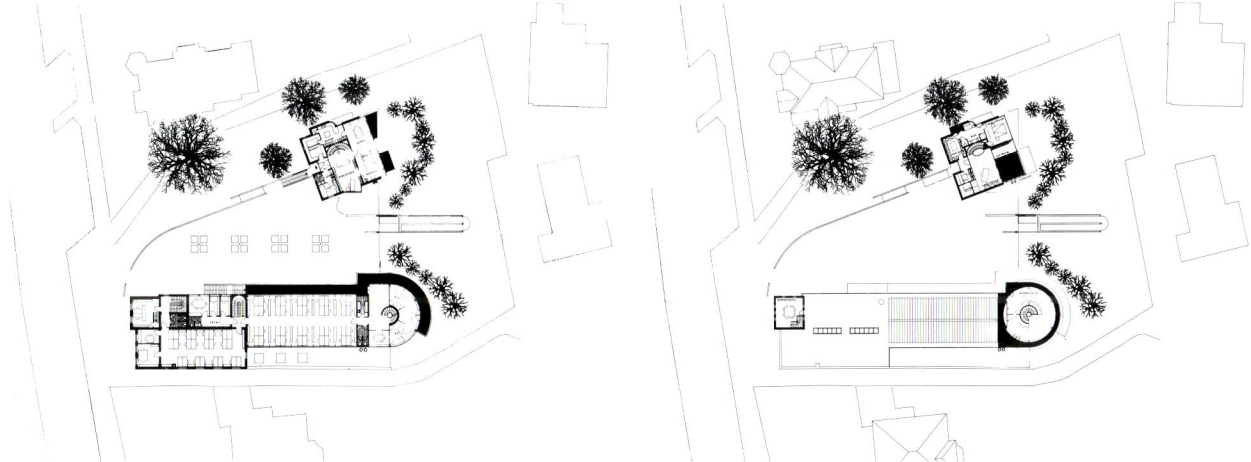

Second floor plan *Third floor/roof plan*

MEINHARD VON GERKAN   103

Airport Parking Garage • Hamburg • 1989–90

The circular parking garage is an integral part of a new departure terminal, providing eight hundred spaces on nine round levels. The levels are reached from two staggered spiral ramps—one up, one down. Vehicles can get to each level directly, guided by a traffic routing system. Lanes on both the ramps and parking levels are one-way, with lane cross-over occurring only at the garage entrances and exits. Pedestrians reach the garage from a separate stair-and-elevator tower. The tower is connected to the garage by lightweight bridges. The required emergency stair tower is on the opposite side of the garage.

While the circle is the dominant geometric form of the garage, an essential design feature is the curtain-like steel grille that unifies much of the building behind one facade. It allows exterior views, provides ventilation, and seen from a distance, articulates the volume of the building. The screen was left off of the entrance and exit stories and the two top parking levels to create a sense of lightness and to reveal the structure. *Meinhard von Gerkan*

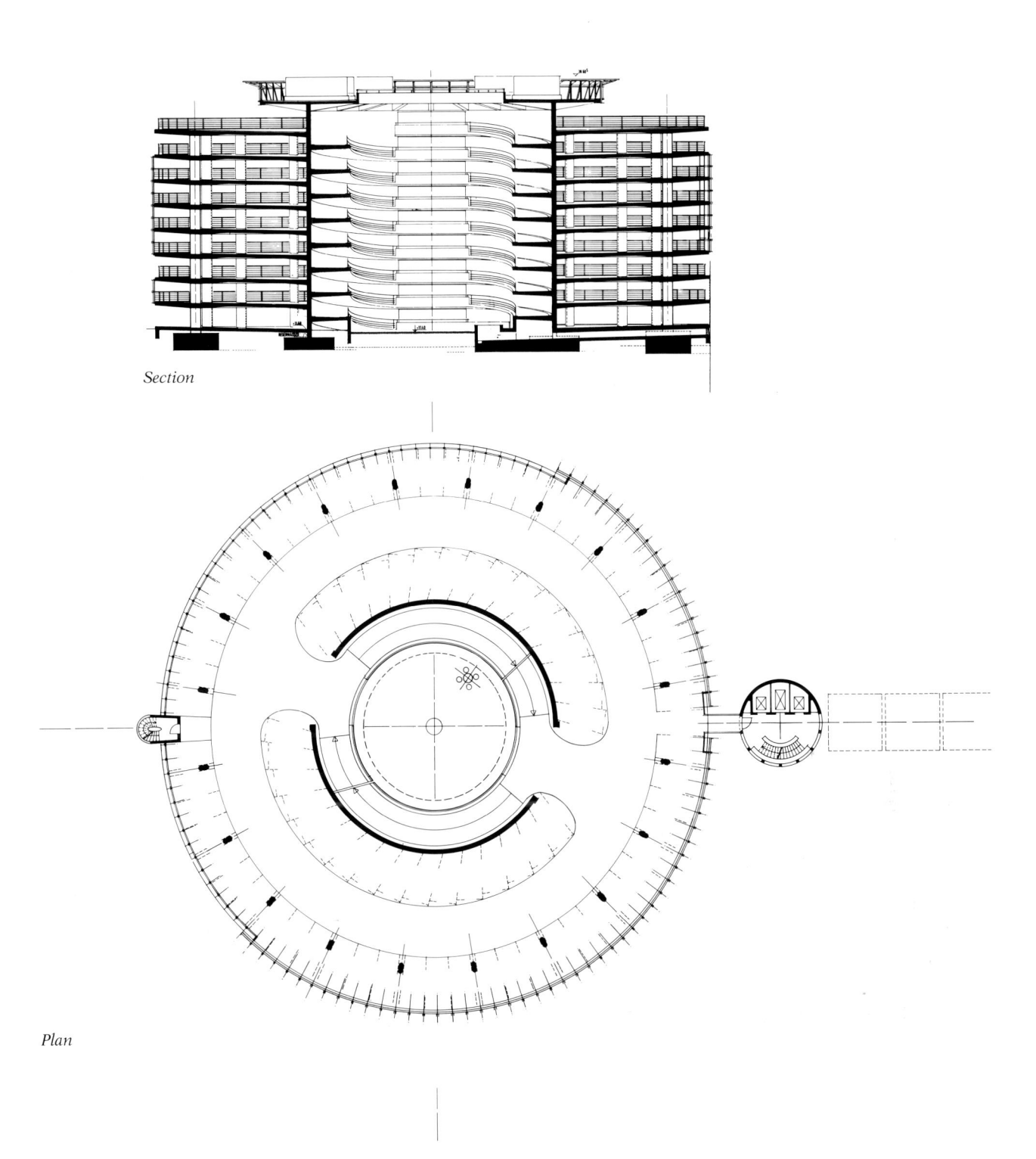

Section

Plan

Airport Terminal • Stuttgart • 1980–91

The geometrical configuration of the new terminal has been reduced to two basic forms: a long wing with a triangular cross section and a rectangular hall with a trapezoidal cross section. These two elements serve as dominant organizational foci, needed in the airport's heterogenous setting.

The tree-like structural design of the hall roof—the dominant design element within the hall—is intended to be a feature unique to this airport. The roof is supported by a closely spaced (four to five meters) grid of "twigs," four of which come together to create a single "branch." Twelve branches then join to form a "trunk," which is fixed into the foundation.

The roof plane ascends sharply from the drive-up lanes in front of the terminal (as an indirect expression of flight) and gradually from the tarmac on the rear side, forming a ridge that acts like a contour of the site and also as a noise barrier between the passenger arrival and plane takeoff sides. Inside, the waiting rooms and passenger corridors are arrayed across the depth of the building; this and the "tree" construction unite the hall into one large unobstructed space. Fit into the peaked cross section is a series of terraces, which form semicircular vaults projecting out into the middle of the hall and lead to restaurants, courtesy and conference rooms, and the viewing terrace, located at the high point of the ridge.

The base of the terminal is clad in natural stone; the joints are a major design feature of the exterior. The recessed window openings emphasize the plasticity of the monolithic base. The interior shading system for the hall—rotating, wing-like blades—allows for varying degrees of light and shade. *Meinhard von Gerkan*

STUTTGART

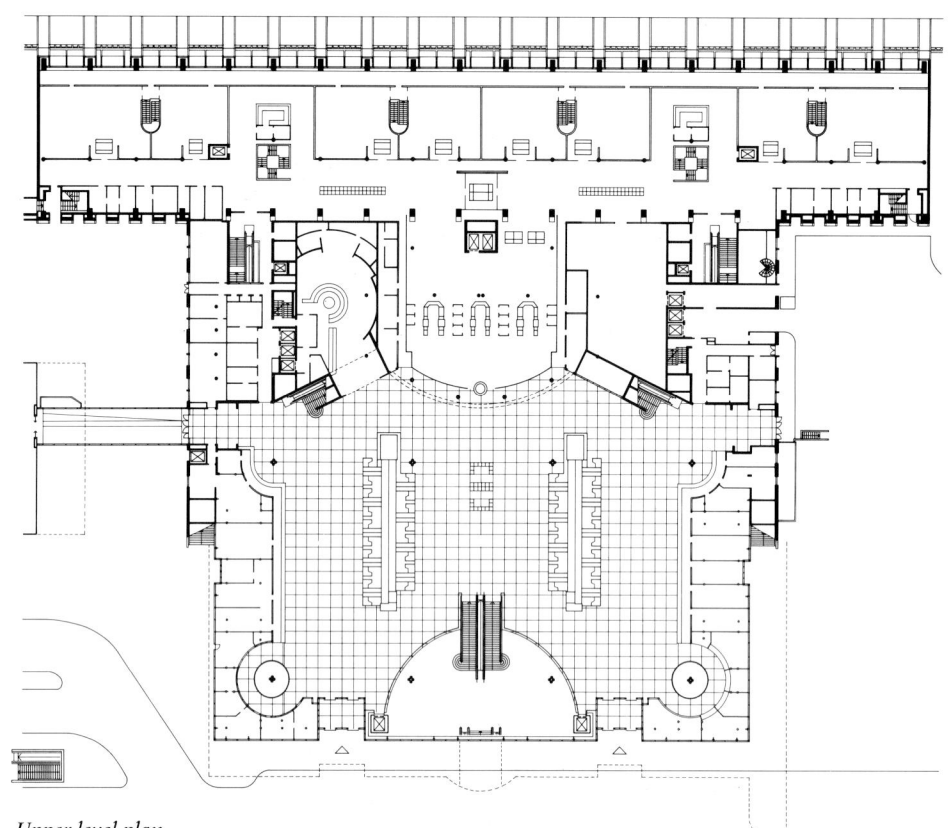

Upper level plan

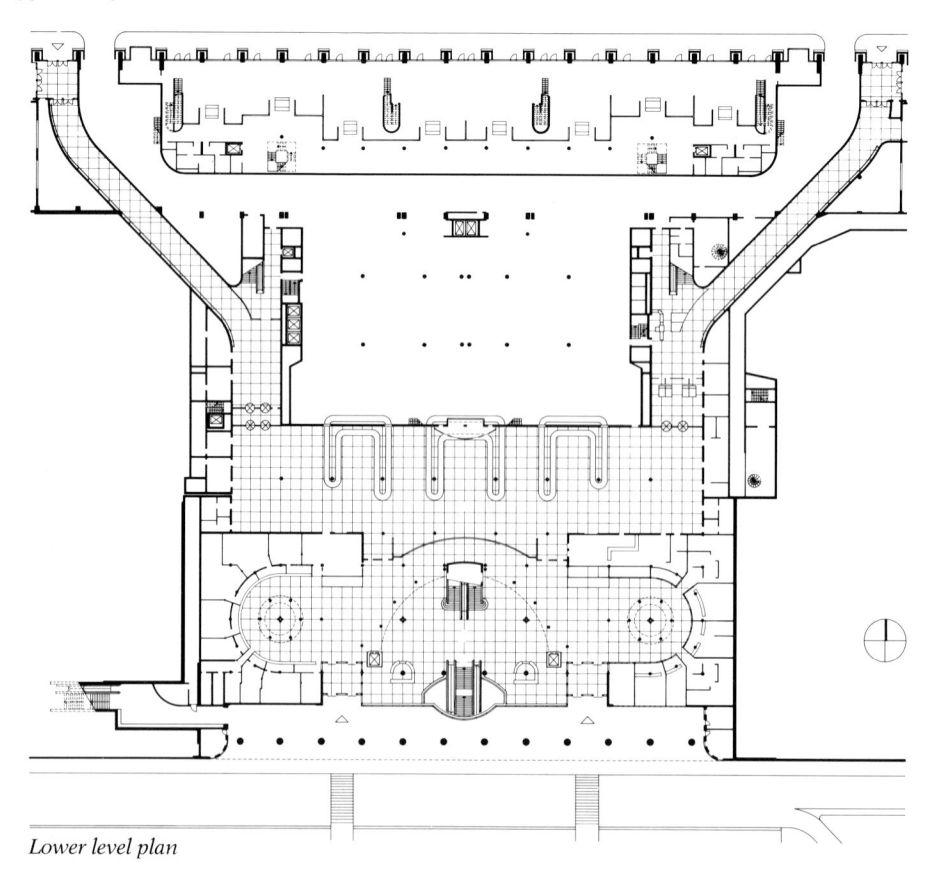

Lower level plan

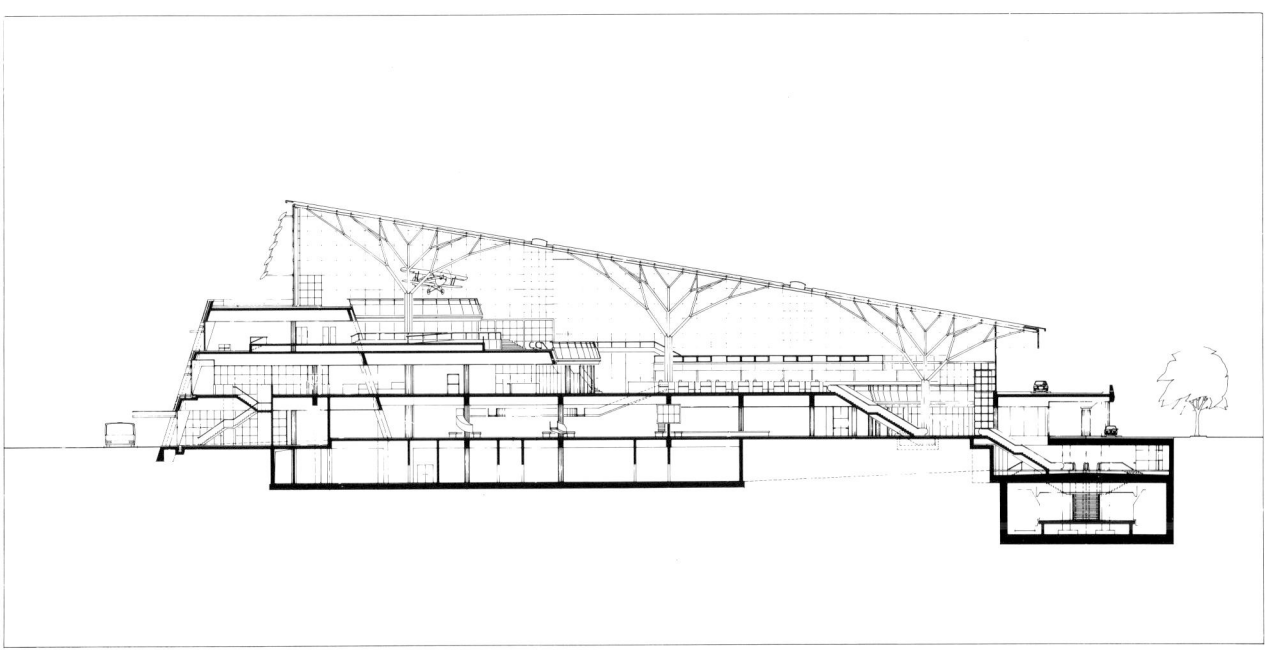

Section

Municipal Hall • Bielefeld • 1987–90

This municipal hall is simply structured and planned. The two halls on the main axis can share the stage area; surrounding them are foyers. The parking garage is attached to the rear. Simplicity also extends to the choice of materials and colors. The white and light gray color scheme renders the building neutral; it remains a backdrop for the various events taking place.

The austere design of the main building creates unity within diverse urban surroundings. The modular window grid of the facade is inset with opaque panels where it covers the entryway stairs; the resulting pattern lends the building a sense of dynamism and vitality. The stairways between the exterior and an interior facade form a transitional zone: they are open to both foyers and promenades. The sightlines to the halls and to the city are left clear. The movement of visitors will be a characteristic element of this public building for those inside as well as for passers-by. The events staged there become an integral part of the city's life.
Meinhard von Gerkan

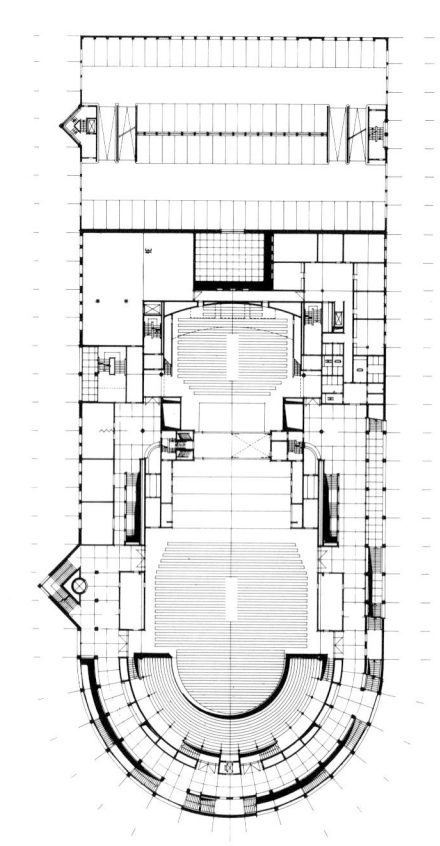

Upper level plan

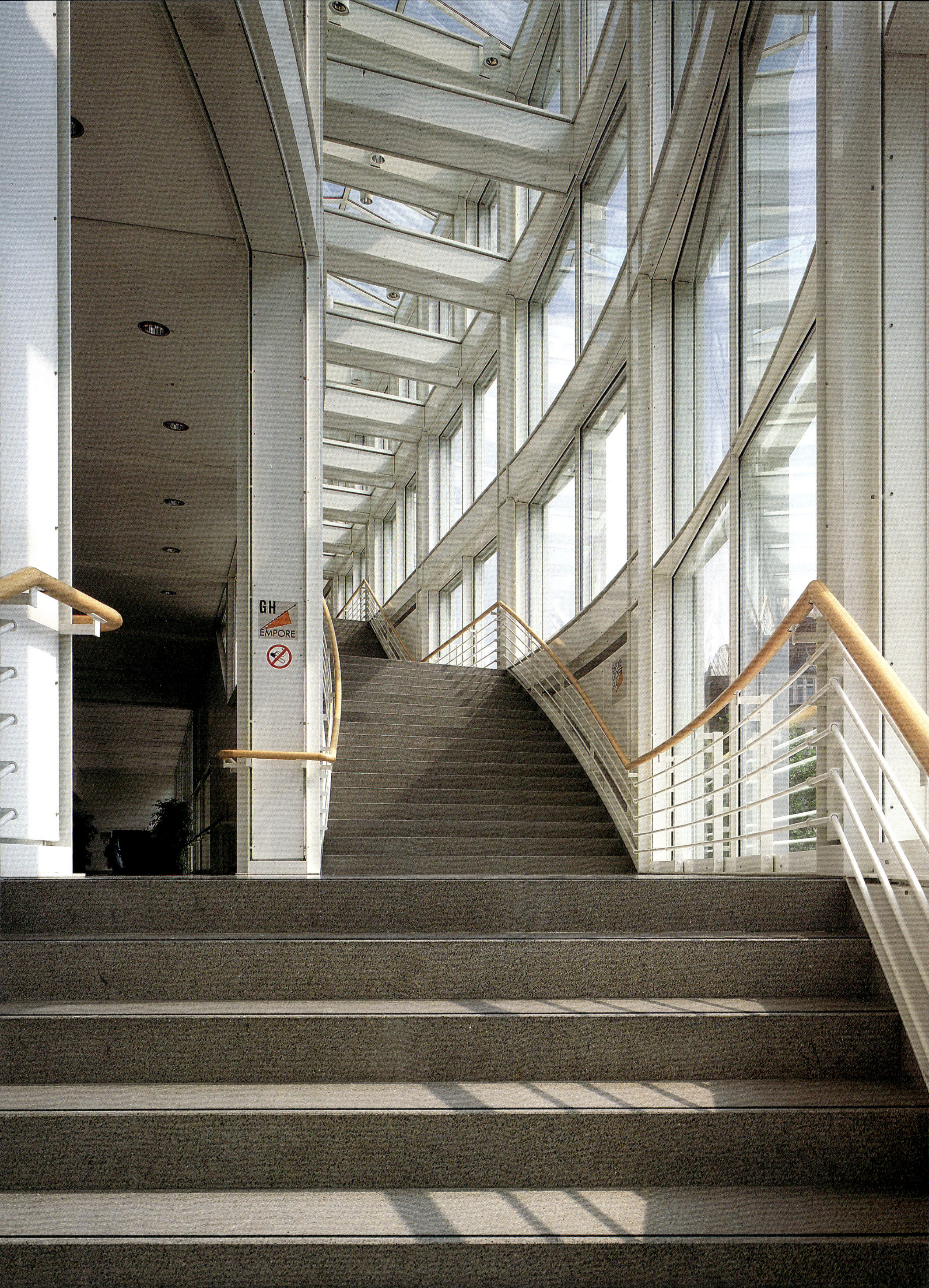
GH
EMPORE

THOMAS HERZOG
Youth Educational Center Guest House • Windberg • 1987–91

Windberg is a small community in lower Bavaria, located in a southern offshoot of the Bavarian Forest where the hills meet the Danube Plain. The original medieval village is surrounded by a monastery which dates from the early twelfth century. Still home to the order of monks that founded it, the monastery now contains a youth educational center as well.

The scheme attempted to resolve several urbanistic issues, especially the scattered post-war housing to the south of the town that had robbed the village of much of its original compactness. The guest house also had to defer to the powerful historical structures, so its design was structured as a very simple shape. In addition, the new building had to be part of the circulation system of the entire complex. Thus it was oriented parallel to the main building and frames the edge of the hill, while preserving the view from the monastery.

The plan was generated primarily by energy considerations. Special attention was paid to the proposed use of each type of room and to the required ambient temperature. The floor plan distinguishes between two different rooms zones: In the southern section of the building, all rooms face south, to take advantage not only of the prettiest view but also of the sun's heating effect. In the northern section, the rooms are used only for brief periods of time and are rarely heated.

It would be surprising if a building that was designed in response to environmental concerns did not result in a different kind of design. In fact, the building represents architecture of our own time. The spirit of the place, a wise use of natural resources, and the users' demands are the main design features. *Thomas Herzog*

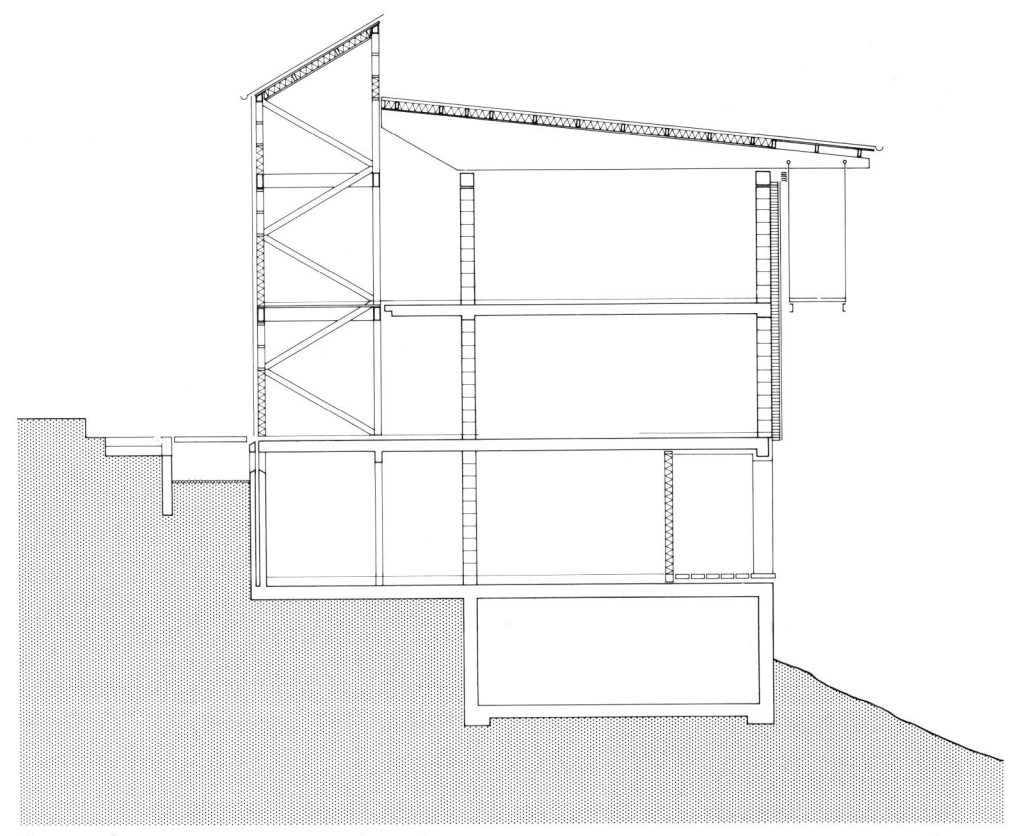

Cross section

Upper level plan

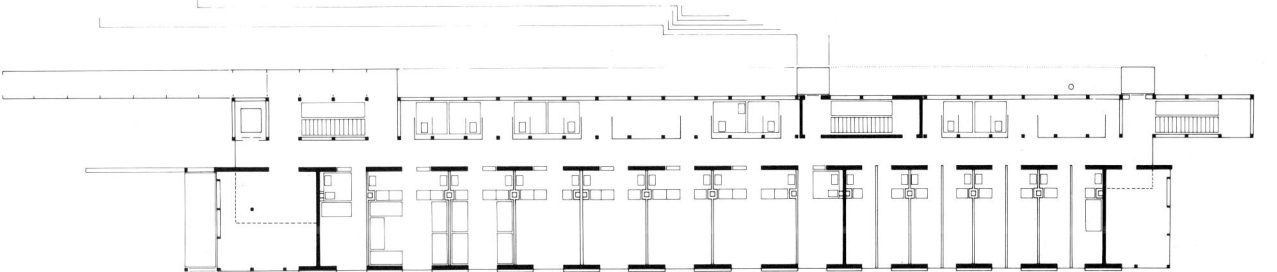

Entry level plan

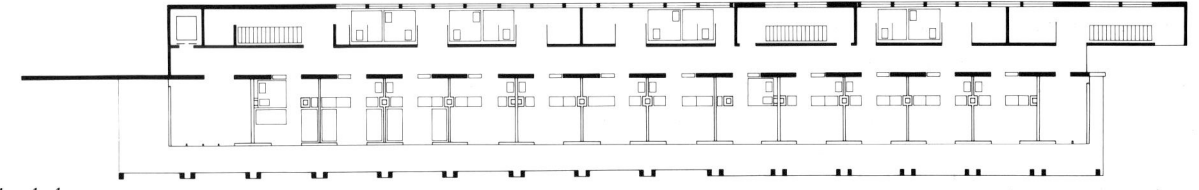

Lower level plan

THOMAS HERZOG 113

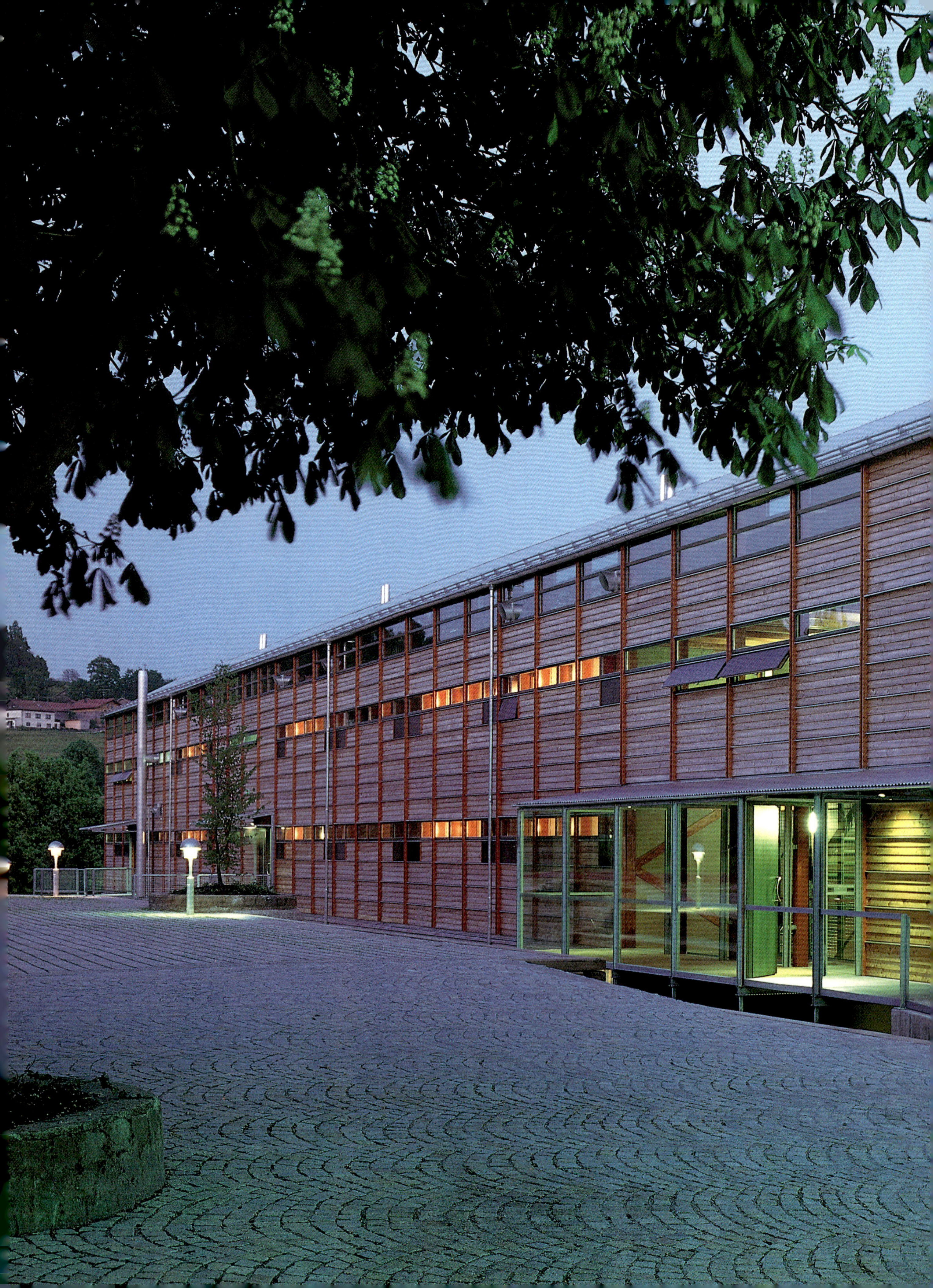

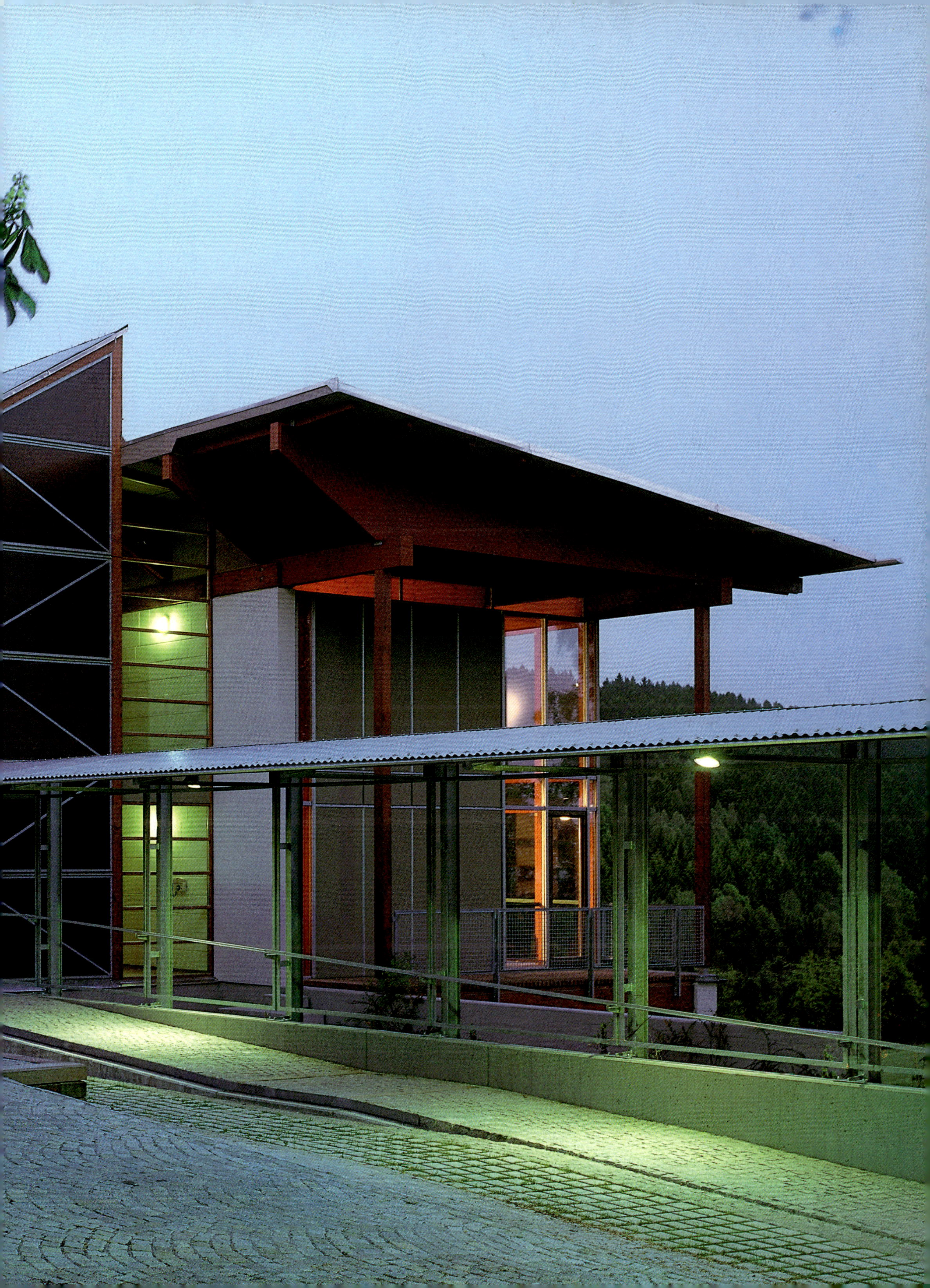

Two-Family House • Pullach • 1986–89

For this project in a small town in Upper Bavaria, the client requested a wooden structure, and asked that special attention be paid to solar aspects of the design. In the rooms that face south, the full depth of the house is apparent; there are free lines of sight to the entrances at the north. The inner structure of the building projects into the space to emphasize the length of the house as well. All common rooms adjoin the southern facade, ensuring solar heating even from the low winter sun all the way through to the virtually closed back of the building. This approach eliminates the problem of transferring heat within the building, as all the rooms are bathed in sunshine.

The plan is divided into parallel zones that expand on successive floors. Similarly, the section widens from bottom to top. The roof consists of an interior surface of insulated glazing, which closes off the rooms, and an exterior surface of single-pane safety glass, which acts as weather protection for the facade and the wood structure.

Thomas Herzog

Upper level plan

Entry level plan

Basement level plan

THOMAS HERZOG 117

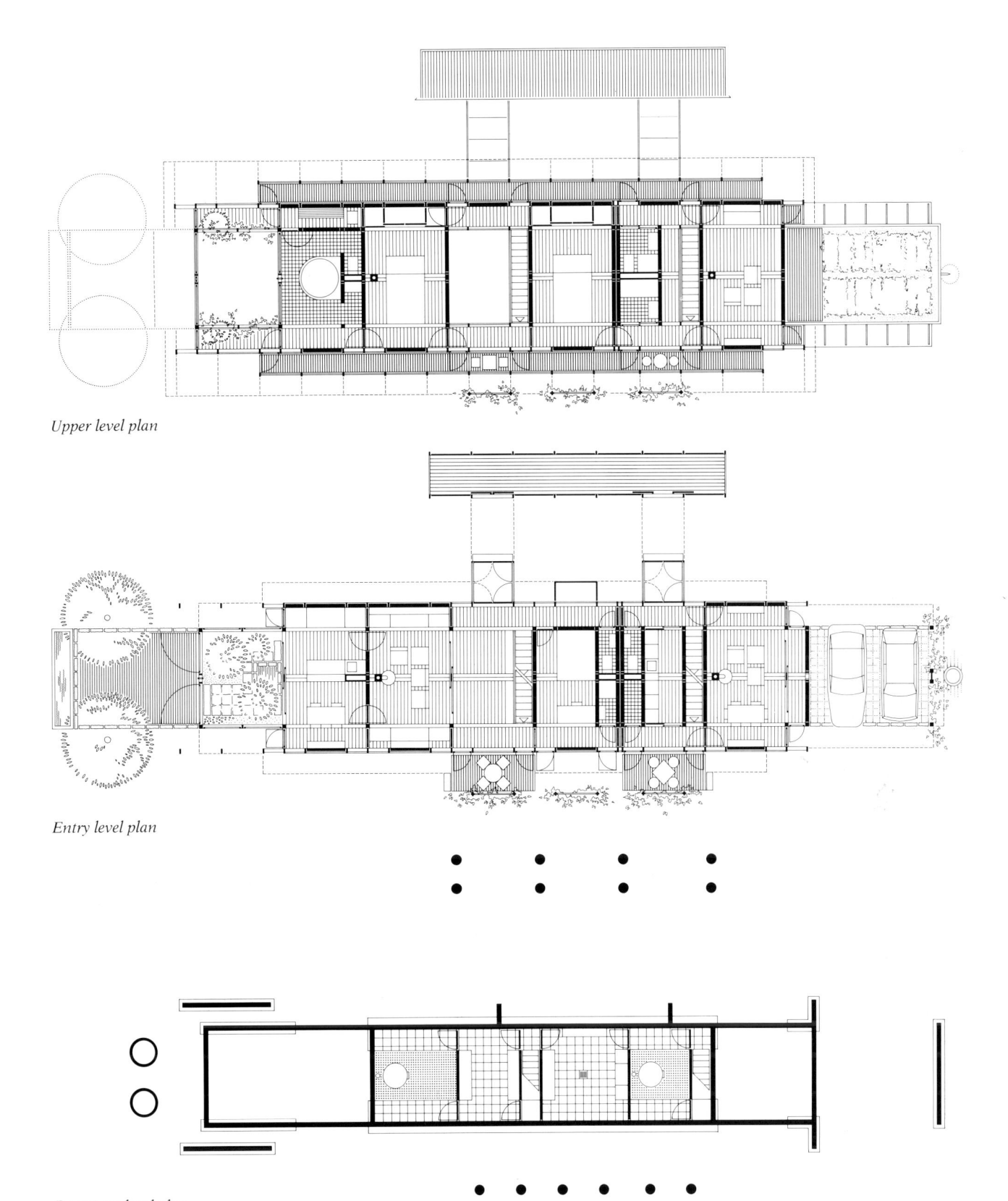

HILMER AND SATTLER
Regional Finance Office Annex • Munich • 1985–91

The annex is a structure added to the perimeter of a block of buildings and as such is subject to certain rules, although these limitations are not necessarily restrictive. The overall goal was to have the building function not as a composition of surfaces, lines, and reflections but rather as a solid structural body in a highly compressed urban setting.

The program, economic considerations, and input from the owner resulted in a conventional double-loaded floor plan with a central corridor. Daylight enters this corridor through rows of windows located above cabinets along its length and through the open corners of the building.

The building has a reinforced-concrete structure. The street facades are covered in terra cotta; the inner courtyard is finished in plaster. This differentiation between inside and outside is typical of the traditional city block. In the inner courtyard, the architecture is comparatively modest. Green is meant to dominate here; ivy and wild grape vines wind their way across the facade. The street facade highlights the building's public function through architectural structuring and refined details as well as the choice and quality of the materials.

The structure of the street facade is based on the classical orders. United by a granite base, the first and second floors form a single entity. This base is topped by three standard floors. A steel-supported roof projects above an attic story. Horizontal moldings and vertical trim regulate the play of light and shadow on the facade and lend plastic emphasis to individual architectural elements according to the established hierarchical order. *Hilmer and Sattler*

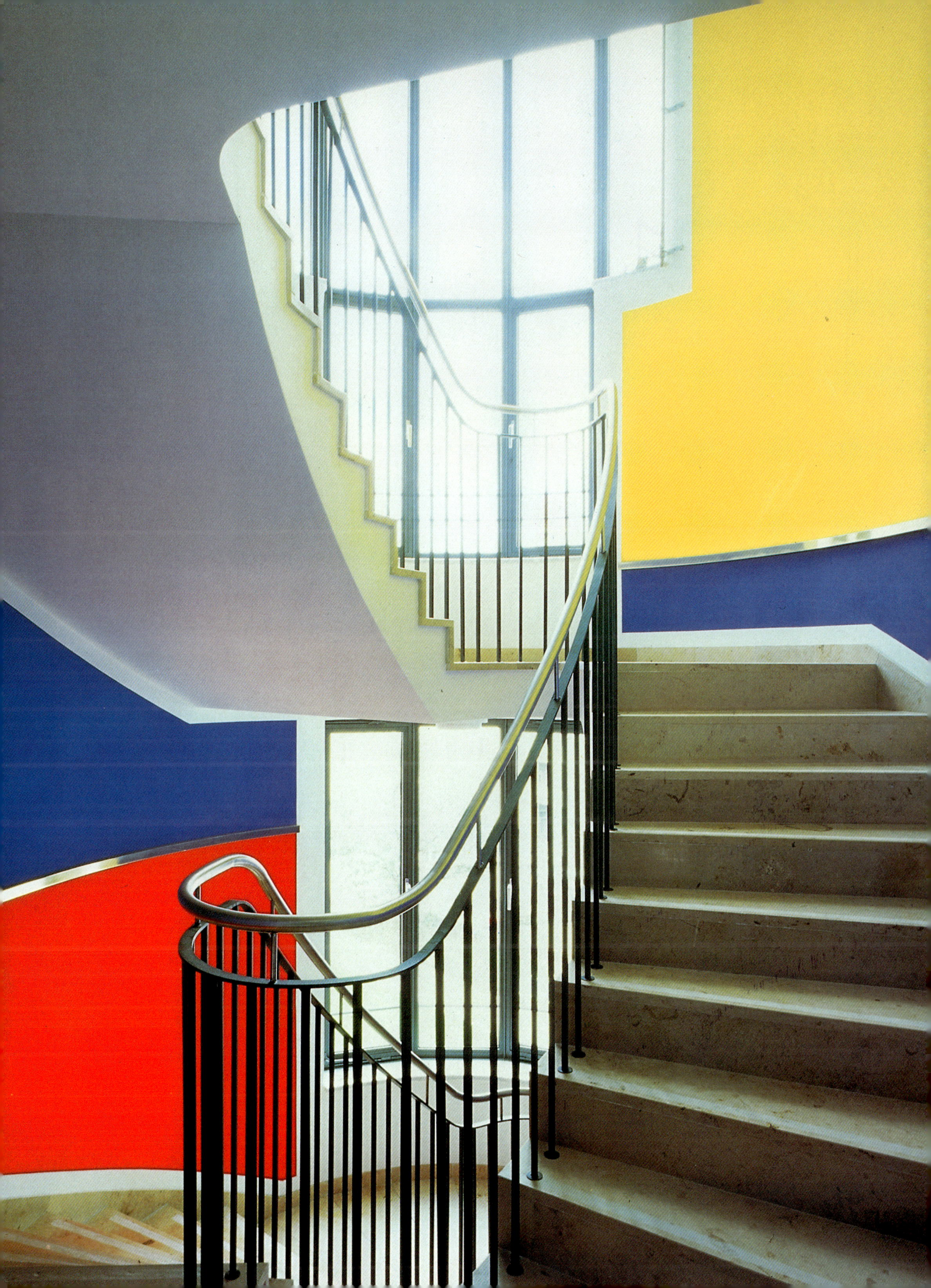

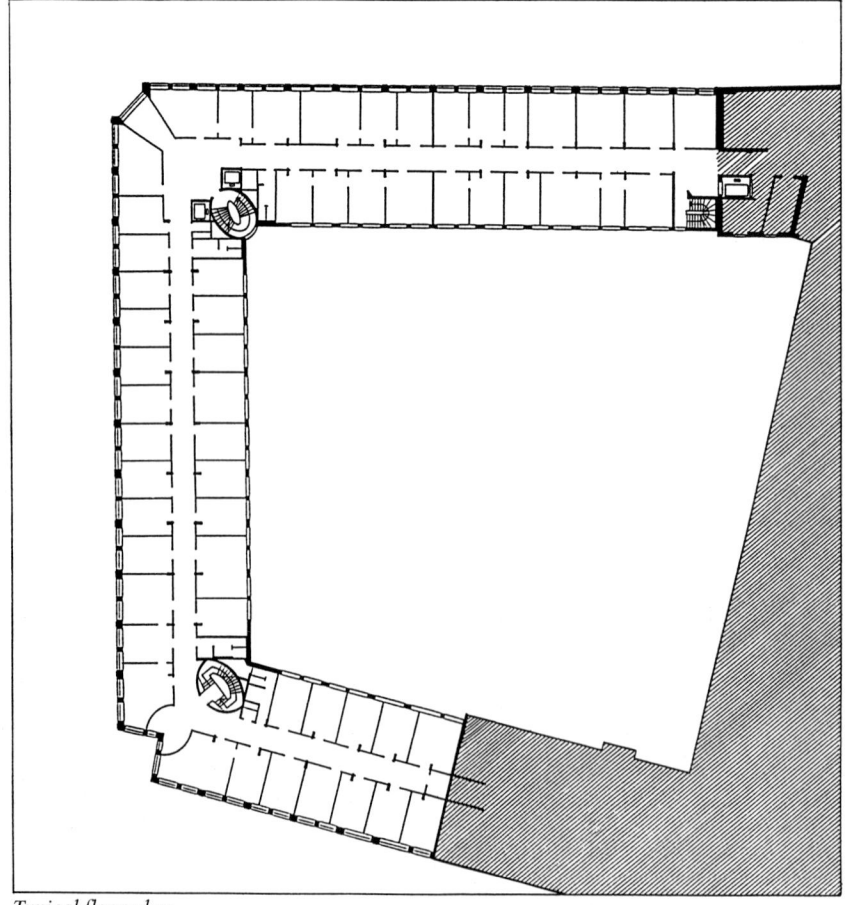

Typical floor plan

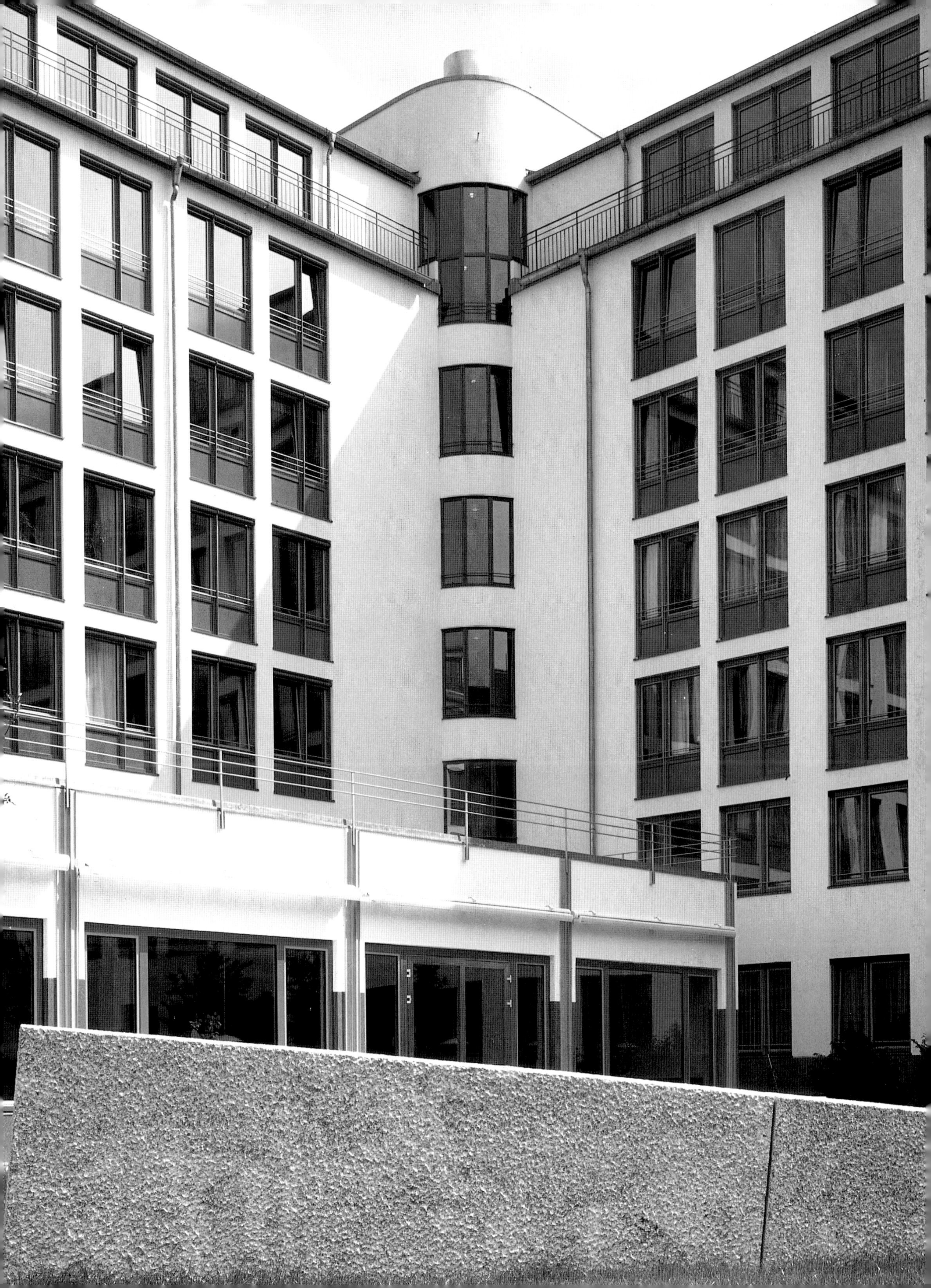

Albgrün Bridge • Karlsruhe • 1983–86

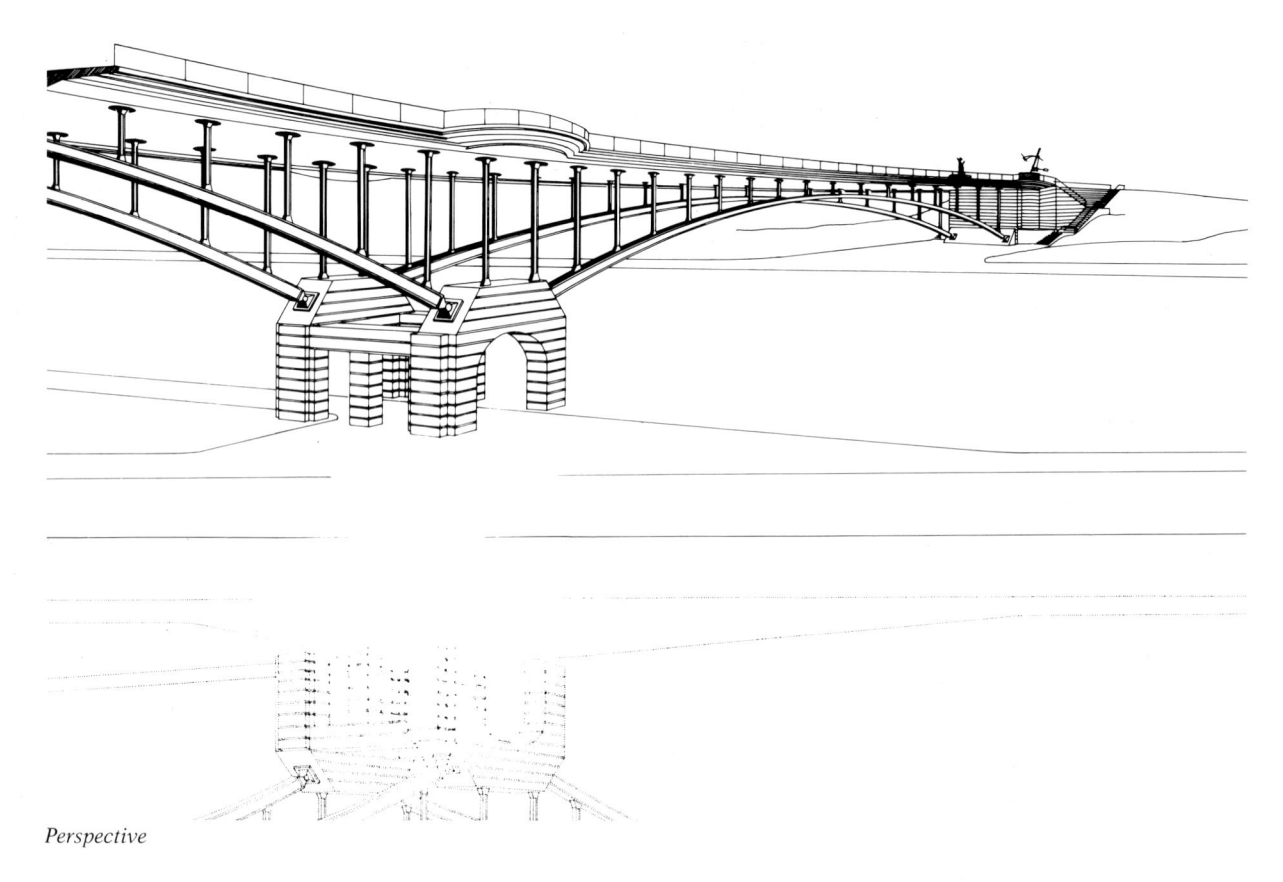

Perspective

Cross section

This design won first prize in a combined design/build competition sponsored by the city of Karlsruhe. The program was to design a bridge as a pedestrian and streetcar link to Neureuth over both a newly planned city park along the Alb River and the southern tangential expressway. The design of the bridge was determined by three factors: the wide arch expressing the "bridging" function; the quirky combination of materials as different as filigree steel and solid concrete; and the architectural treatment of the plinths and abutments. The structure is composite steel and concrete. Arched steel span girders bear a concrete slab over structural steel columns. The beginning and end of the bridge are marked with two pairs of sculptures. *Hilmer and Sattler*

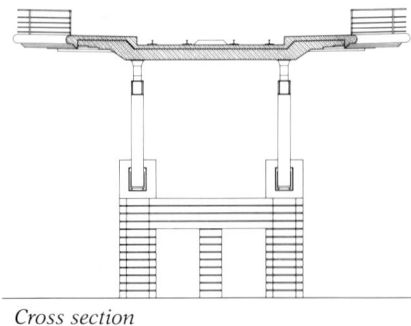

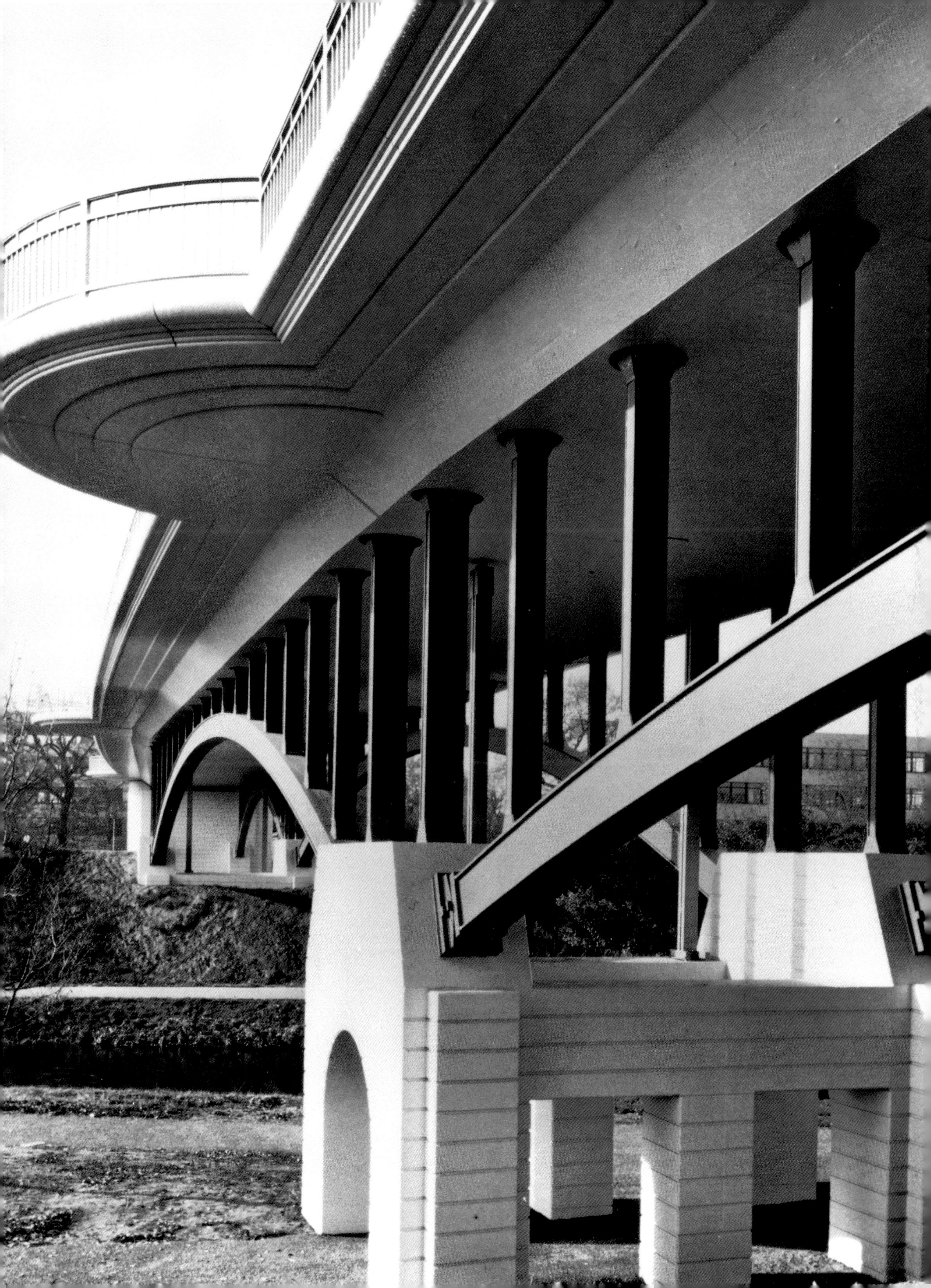

JOCHEM JOURDAN AND BERNHARD MÜLLER

Landeszentralbank • Frankfurt am Main • 1978–80

The Landeszentralbank was designed at a time marked by a new sensitivity to the historical city. Recognizing the past of a city or a house is an essential expression of our architectural culture.

The design was intended to repair the area of the city around the main railway station, to express the city's many varied qualities, to preserve the historical buildings in the area, and to articulate public space. Thus, the Landeszentralbank includes old and new buildings. Streets and squares were newly planned; the surrounding nineteenth-century buildings defined the maximum height. A sequence of inviting built and open spaces, passages and arcades was created: an architectural progression with different expressions, views, orientations, and uses. The treatment of the stone surfaces emphasizes the plasticity of the relief and intensifies the physical and visual experience.

The monumental column at the south corner of the court facade has the diameter of one of the Doric columns of the Parthenon, but remains a fragment. The column has no base and, instead of a capital, has an iron construction: it has been reduced to a pure symbol. But it is also pivot, joint, and network of paths, beginning and end of the arcade. Fit asymmetrically into the ground plan, it is meant to disturb the equilibrium of the composition.

The structure was dependent on the open plan. The reinforced concrete frame allows the creation of independent rooms as well as figurative room images, and also of special areas like the main hall and stairwells. The supporting skeleton develops Le Corbusier's theory of the free plan; flowing and aperspectival space versus limited and perspectival space overlap in a succession of exciting, poetic places. *Jochem Jourdan*

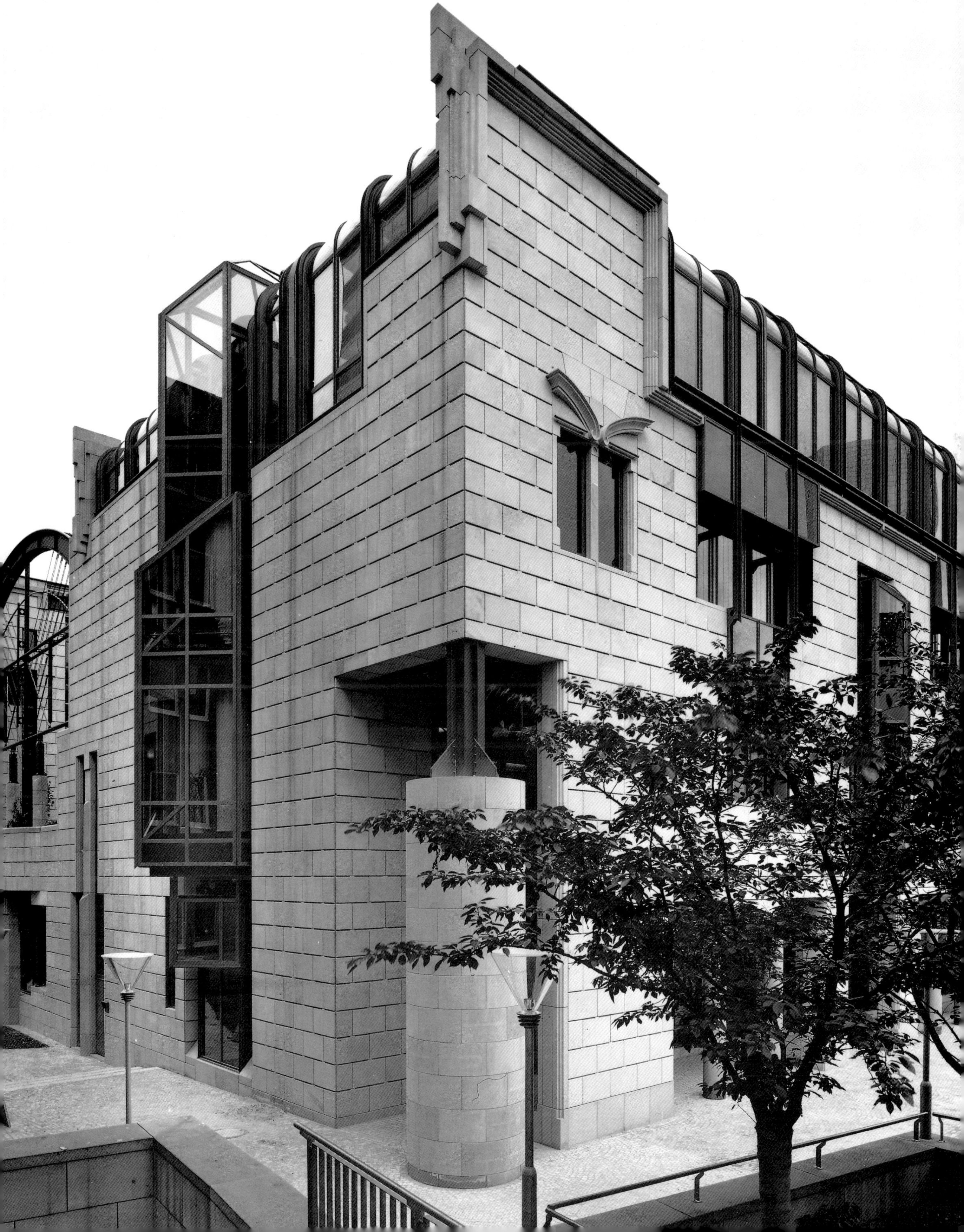

126 JOCHEM JOURDAN

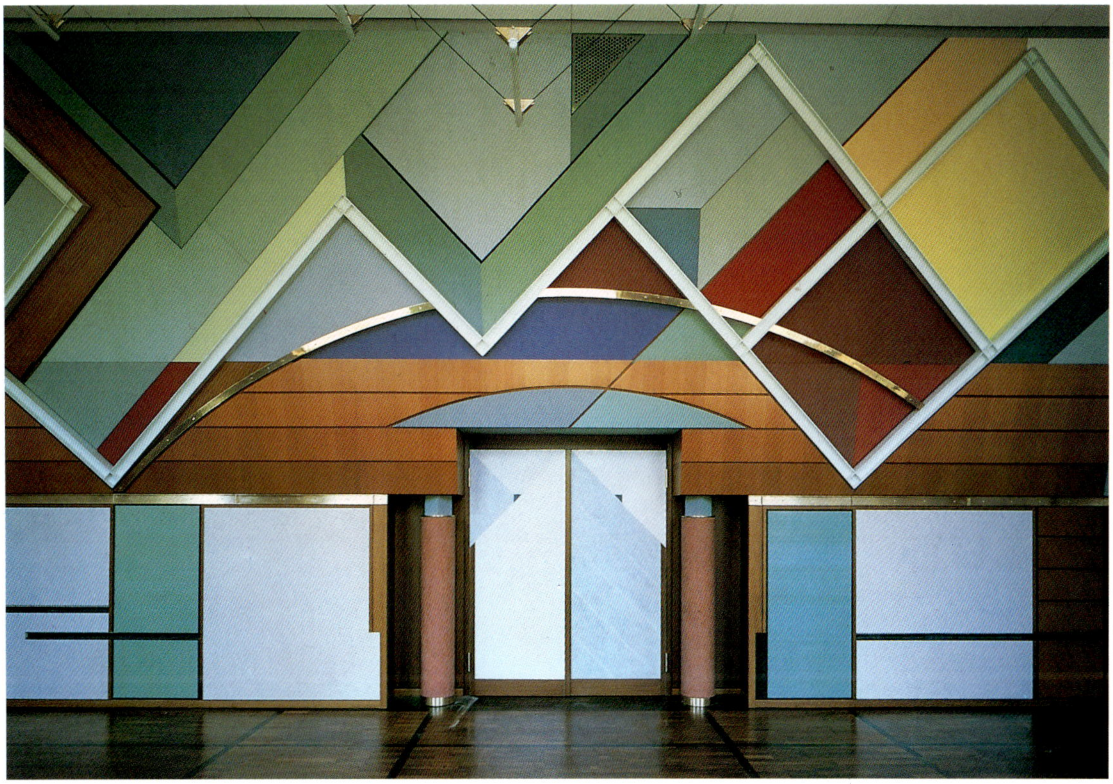

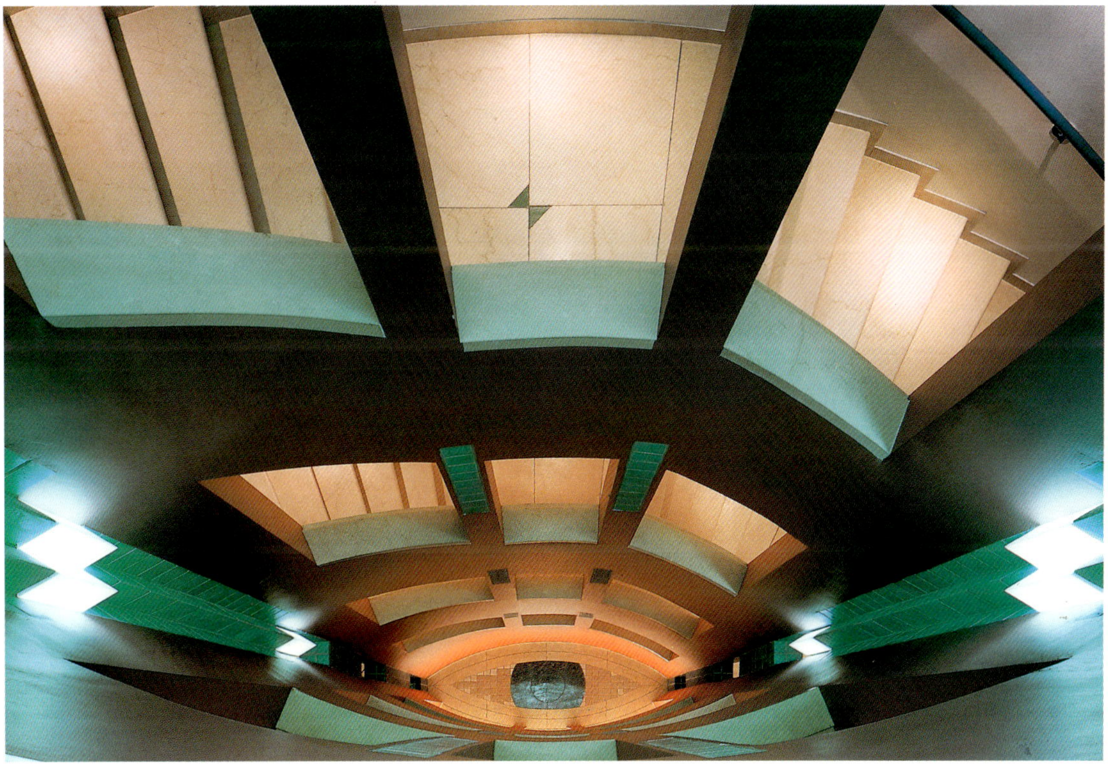

128 JOCHEM JOURDAN

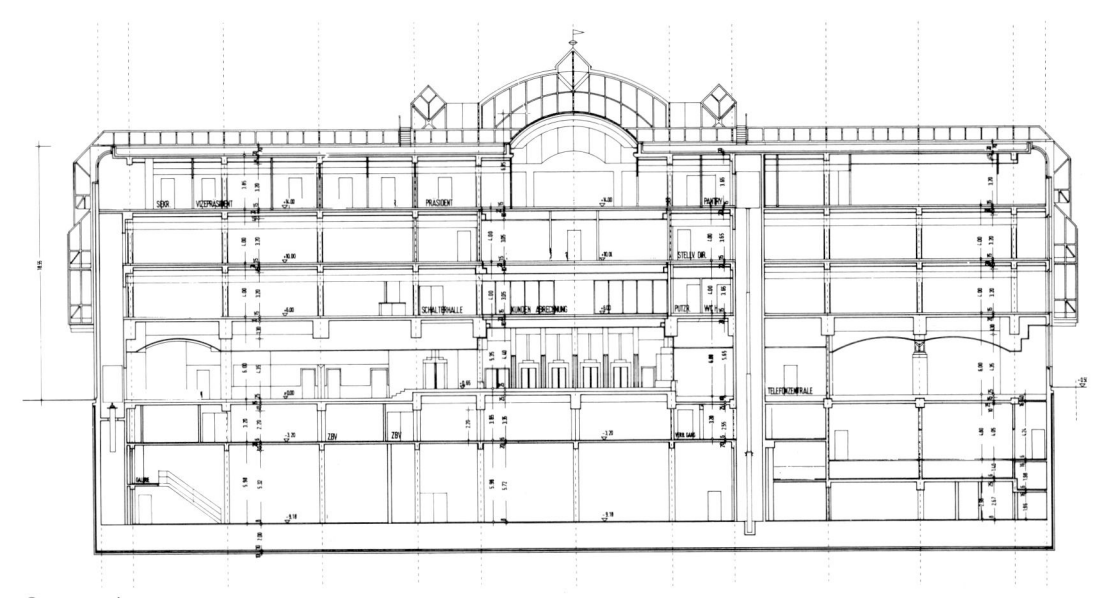

Cross section

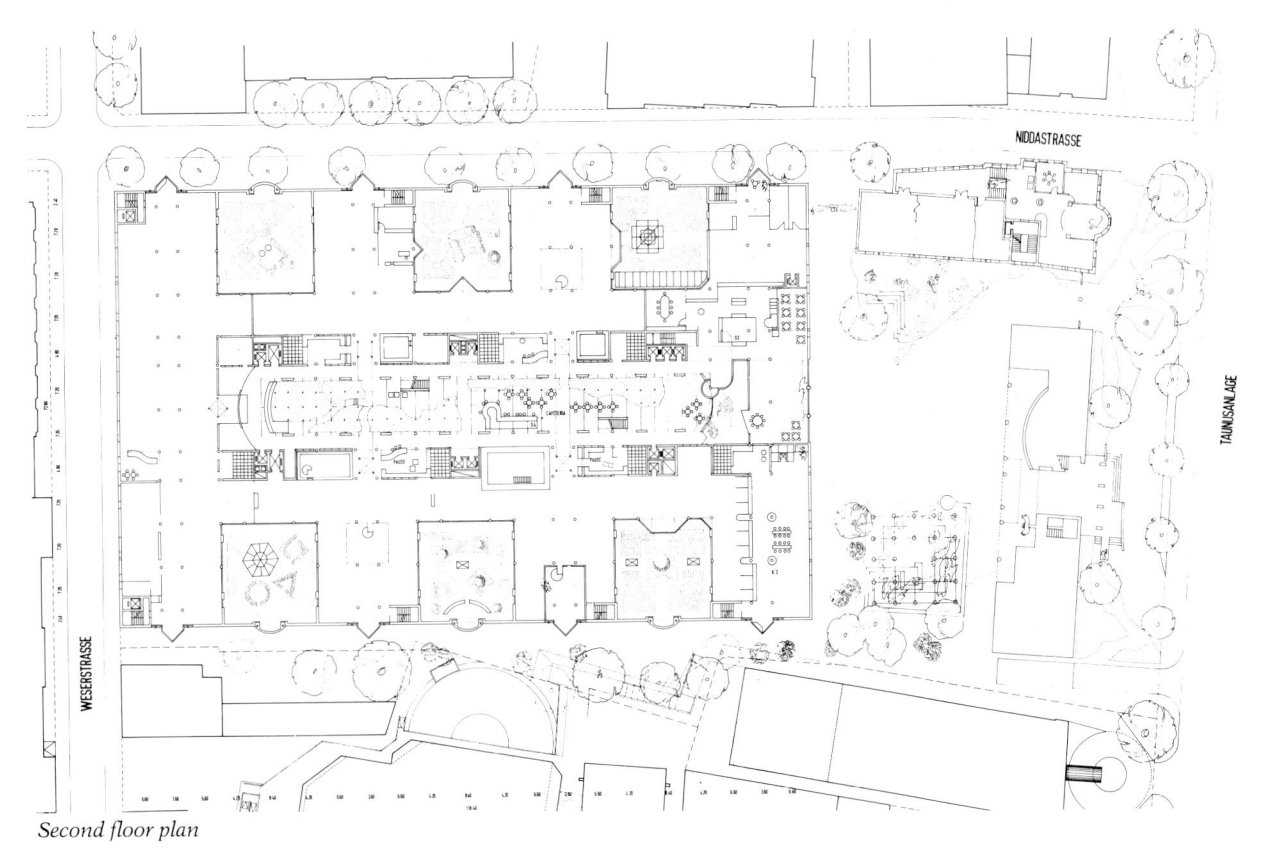

Second floor plan

Documenta Hall • Kassel • 1989–92

The Documenta Hall does not have the character of a museum; it is a transitory place, a place for contemporary and future ideas about and concepts of art. Instead of finding only objects with an already determined value, the hall is a place where people are confronted with a single question: What is art? Thus the architectural approach focused on the hall as a workshop, with all possible informality and freedom, as a place for unbiased discussion strongly committed to art: a shell. It required external restraint, not vividness, an architecture without statuary qualities or the permanence of a traditional museum.

Architecture is always urban design: creating a composition of solids in space, shaping intermediate spaces, working with what is available or transforming it into something totally different. A given architectural approach is revealed in its treatment of the city and the site. The definition of exterior space is enlivened by the composition. In terms of city planning, the positioning of the hall parallel to the Staatstheater on the Auekante was decisive—it makes the building an integral part of the area—and the design is based on the relationship of the Auekante to the Friedrichsplatz. The sloped outdoor urban space and the inside room sequence are dialectically opposed. The view of the landscape from the dynamic, side-lighted hall intensifies the path to the Friedrichsplatz and makes it appear to continue as a route for visitors inside.

Entry to the Documenta Hall is from the Friedrichsplatz. The entry canopy follows the rhythm established by the entrances to the Red Palace, the Fridericianum, and the Staatstheater, which all face the square. The flexible planning—exhibition rooms that can be subdivided several times—enables both the building and individual areas in it to be used easily after the Documenta. The small exhibition rooms can be used for film screenings, lectures, poetry readings, or small-scale exhibitions; the large hall can be used by the Staatstheater for rehearsals.

Jochem Jourdan

JOCHEM JOURDAN 131

Lower level plan

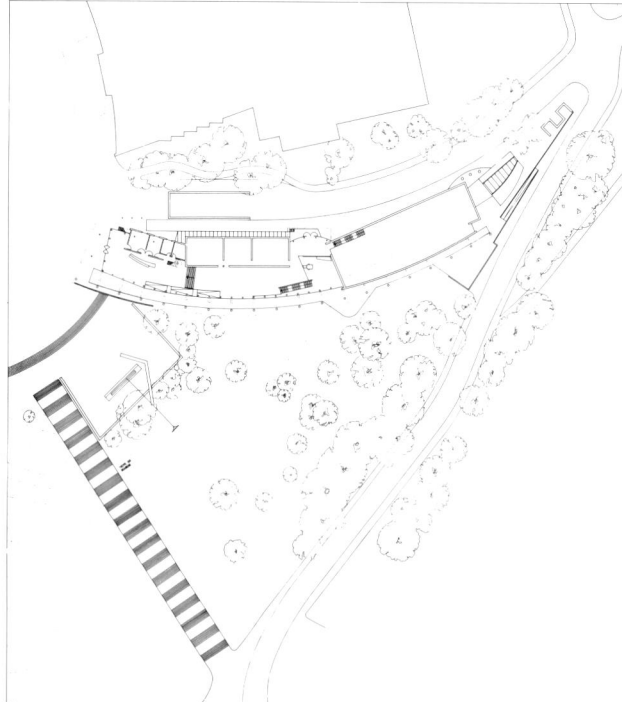

Entry level plan

132 JOCHEM JOURDAN

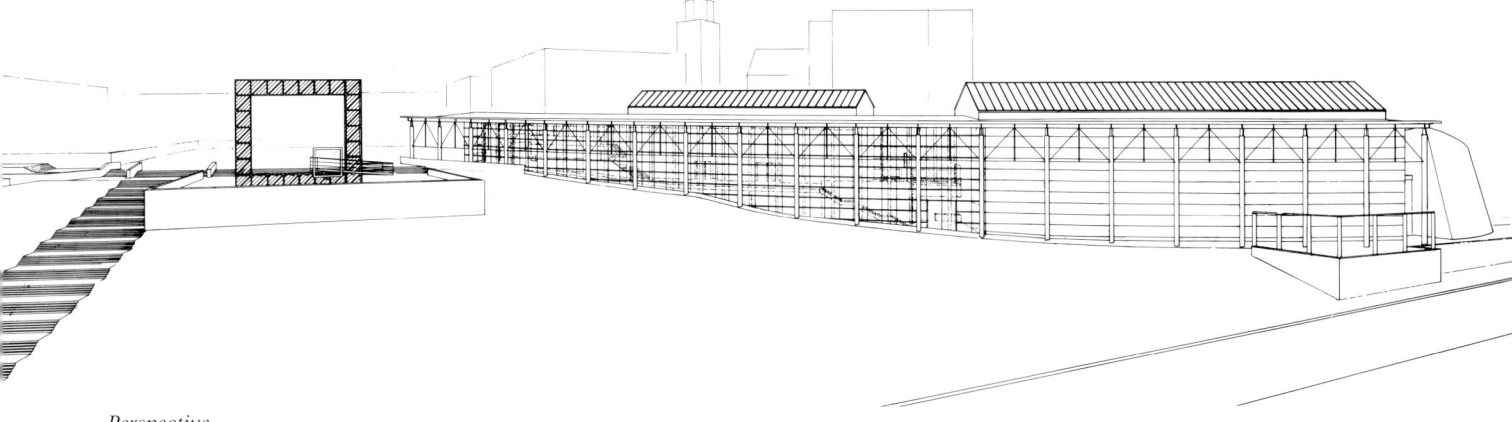

Perspective

KAUFFMANN AND THEILIG
Office Complex • Ostfildern-Kemnat • 1988–90

The new building had to solve the structural and urban problems of a less-than-spectacular site. Two office buildings were on the property: a four-story building from the 1980s to the north and a plain, two-story building from the 1960s to the south. The new office building was integrated into this ensemble; now all three are set on a common base formed by a new underground garage and appear to share a single foundation.

The new building features a central, double-loaded, north-south corridor, which flares into an open inner courtyard reminiscent of a winter garden. The restrooms, maintenance room, and employee kitchen are positioned around the open space; a stair-and-elevator tower links the open corridors leading into the glass hall. The courtyard introduces natural light to the corridors and in turn to the offices; thus the two office sections are lighted from both front and rear. These sun-drenched, mediating spaces have a quality difficult to envision from the heterogeneous surroundings.
Kauffmann and Theilig

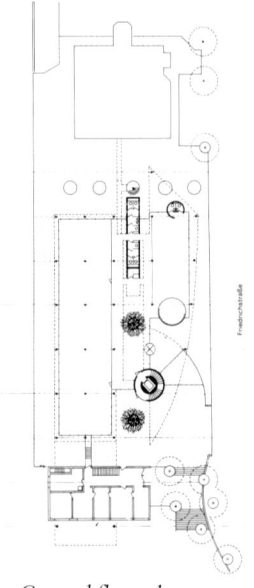

Ground floor plan

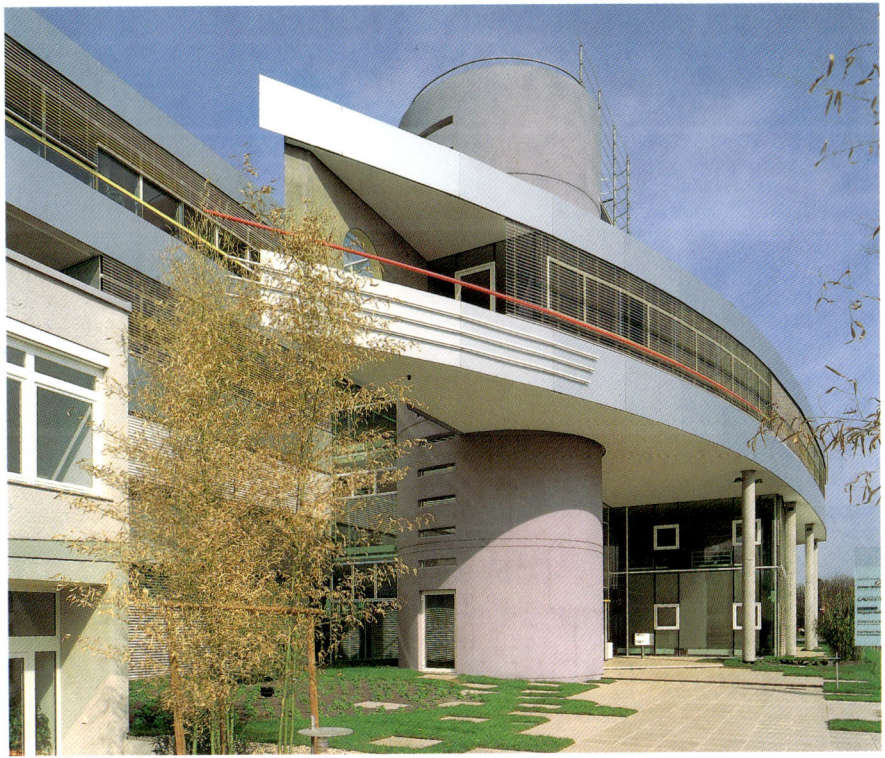

KAUFFMANN AND THEILIG 135

Exhibition/Office Building • Maintal-Dörningheim • 1989–92

The architecture of this new office and exhibition complex for the Dötsch Company was based on the desire to display modern office products in an appropriate setting while creating a progressive and exemplary work environment for all employees. The requirements shaped the architecture; the architecture aided in achieving this dual objective.

The building is located in an unattractive neighborhood. A haphazard industrial area lies to the north, east, and west; to the south is a major thoroughfare, from which the building can be seen. The property outline is illogical: probably, parts of old field boundaries were pieced together, unintentionally creating a parallelogram, which was then repeated in the adjacent structures. The upper, circular section of the building breaks from this pattern.

Though the ground-floor sales and exhibition area does follow the basic parallelogram, the building is composed so that there is no sense of that shape: a wood roof shell on a steel load-bearing system creates a floating plane. Room-height glass panels create seamless transitions from exterior to interior. The view of the dreary surroundings is mitigated by closed, built-in elements in the facade.

The ground-floor areas and the upper-story offices are connected by a spacious, open area covered with a filigree glass structure: a casual gathering space and also a place to understand the architecture of the complex. There are a variety of distinctly crafted stairways, perfect vantage points from which to experience the interior space. Thus, a new center of the building is created, a new orientation point which counters the mediocre surroundings.

The building that emerges has three overlapping layers, each formally and structurally independent of the others: a glazed rooftop conference area, the round office section, and the exhibition space. The building program is reflected in the form and even in the smallest details: modern technology without technological exaggeration, appropriateness and functionalism without functionalistic one-sidedness, joy in the way objects perform and also in how they look.
Kauffmann and Theilig

Third floor plan

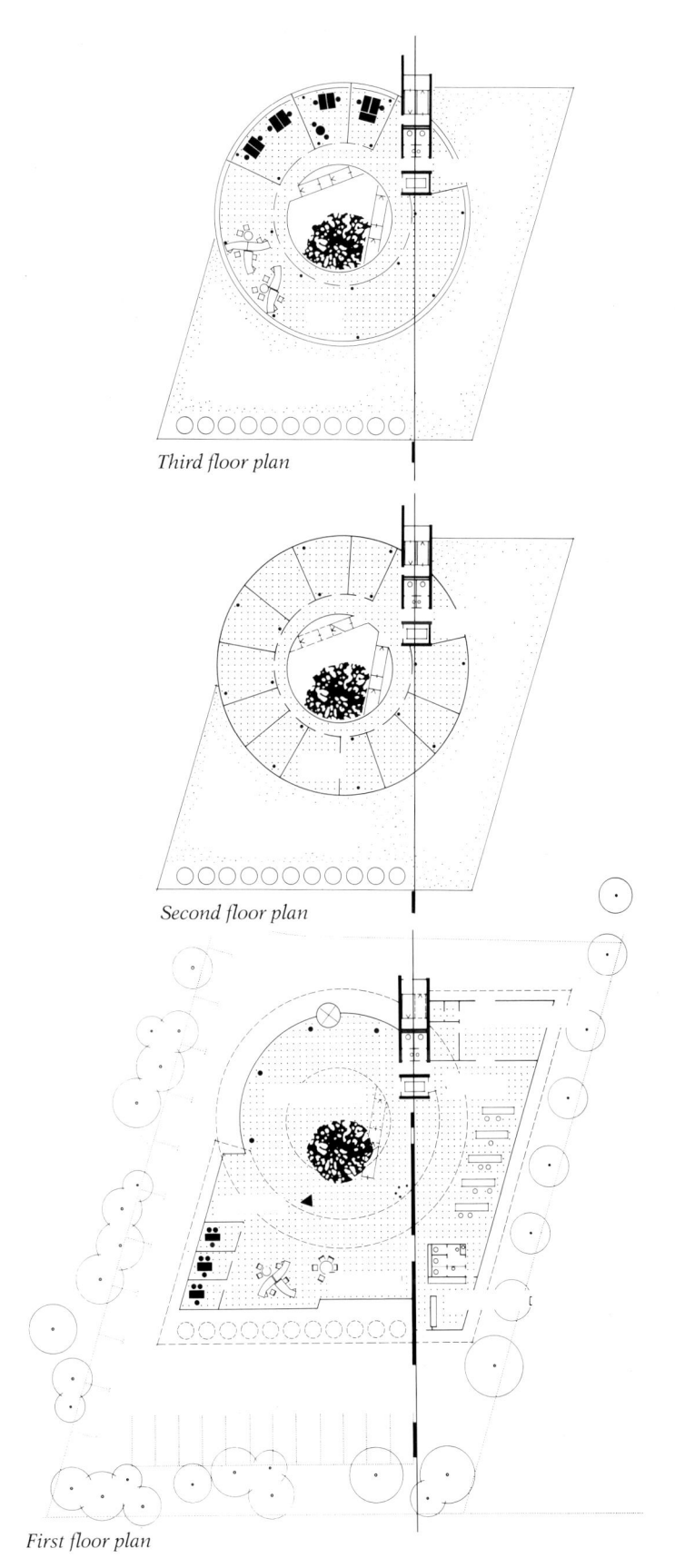

Second floor plan

First floor plan

138   KAUFFMANN AND THEILIG

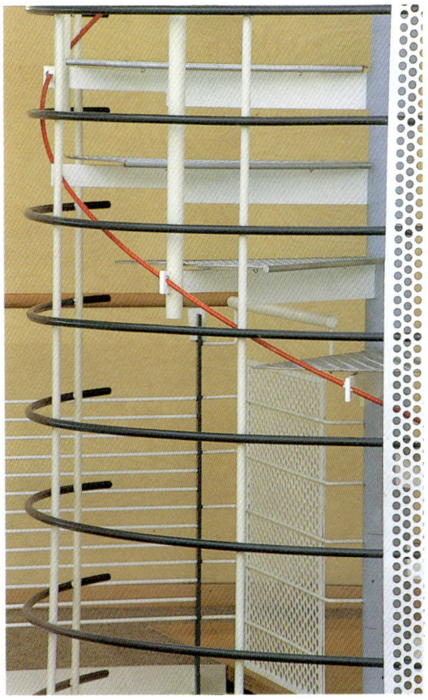

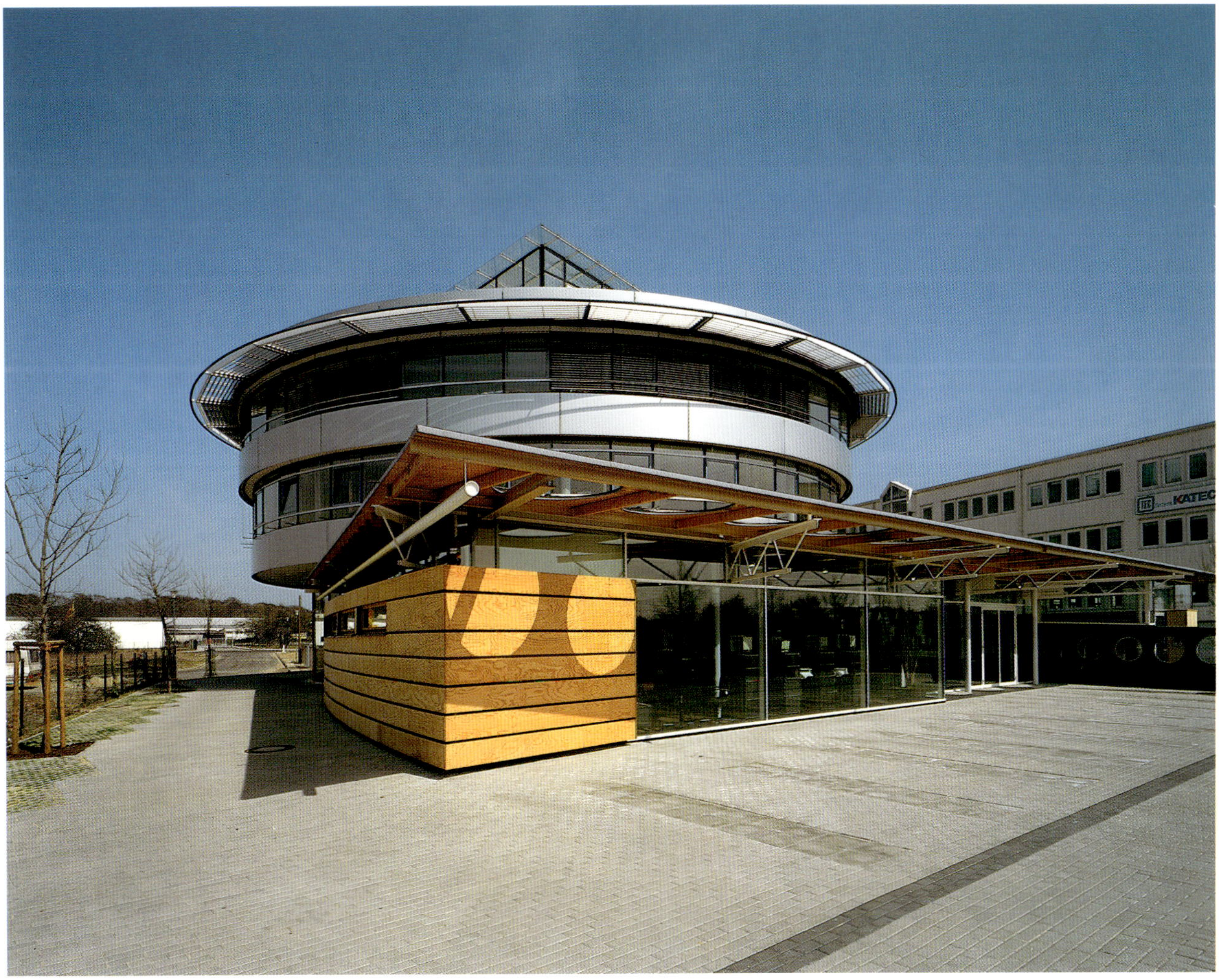
KATEC

UWE KIESSLER
Technical Center • Lüdenscheid • 1986–88

The Erco lighting plant is located at the edge of Lüdenscheid on a site overlooking the forested countryside. It consists of two major elements: a huge production shed lighted from the north and dating from the 1960s and the new technical center. The breakdown of the parts exemplifies the nature of industrialization in the late twentieth century. The production is as automated as possible; the technical center contains the research and development areas, without which the firm's products would quickly become outdated and the factory useless.

The technical center consists of a low central tower with two wings. The western one accommodates customer and design services; the much larger eastern wing, a tooling shop and areas for prototype development and testing. The tower contains central activities: archives, publicity, marketing, administration, and management; accounting is located in a 1960s slab to the south of the production shed and is connected to the new building by a bridge between the top floors and a glazed corridor at ground level.

A manipulation of section and an exploitation of visual connections are characteristic of the whole building: a spatial generosity makes the building much more than a machine for working. Split levels and double heights are frequently employed in the two wings to bring daylight into the middle section and to provide spatial variety and social continuity. Even the most conventionally factory-like part, the tooling shop, is filled with daylight from its great glazed roof, and the highly skilled craftsmen who produce the lamp patterns used in the production shed work in an atmosphere that is more like a cross between an office and a conservatory than a conventional workshop. *Peter Davey*

UWE KIESSLER 141

Upper level plan

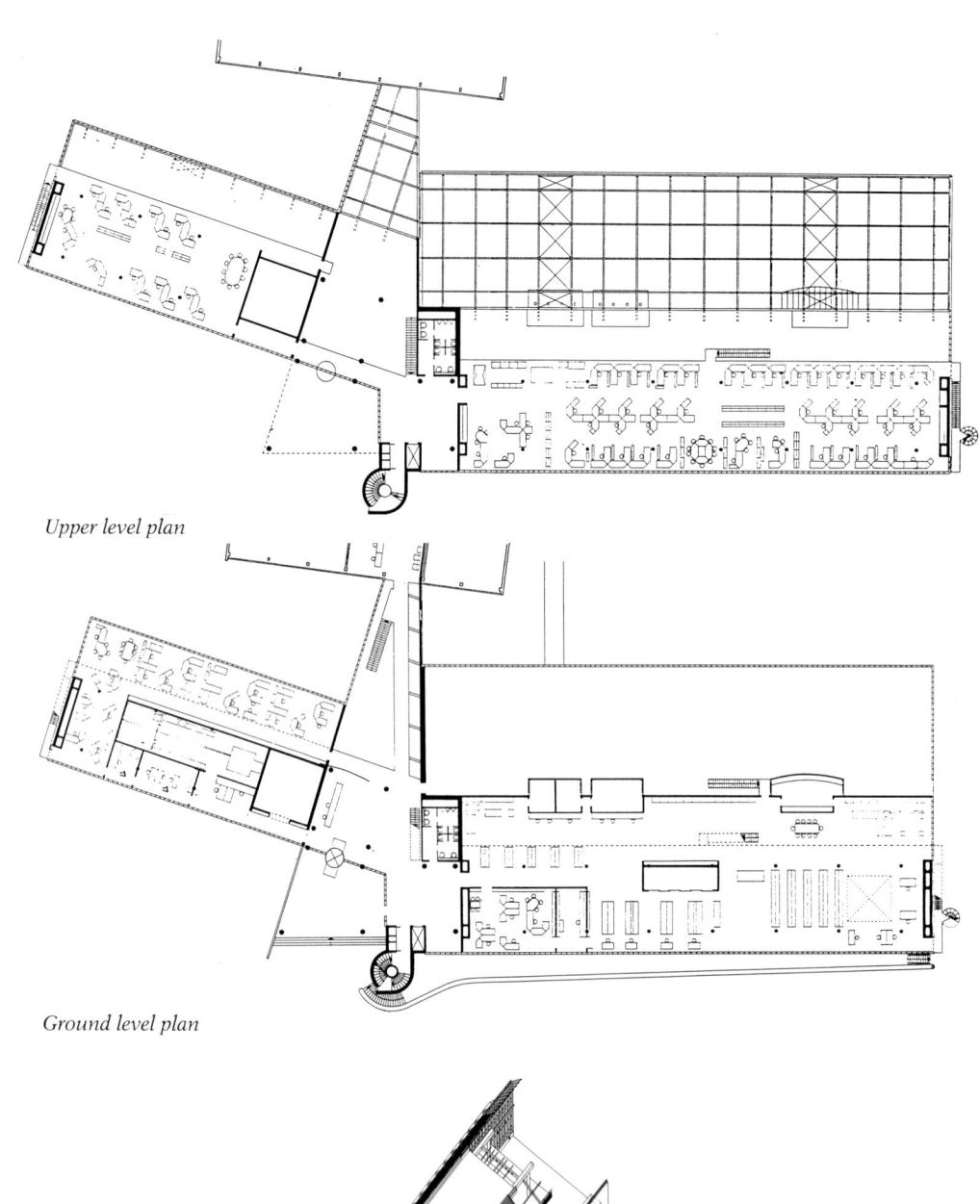

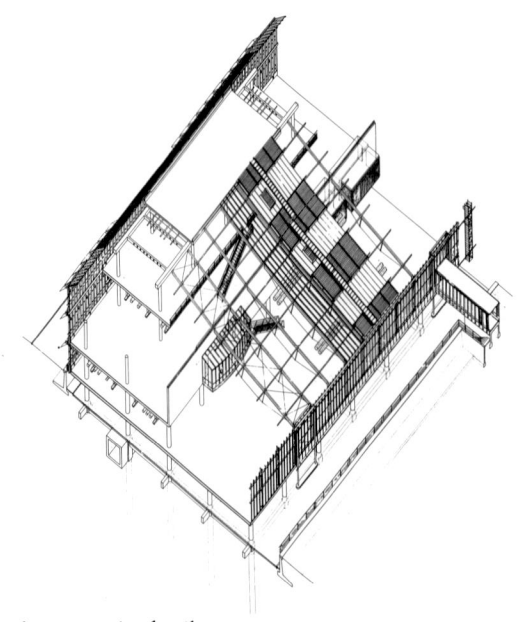

Ground level plan

Axonometric, detail

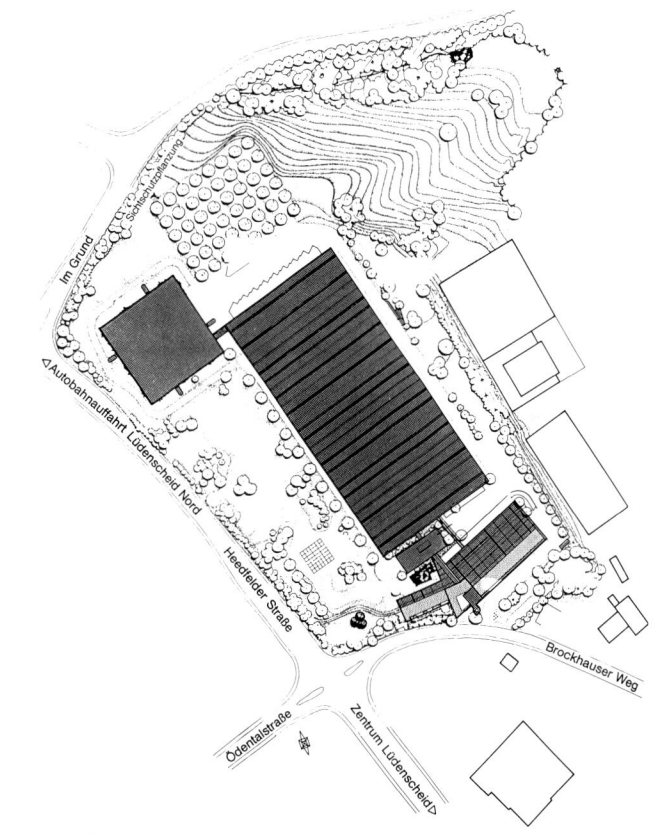

Site plan

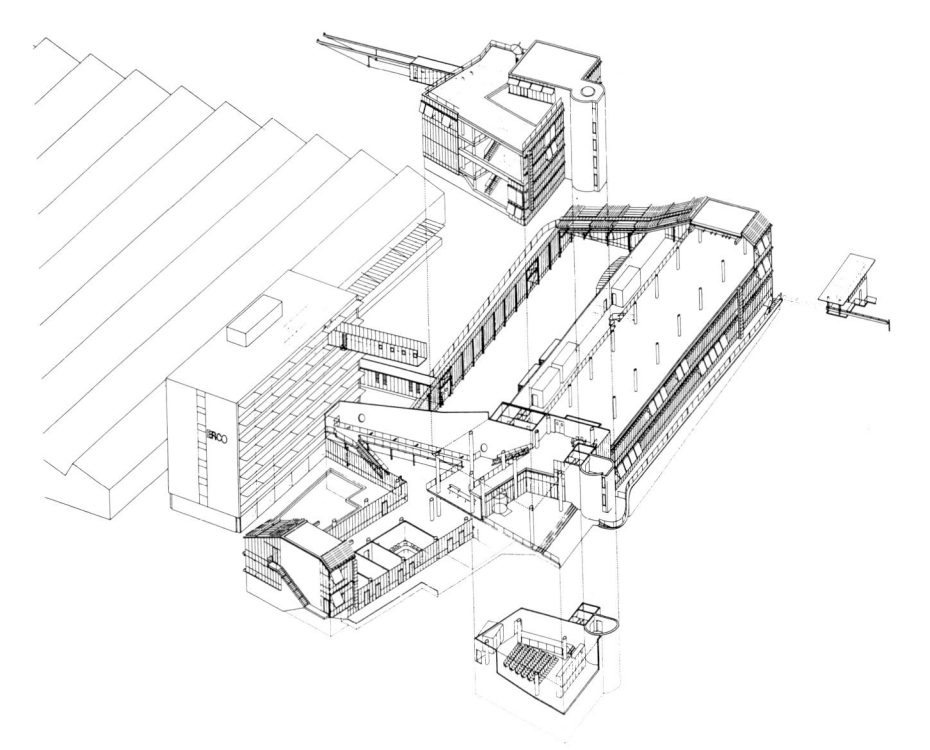

Exploded axonometric

JOSEF PAUL KLEIHUES
Hospital Addition • Neukölln • 1968–78

The addition, on a long, narrow site parallel to the beautiful old hospital complex, took twelve years of planning. The old buildings had no common structural characteristics; thus, great attention was given to an appropriate scale and height. While forty-nine thousand square meters of usable space were produced, the new building remains below the height of the adjacent nurses' housing and residential blocks.

Quite independent of the rather low height, unusual for hospitals of this type, the volume of the addition responds to special demands regarding scale, architectonic detail, and appearance. A large building corresponds to both the functional requirements and the wish to guarantee the unity of the parts through measurement, number, material, and color. Moreover, the grid of the facade intentionally confuses the reading of stories or functional units so that scale is maintained even in relation to the overall area. *Josef Paul Kleihues*

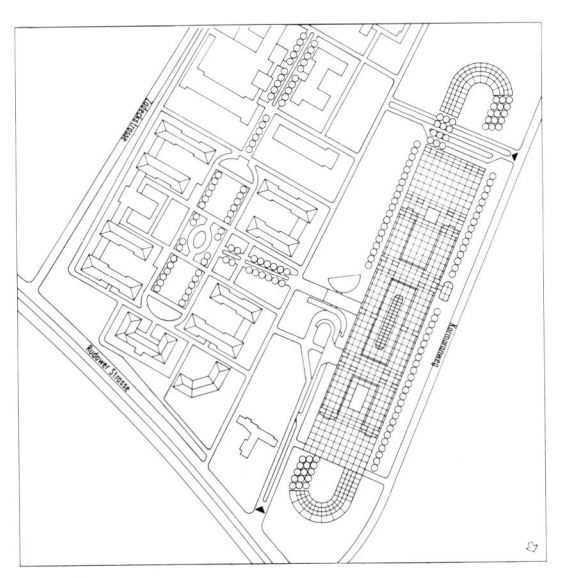

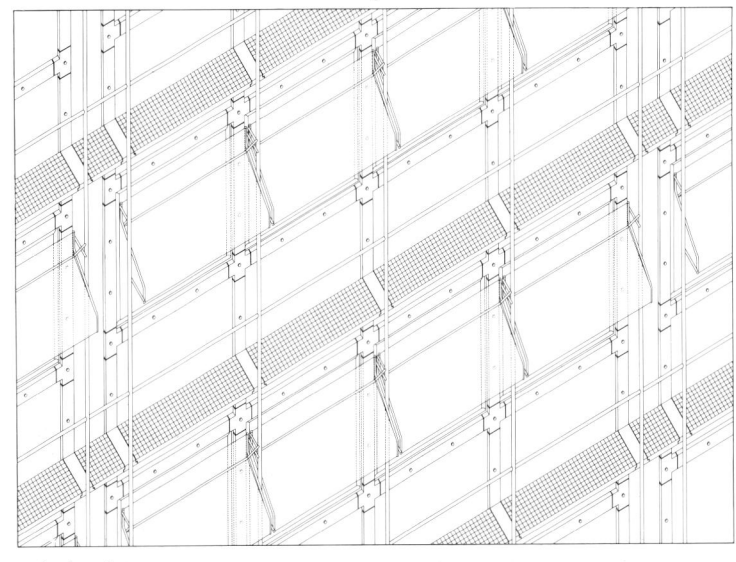

Site plan

Facade detail, isometric

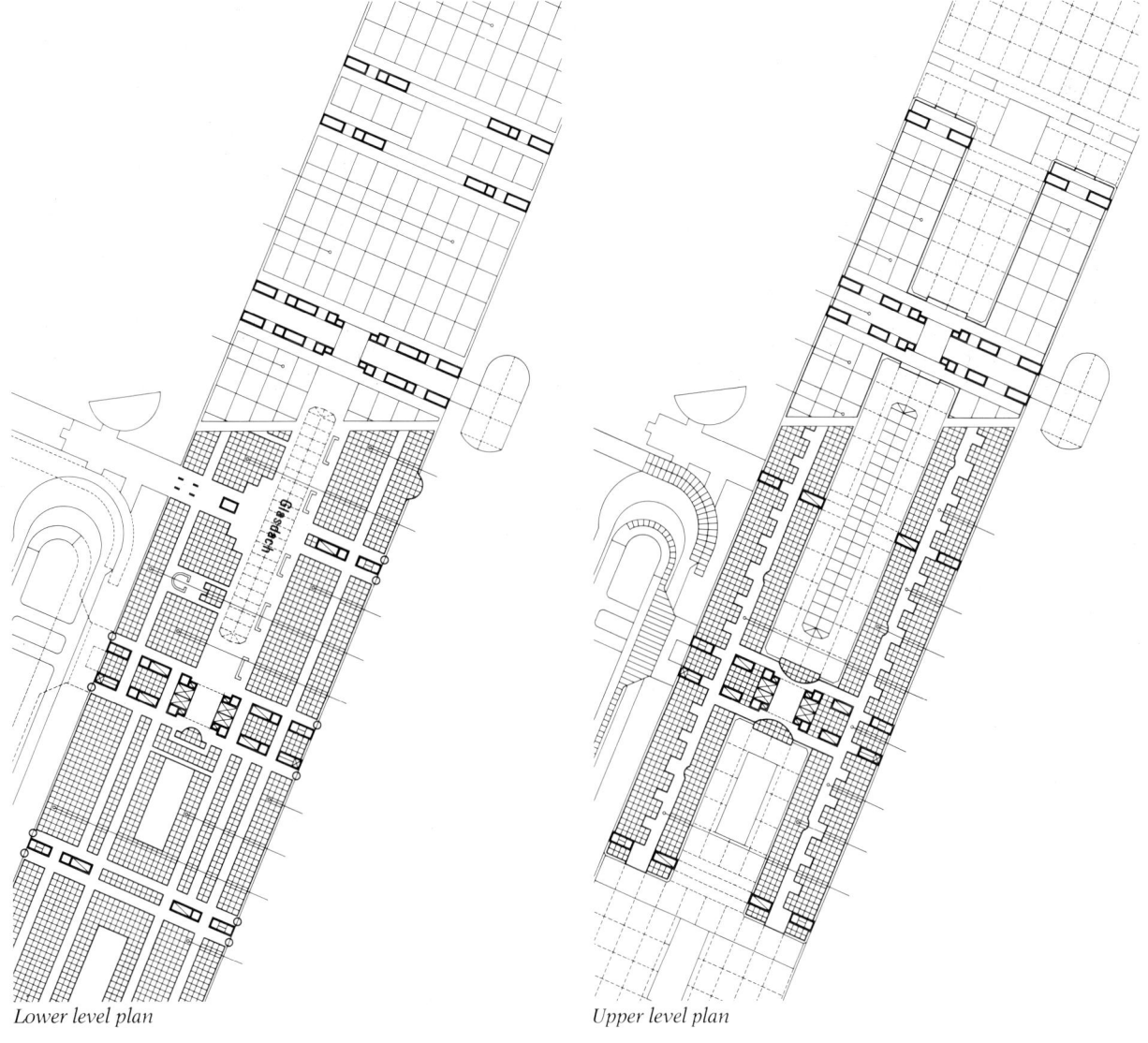

Lower level plan

Upper level plan

JOSEF PAUL KLEIHUES 145

Pre- and Early History Museum • Frankfurt am Main • 1981–89

The Museum for Pre- and Early History provokes dialogue between traditionalism and modernism and entertains both the intellect and the senses. As a culturo-scientific institution it satisfies functional demands; as a culture-purveying institution it presents a spatial and atmospheric quality of experience. Functionalism and experiential quality are not alternatives; together they produce an important interplay. This is matched by the spatial-architectonic design of the exhibition areas, the spatial-functional arrangement of the storeroom, restoration, and administration areas, and the urban-planning arrangement of the new building within the context of the surrounding historical fabric. Priorities in this building were: that figures and dimensions and geometrical laws be more than just happy coincidences; that the architectonic form permit a clear statement; that the choice of materials have priority over the choice of colors; and that there be no aesthetic alternative to craftsmanship and proper attention to structural detail.

The facades of the building are not only the closed street walls, presenting an image of stone interlocked by a grid of steel bolts, but also the glass walls that open up the exhibition rooms, presenting transparency emphasized by narrow aluminum mullions. The dimensions of interior planning that unite the new and the historical components with the reddish sandstone floor grid simultaneously determine the geometry of the plain aluminum exhibition showcase bases and the steel plinths for the stone monuments. The conscious reduction to these three materials and the fact that all walls are painted white emphasize the various exhibits from the museum's collection. The grouping of the showcases results not only in topical rows but also in avenue, courtyard-shaped, and other freer configurations which simplify orientation and enhance the museum experience. The general aim of these compositions of similar and differing elements is not just to present the exhibit as an object but, wherever possible, to put across its aura.
Josef Paul Kleihues

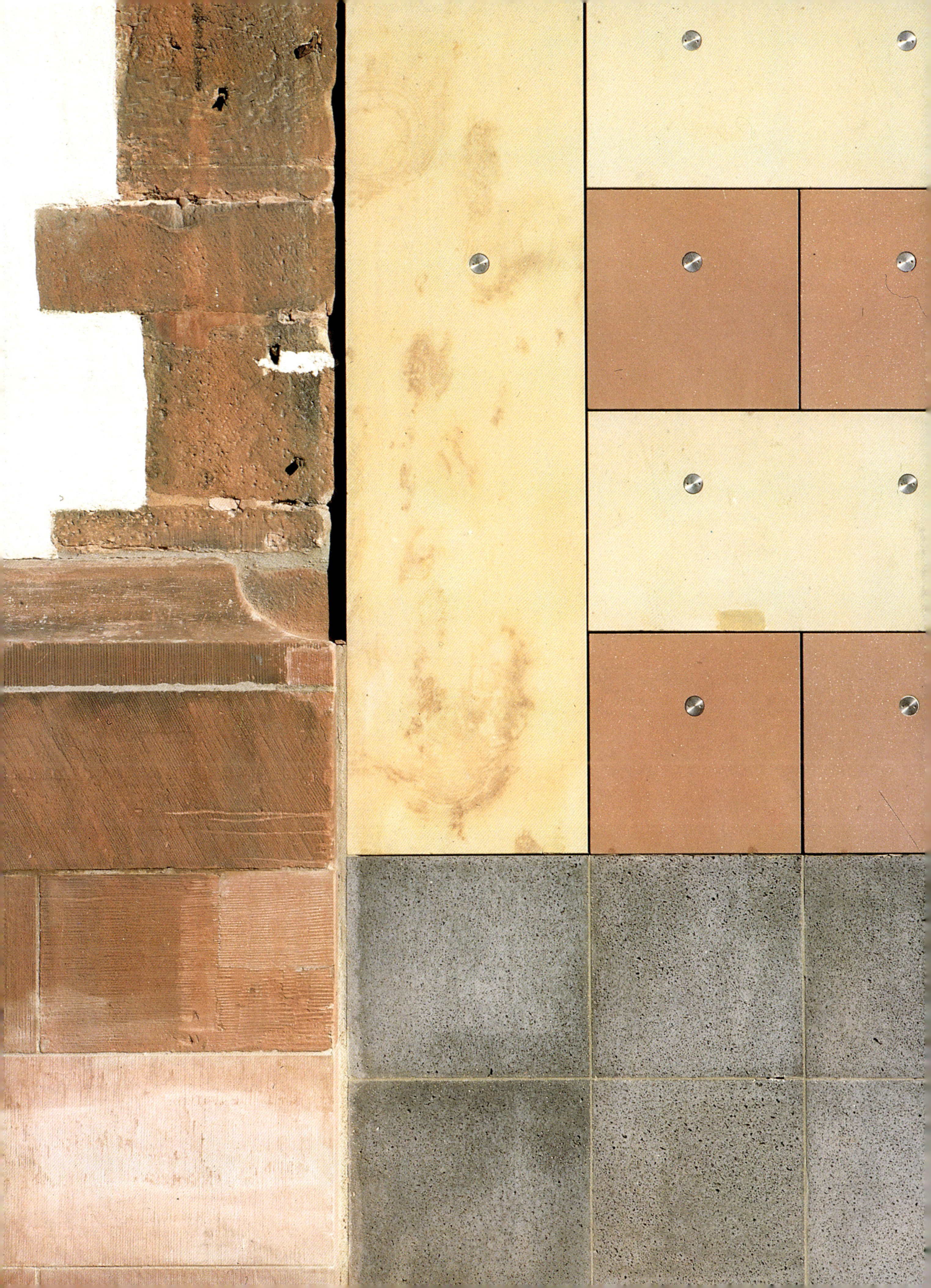

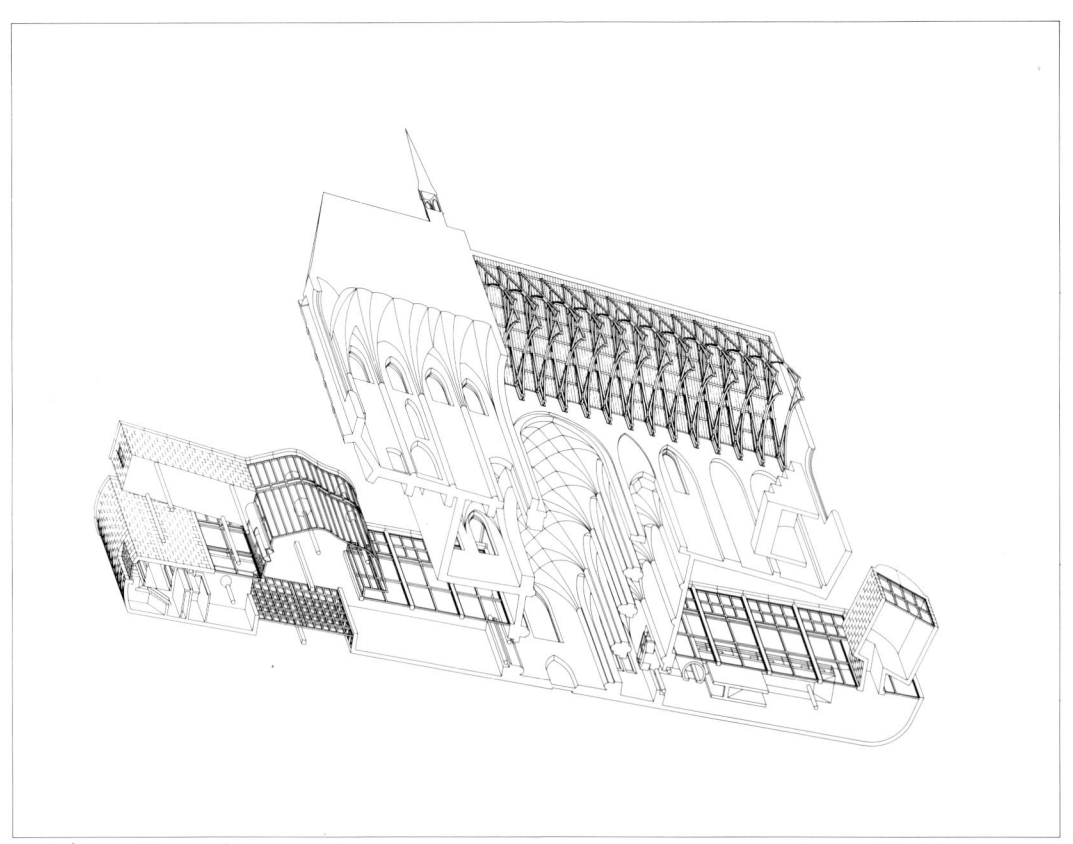

Worm's eye axonometric

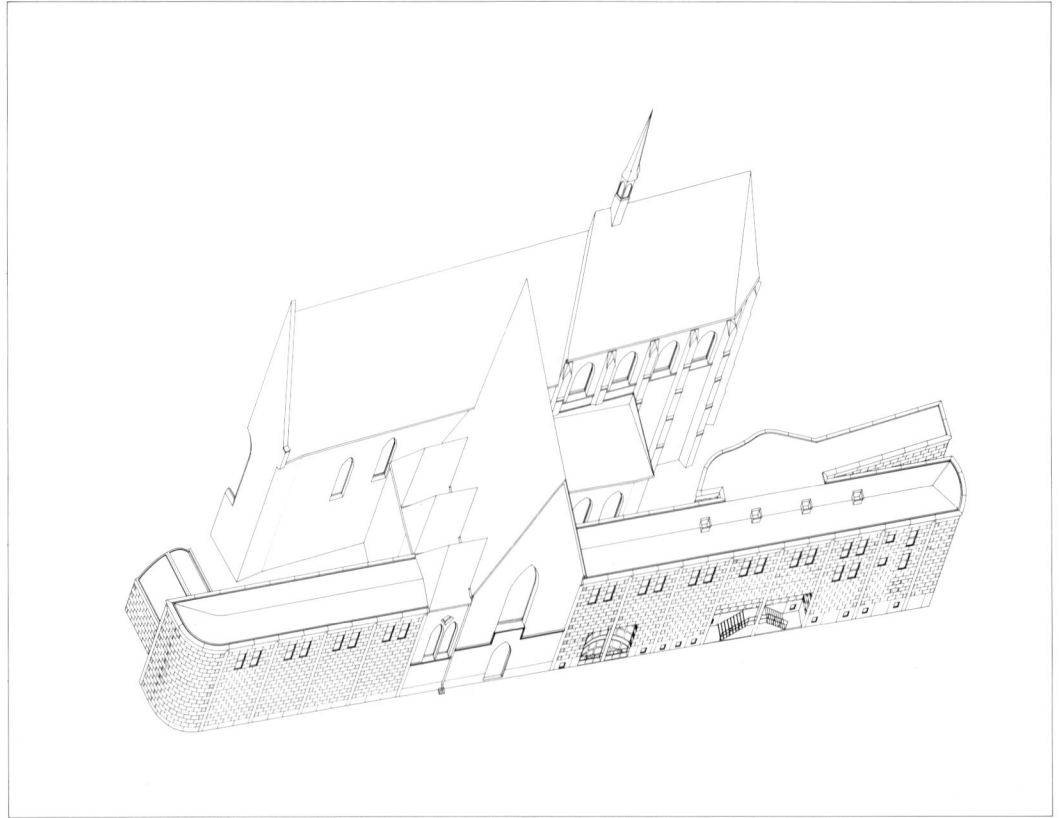

Axonometric

148   JOSEF PAUL KLEIHUES

Cross sections

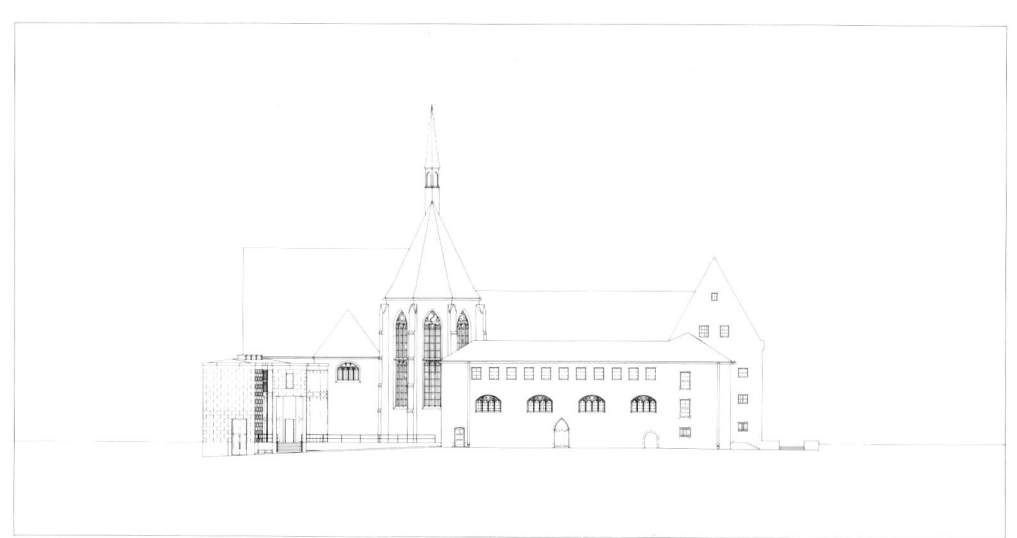

Elevation

Elevation

JOSEF PAUL KLEIHUES 149

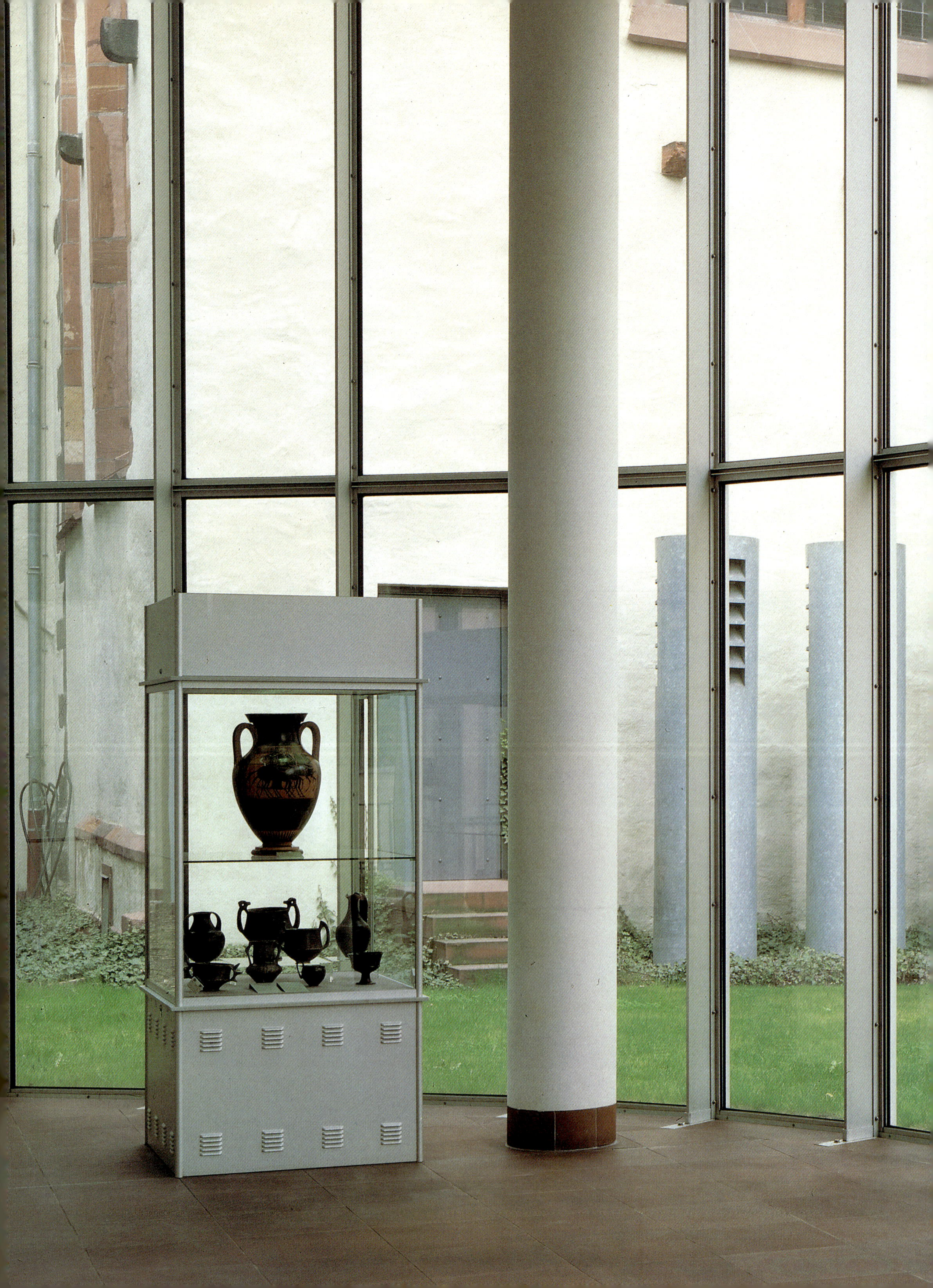

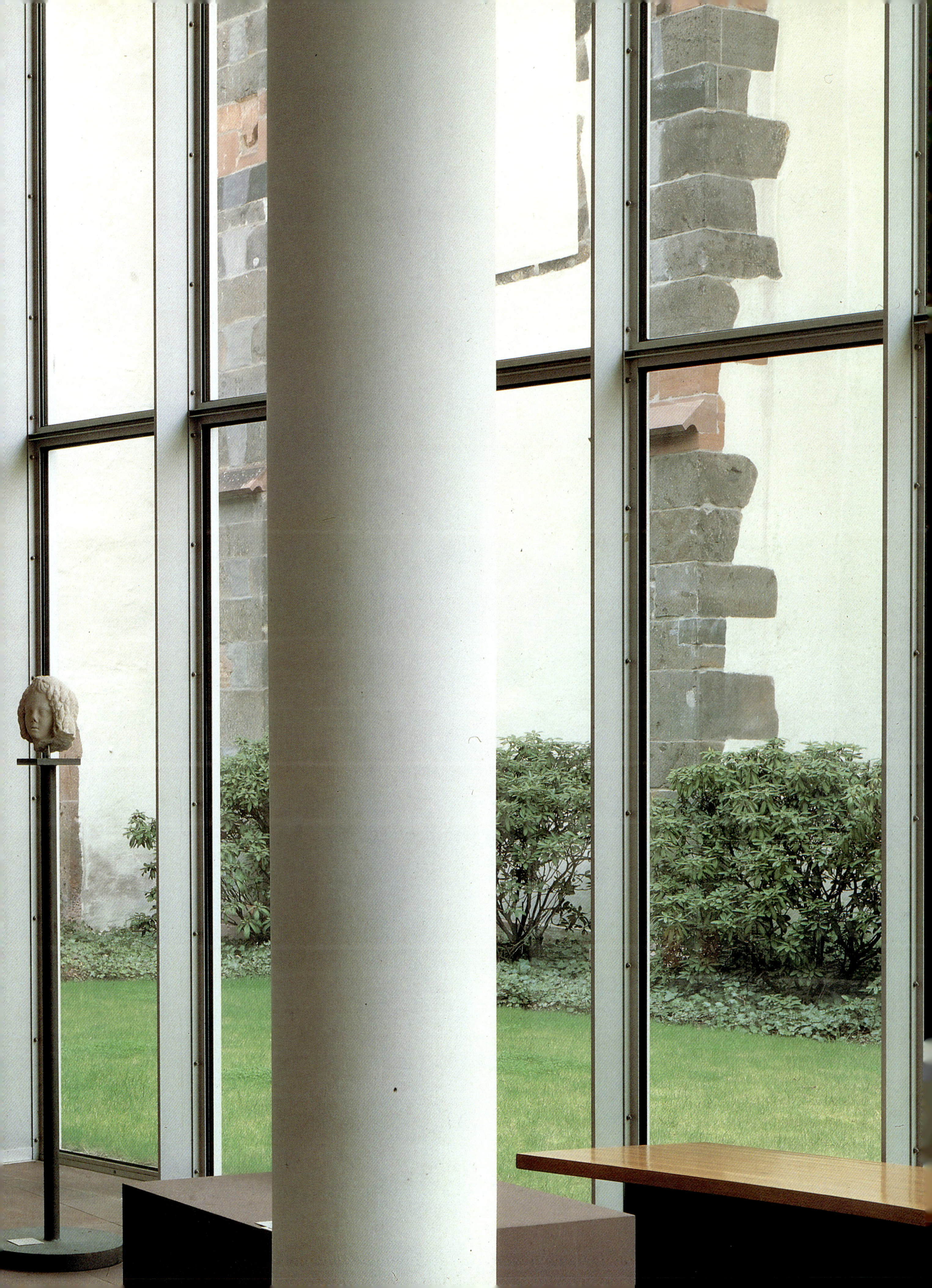

Municipal Gallery • Kornwestheim • 1990

The parallelogram, semi-circle, and square are the geometric figures in this floor plan; they determine the stereometry of the gallery's volumes and spatially rearrange its heterogeneity. The architectural image corresponds to the different structural parts; it is restrained in detailing and color: plinth, columns, walls, and pillars are clad in travertine, and the window frames are white.

Long and stretched out, the temporary exhibition area on the ground floor has an open plan for easy movement from piece to piece. The walls can be adjusted to create different kinds and sizes of spaces. The east wall, which runs the length of the room, is lighted from above. By placing partitions perpendicular to it, naturally illuminated display cases can be created. The space, with a view of the market square, also receives light laterally, from the front of the building. Shades and artificial lighting make possible varied effects. The second floor houses the Henninger Collection.

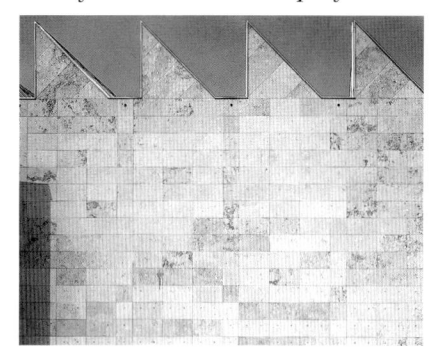

The semicircular lecture room lends itself to a number of uses. The stairway to the upper story opens invitingly toward the entryway and narrows perspectively as it approaches the upper story. This light-drenched space characterizes the enchantment of this small, beautiful gallery.

Josef Paul Kleihues

Ground level plan

Elevation

JOSEF PAUL KLEIHUES

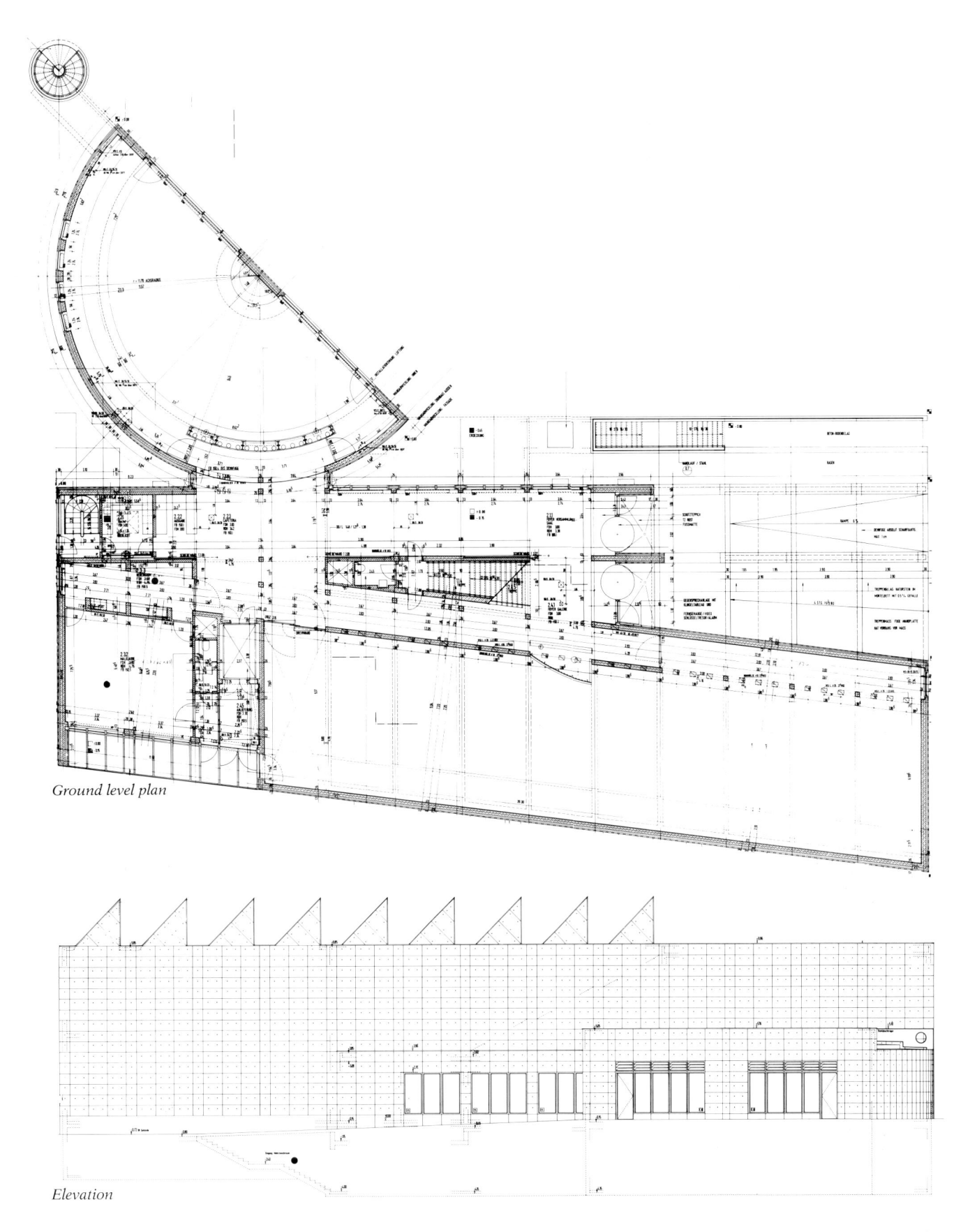

HANS KOLLHOFF
Housing Project • Berlin-Charlottenburg • 1983–87

The curved wall of this competition-winning design—like the impulsive yet precise brush stroke of a Japanese character—together with the Charlottenburg Castle, a pavilion designed by Karl Friedrich Schinkel, and a bridge, creates a particular overall composition in the city plan. A pure line emerges confidently from the heterogeneous buildings opposite the castle and embodies Schinkel's principle of the orthogonal relationship of axes.

During the first phase of planning, the decision was made to integrate, rather than demolish, a turn-of-the-century house on the Luisenplatz site. The result is a rigorous superimposition of the new curve and the older, angular house shape, forming an entirely new composition. The cubic form of the old house is squeezed out of the slab and monumentalized so that the contradictory character of nineteenth-century architecture is pushed to its limits. The trapped building unit gesticulates wildly as it emerges from the perimeter block surface. The stimulus provided by the compartmentalization of Berlin apartment houses is thus employed conceptually.

The contrast between the superblock housing and the baroque Charlottenburg Castle is also interesting. Its scenic potential is exploited in the wing-shaped roof, the large window, and the choice of heavy blue industrial brick (also used in some of Peter Behrens's industrial buildings). This integration implies very definite notions of living in the city: apartments open to the outside world (in this case, the sun, the castle, and its garden); individual expression in the facade in spite of its elegant and reserved nature; a generous outside area for each apartment; and a kind of common porch on each

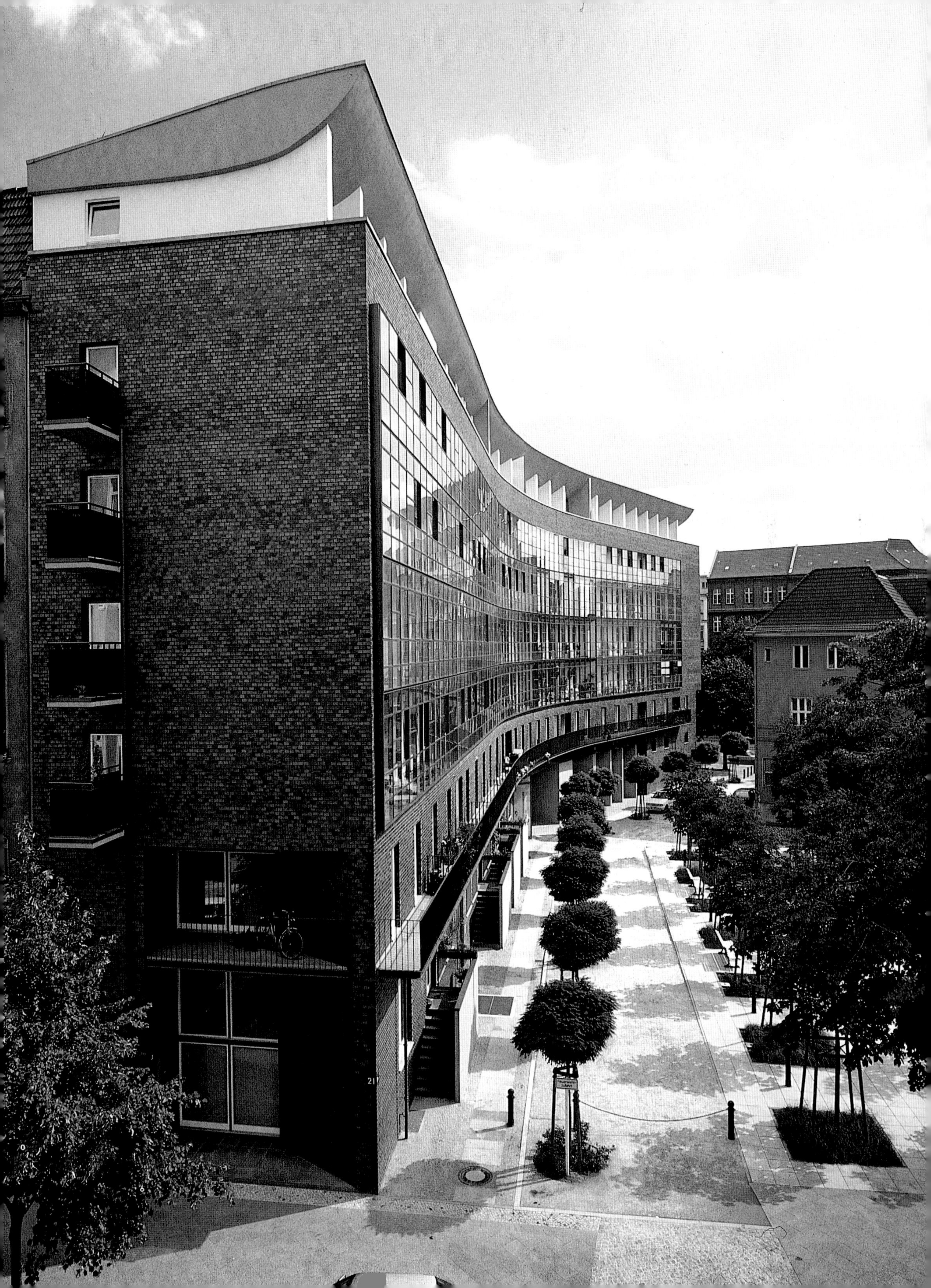

floor, to suggest the possibility of circumambulating the house. The process of adaptation to the site—orientating the apartments to the water, castle, or road, considering the need for sun and natural light—creates a greater degree of differentiation in the detailing, which in turn provides a welcome impetus to transform the basic figure even further. Thus instead of compromising on necessities, architectural inspiration was drawn from these chance factors. The abstract, curved slab becomes a complex composition, in which figural identification of the various areas is effected precisely at the level of detail.
Hans Kollhoff

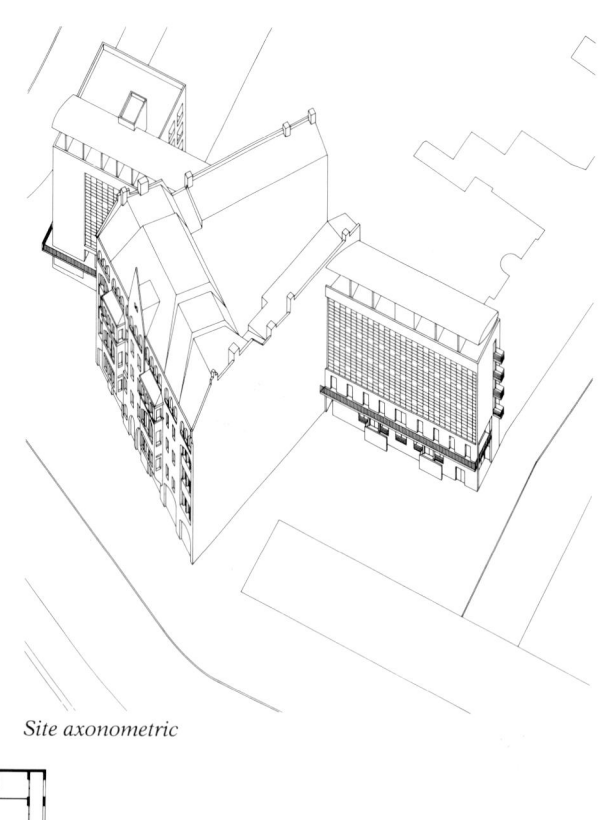

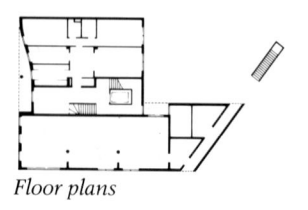

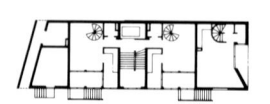

Site axonometric

Floor plans

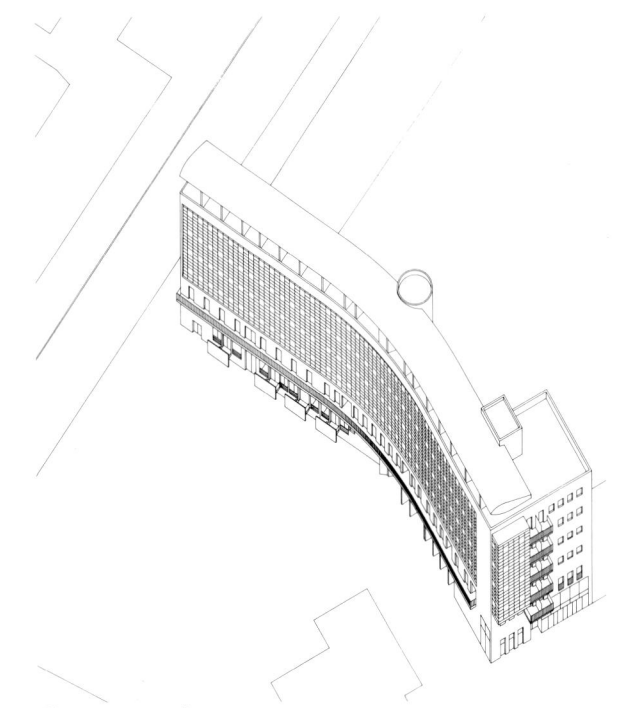

Site axonometric

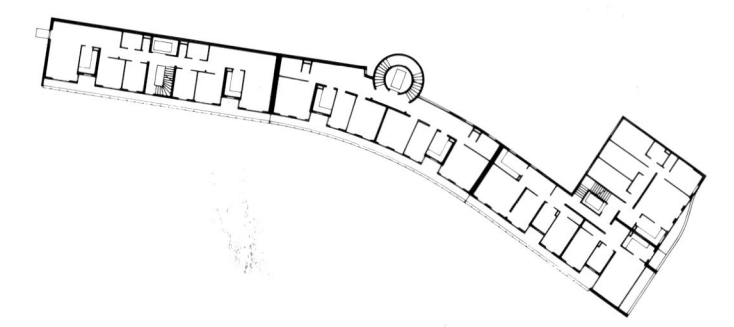

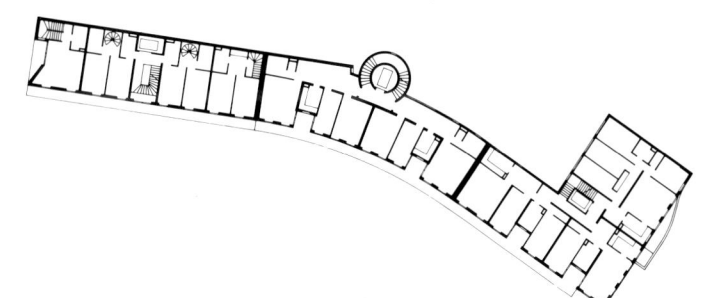

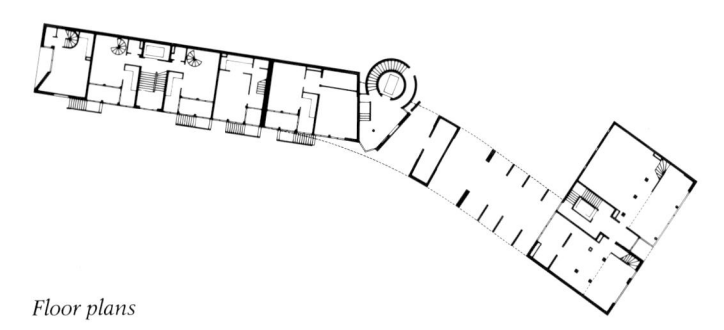

Floor plans

HANS KOLLHOFF 157

Potsdamer Platz Competition • Berlin • 1991

While it is possible to restore Potsdamer Platz to its historical dimensions, this should not be achieved by reconstructing the original square or by sacrificing it to modern pluralism. In this project, a compact base for seven high-rises was sited between the Potsdamer Platz and the green parkland of the new Tiergarten, which serves as a link to Potsdamer Park and Gleisdreieck Nature Park. In the middle of the square is a carpet of green, traversed by Leipzigerstrasse. The base is patterned after the once dominant building type in the square: it is of standard Berlin eaves height (also referring in this way to the edge of the Leipziger Platz and the front of the Tiergarten) and is divided into base, middle, and roof, with vertically ordered windows, and delicate, yet solidly built, natural stone facade relief. It will have large glass expanses for entryways and shop windows; aside from spacious entry halls, foyers, patios, and winter gardens, the base will accommodate all other functions that require a lot of room.

Hans Kollhoff

Site/typical floor plan

RÜDIGER KRAMM
Housing Complex • Darmstadt • 1989

Although the staircases of this housing complex on Bessungerstrasse seem to behave in a deconstructivist manner, the formal exploration aims primarily at a determined value of use: the inserted, free-form staircases divide the monotony of the straight line into practically independent sections, and permit individual access to almost every apartment. The common zone in front of the apartments is located not in covered stairwells but in transparent areas that provide visual contact to the street, bringing it almost to the entrance doors. The front facade of the building bends slightly, a clever interruption of traditionally austere Frankfurt housing. In addition, the garden entrance is located just at the point of the bend, illustrating the inhabitant-oriented freedom.

While the common spaces can be individually transformed to please particular inhabitants, the design is never really spoiled, possibly because it does not insist on originality. High modernism had the unfortunate effect of patronizing the public by predicting its habits. This divinatory effect should no longer be expected from architecture. The architect should not follow an absolutist utopia, but should face the problems of urban and social planning to derive individual designs. The architect steps back, but his hand remains visible and timely.
Klaus-Dieter Weiß

Cross section

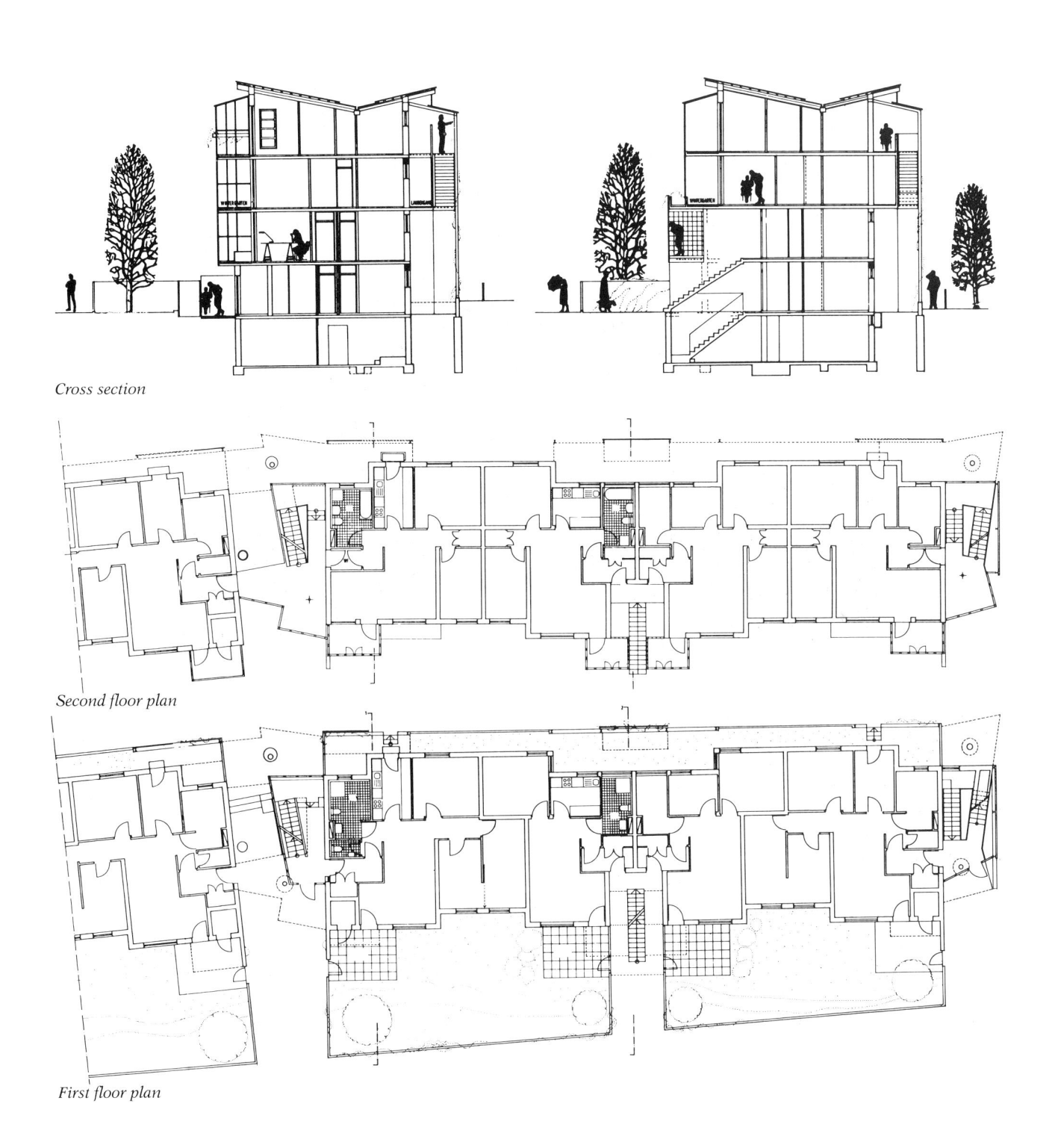

Second floor plan

First floor plan

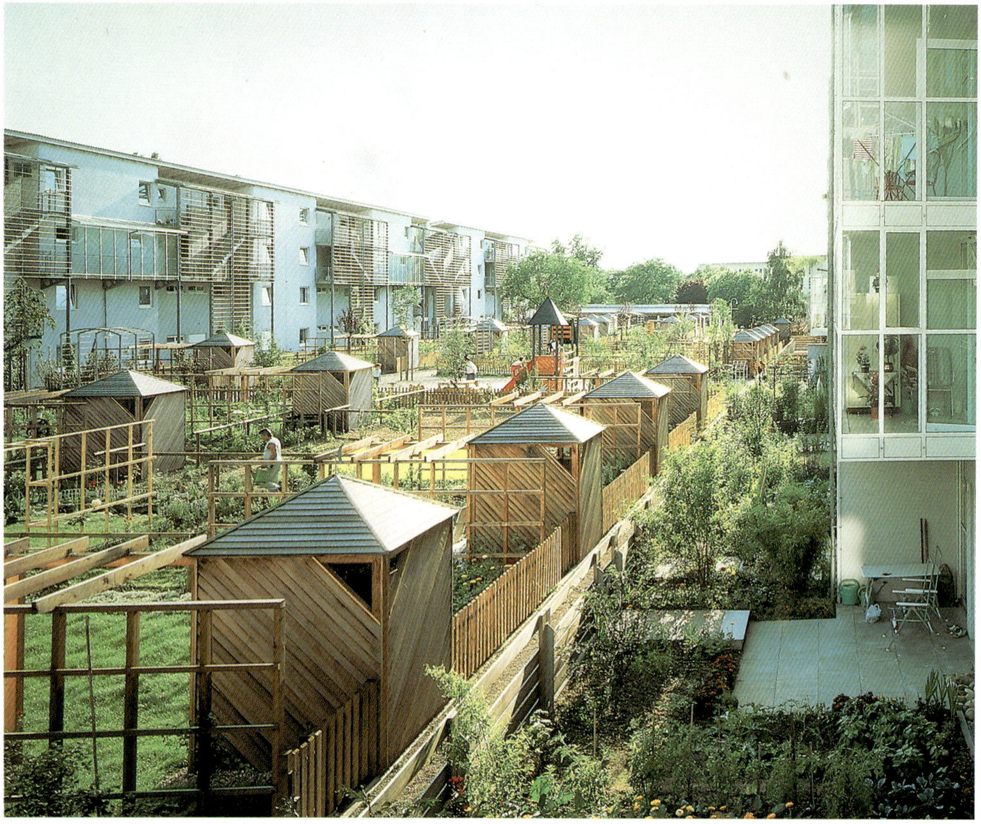

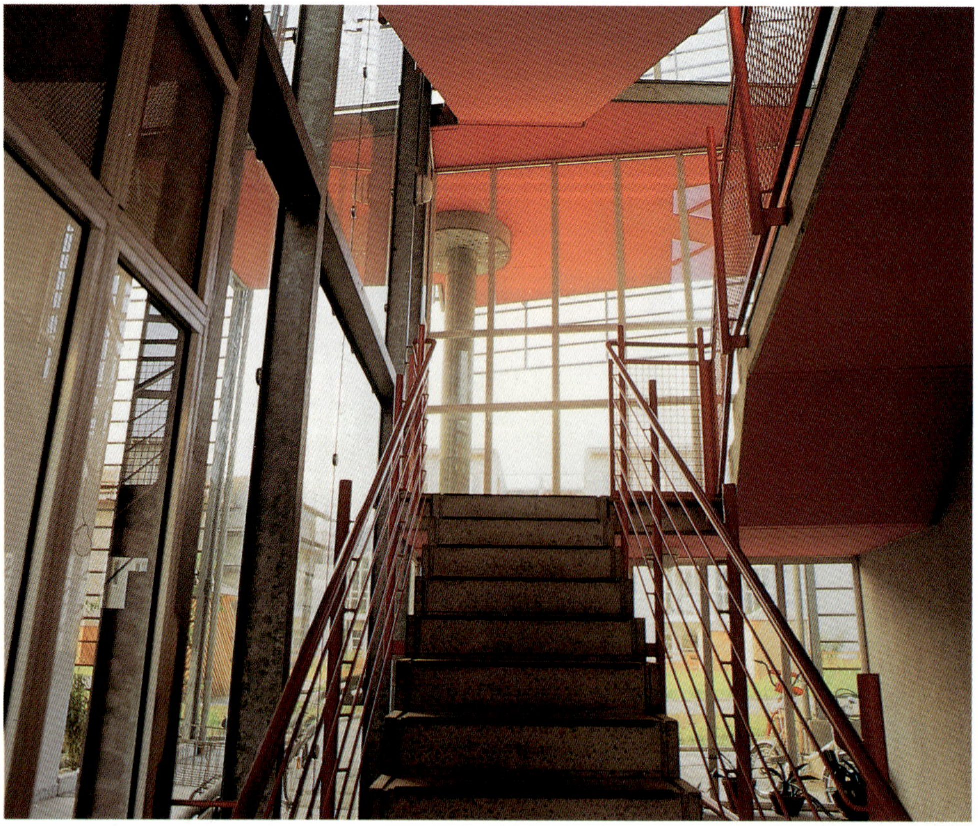

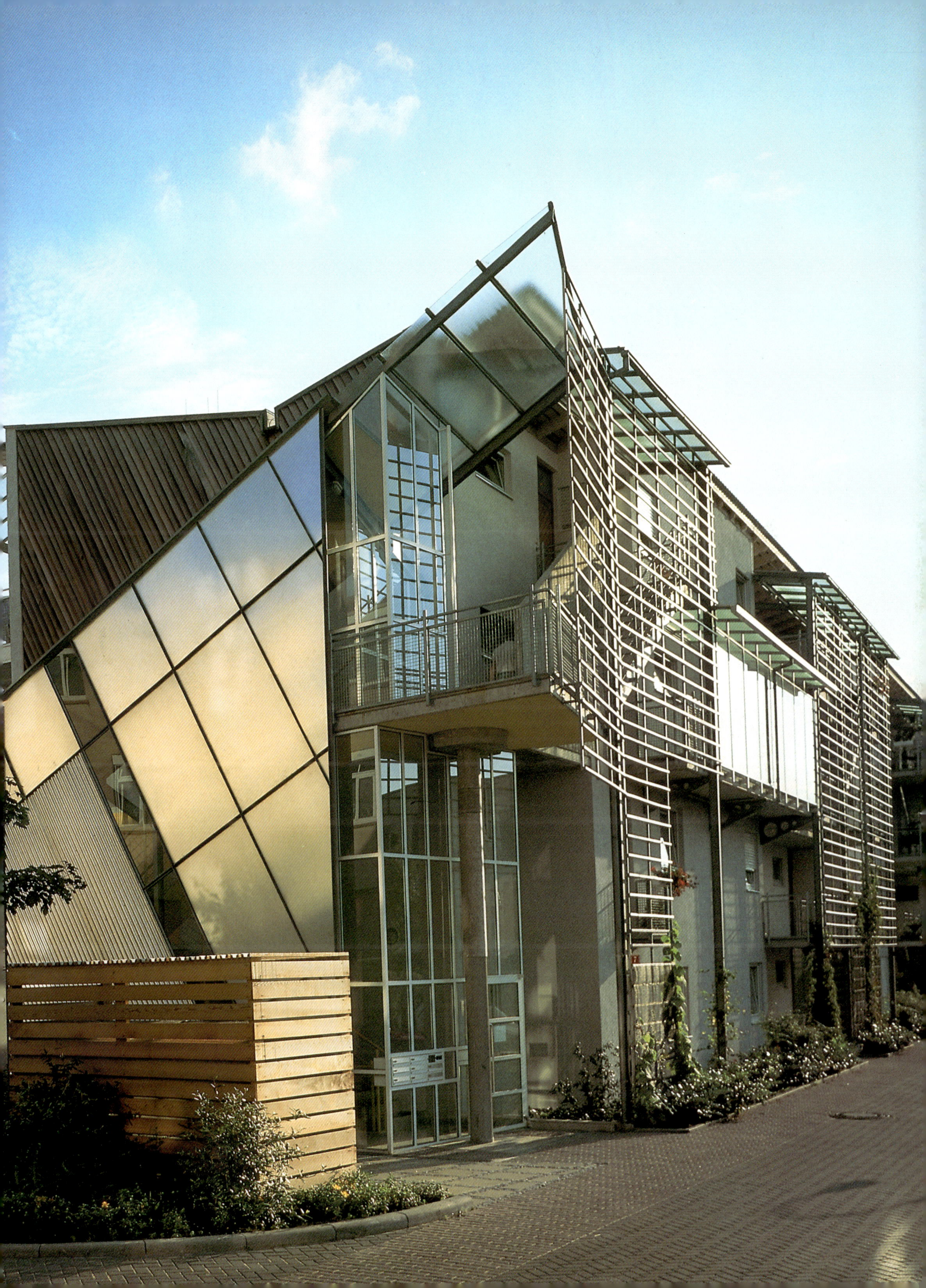

Public Housing Project • Frankfurt-Bonames • 1989

Perspective

The one-hundred-unit model housing project planned for Frankfurt-Bonames provides residents with a range of choices, offering one- to six-person apartments. This housing creates options specifically, though not exclusively, geared toward single parents.

Not just functional considerations but objectives like energy conservation and use of passive solar energy, both apparent in the exterior design, inspired the architectural approach. The strict north-south orientation makes the segmentation of the building into core, middle, and buffer zones very effective. Winter gardens and staircases are unheated buffer zones that protect the compact main part of the structure. The savings effect is admittedly, though unavoidably, reduced by the design goal of minimizing the ratio of exterior surface to enclosed spatial volume. Provisions have been made for a central heating plant as part of the model project. As there is a nature preserve to the south of the site, the slightly inclined and formally distinct monopitch roofs will be planted with tough grass to reduce the water supply to the planned cisterns.

Klaus-Dieter Weiß

Fourth floor plan

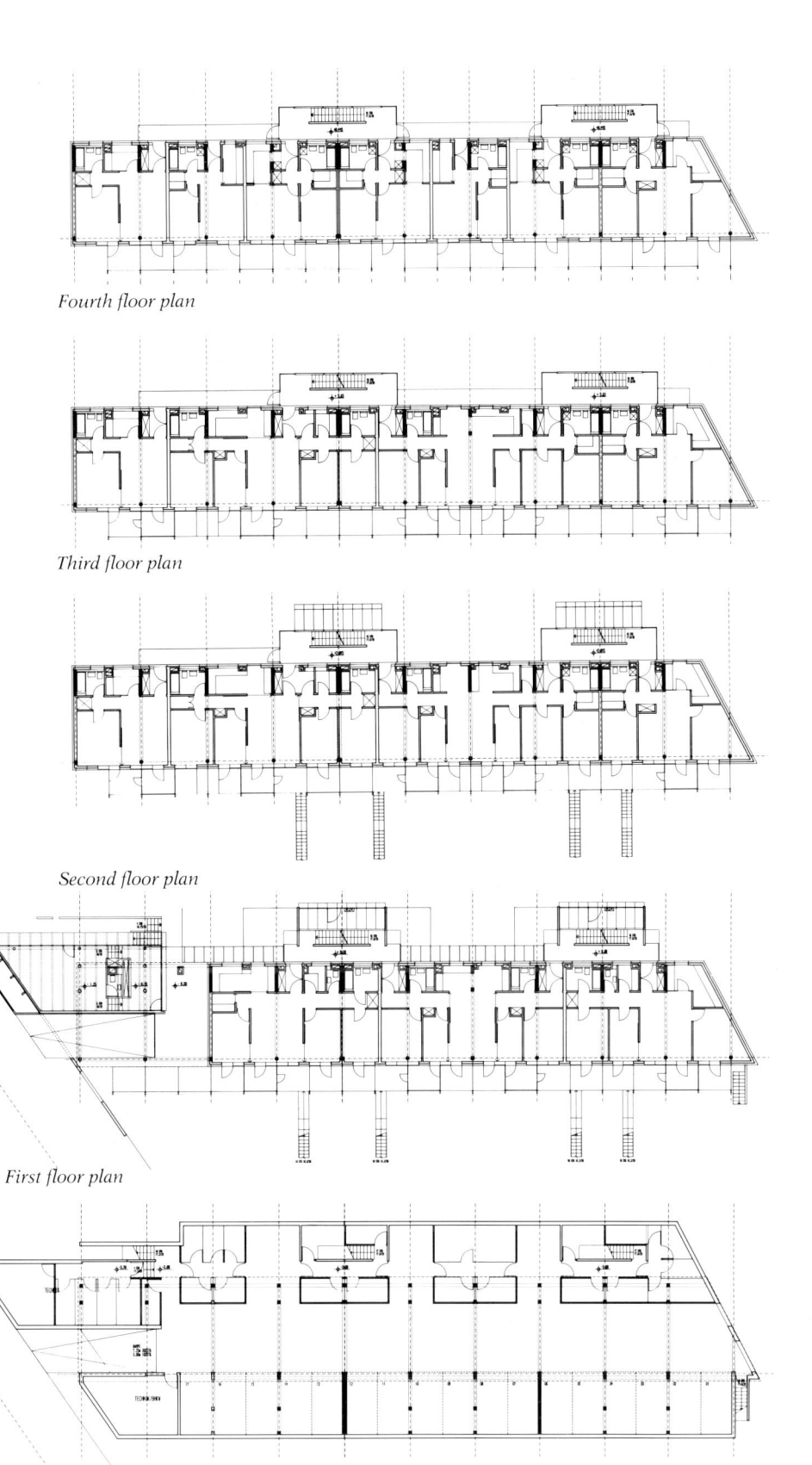

Third floor plan

Second floor plan

First floor plan

Basement floor plan

Zeil Shopping Arcade • Frankfurt am Main • 1992

The Zeil, or Les Facettes, shopping arcade offers a completely new spatial approach to circulation. A spiral path, rising vertically, creates a masterful space in a startling architectural setting. The heart of the arcade is the central hall, its serpentine paths cutting though all the stories, its glass facade and roof establishing a direct link to the exterior, its interior brightly lighted with direct and reflected natural light. The architecture is exhibited with the discrimination of a museum, presenting shop windows like paintings, drawing shoppers into restaurants and onto roof terraces, hawking its wares almost as an afterthought. The broad ramps, imperceptibly opening up to the third dimension, have an affinity with Frank Lloyd Wright's Guggenheim Museum. Arranged on the ten different levels are some seventy shops, all accessible without abrupt changes in level. Everywhere, elevators and escalators provide shortcuts and crossovers. Unlike the homogeneous, level flow of passers-by in the neighboring pedestrian zone, this vertical orientation reveals a city obviously made up of individuals, in this case, individual shops and individual people.

Walking, shopping, errands, recreation, and culture combine here in a kinetic stage play, heralded by the facade itself. The ever-changing, multilevel facade does not serve the advertising and business ambitions of the seventy individual tenants, but stages a performance, constantly redefin-

Perspective

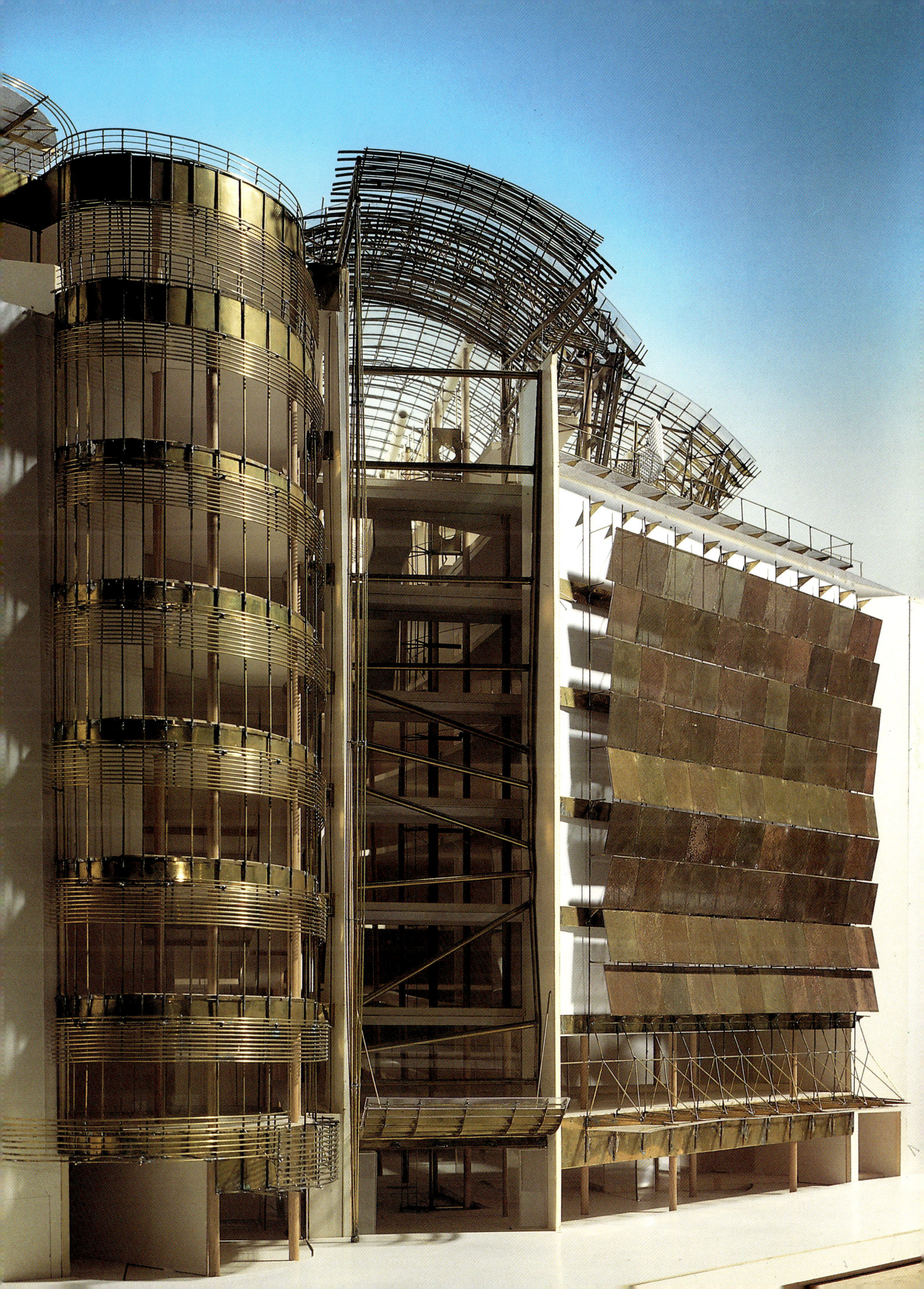

Transversal section

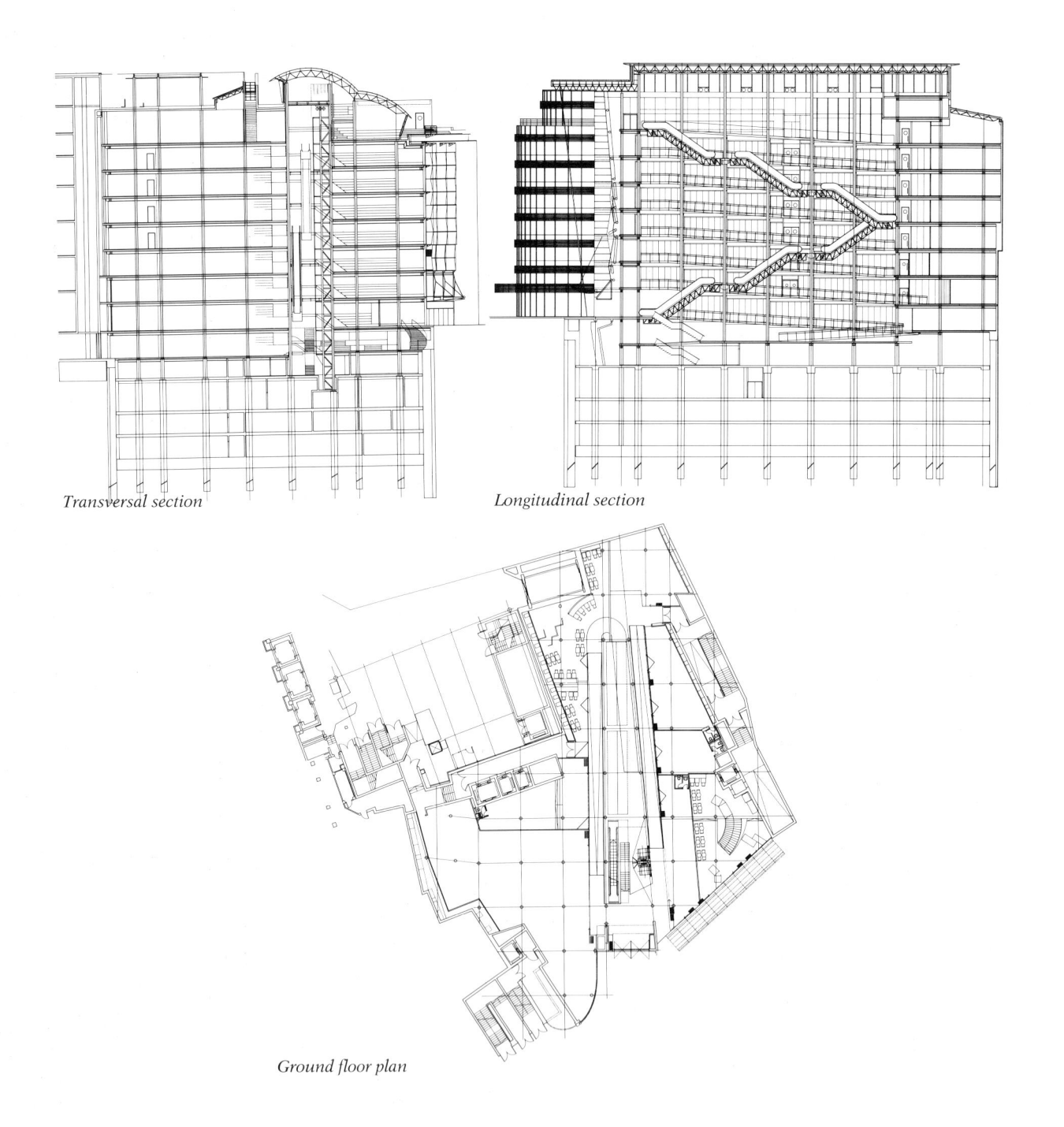

Longitudinal section

Ground floor plan

ing boundaries through movement, color, and light effects. Depending on the time of day, the prevailing weather and light conditions, as well as the ambient sound, the appearance of the facade may change from opaque to transparent, from blue to yellow; these light and color effects rush over the building's second skin, which is composed of numerous perforated-plate elements masking computer-controlled lights and monitors. The artistic character of the shopping arcade extends to the space outside the building. A non-reflective glass skin in front of the vertical ramp-and-escalator axis establishes a visual link between the exterior and the interior. The arcade is sure to become a very lively part of Frankfurt's public streetscape, by day and by night.

Klaus-Dieter Weiß

Interior perspective

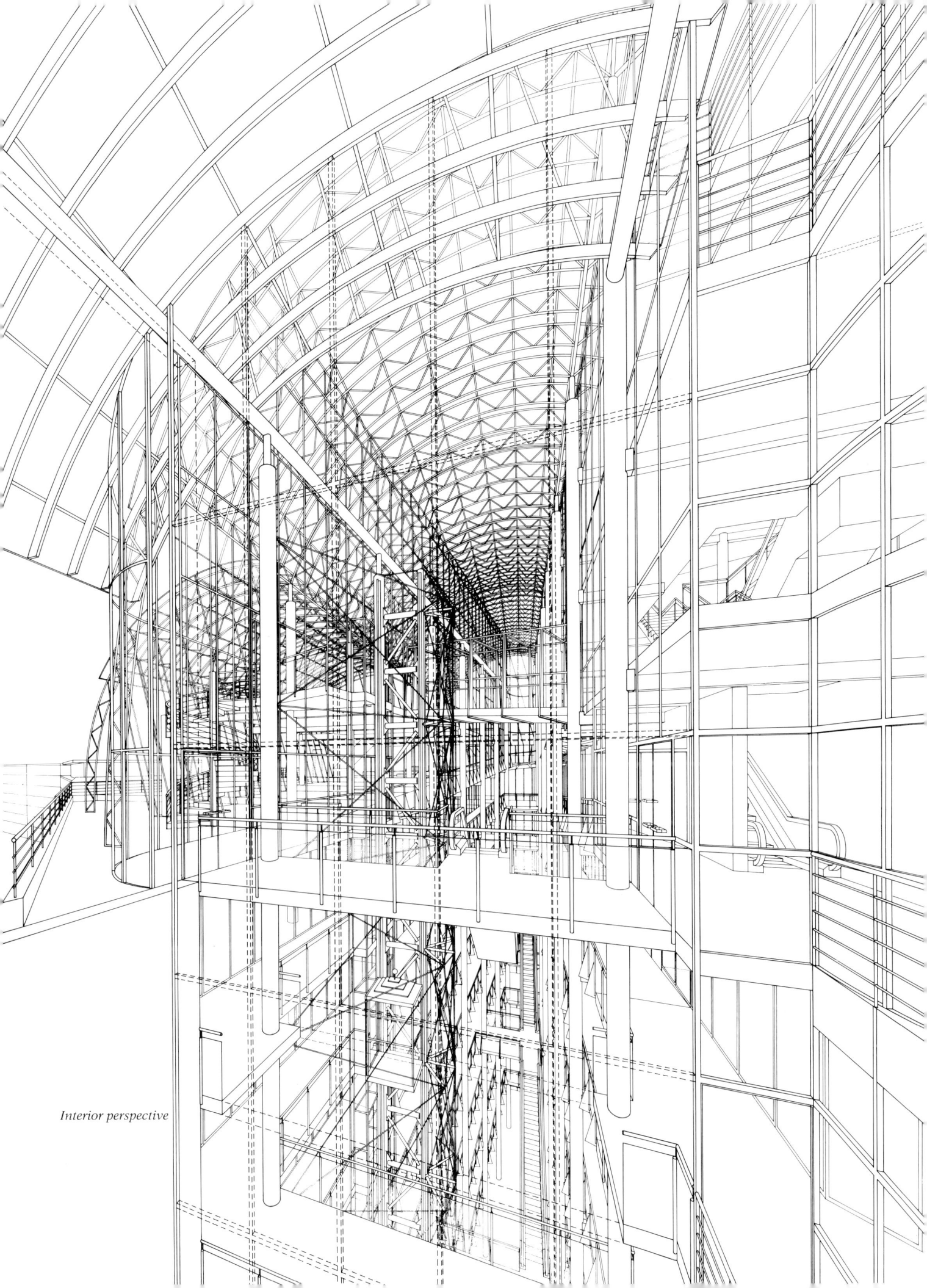

CHRISTOPH LANGHOF
Pressehaus • Berlin • 1992–

The property for the future Pressehaus, a media and press complex for a publishing firm, is on the Stresemannstrasse at the precise intersection of the two former halves of the city of Berlin, two hundred meters from Potsdamer Platz. In the immediate area, the lots are still mostly empty. However, preliminary decisions have been made on the fundamental city planning issues involved, and work on the key buildings and blocks is expected to be largely completed by 1995.

The new press complex is meant to reflect corporate publishing culture; it will also provide office space for non-media tenants. Its design will be a clear departure from the conventional office building. The ground floor will be allocated exclusively to primary uses for the publishing house: an entryway zone—lobby, foyer, hall—cafe, gallery, bookstore, and meeting and presentation rooms. The major design component of the complex, emphasizing its building-as-a-marketplace theme, is a central domed hall. The office areas will be open in plan with as much natural lighting as possible. The roof story will accommodate additional meeting, presentation, and exhibition rooms, a roof garden, and a library for the building owner. *Christoph Langhof*

CHRISTOPH LANGHOF 171

Horst Korber Sports Center • Berlin-Charlottenburg • 1987–90

The sports center has two parts: a sports hall with changing and weight-training rooms to the south, and a multipurpose building with administration and seminar rooms, sauna, cafeteria, medical center, and hotel to the north. The south part of the building is long and low, with a curved front; it is partly supported by pillars. The hotel is tall and narrow; all the rooms face south. Above ground the two parts are separate, facing each other, and joined by a corridor that contains the entrances to the building. Below ground, the two parts form a single building.

It is almost impossible to judge the size of the sports center from the outside: its dimensions can be gauged only from the air. The building is largely hidden by trees, and is partially inserted into the sloping site. It was necessary to fell only a few trees to make room for the center.

The changing rooms are on the basement level, which normally does not receive daylight. Thus the stairway leading there has south-facing windows, so that some light can reach the players' quarters. Spectators come from the parking on Glockenturmstrasse through the trees to the sports hall, and from there descend to the stands, which are above the players' quarters. Up to 3,450 spectators can be seated, and the hall can be divided into two or three sections to accommodate simultaneous matches. During training, the telescoping stands can be moved back into the walls; thus, the size of the training area is much greater than that of the actual playing courts. The roof of the hall, formed of 420 transparent, dome-shaped lights, is curved on both sides and hovers over the floor. The roof lights ensure that the hall lighting is regular, non-dazzling, and natural—ideal conditions for high-performance sports. During good weather the roof lights can be opened to give the effect of playing in the open air. *Christoph Langhof*

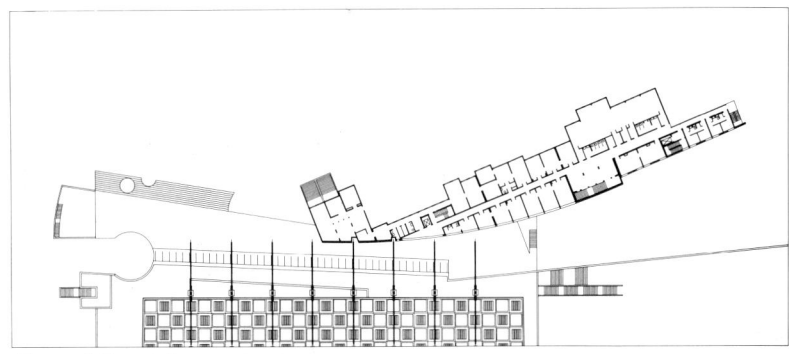

Second floor plan

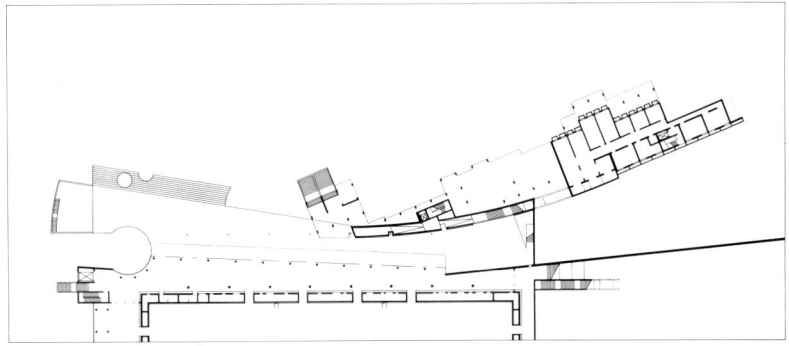

Mezzanine floor plan

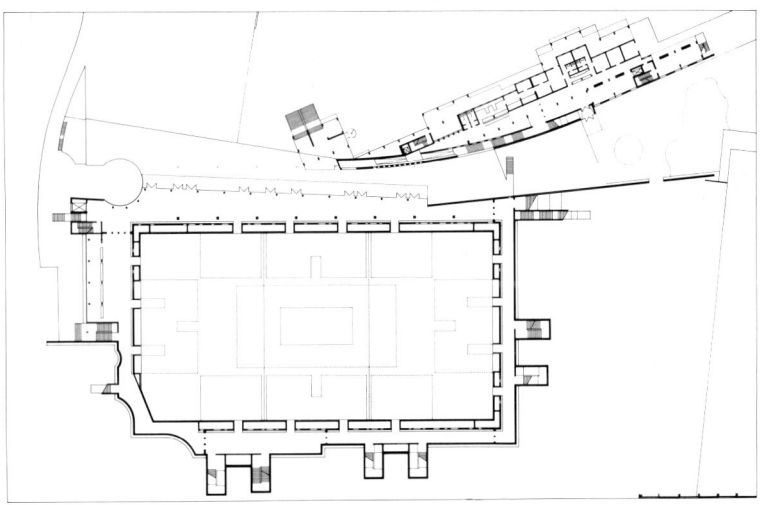

First floor plan

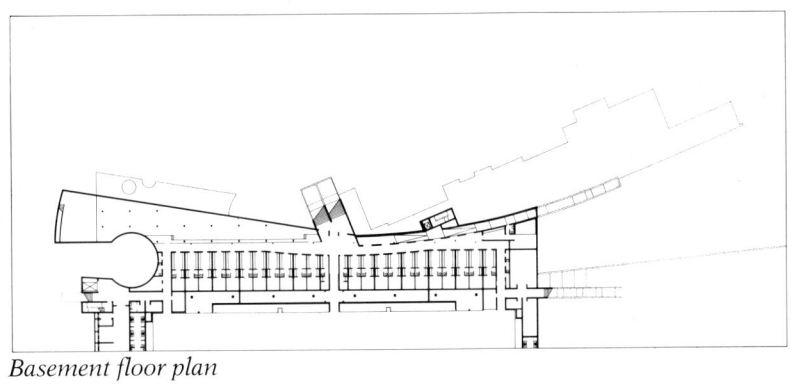

Basement floor plan

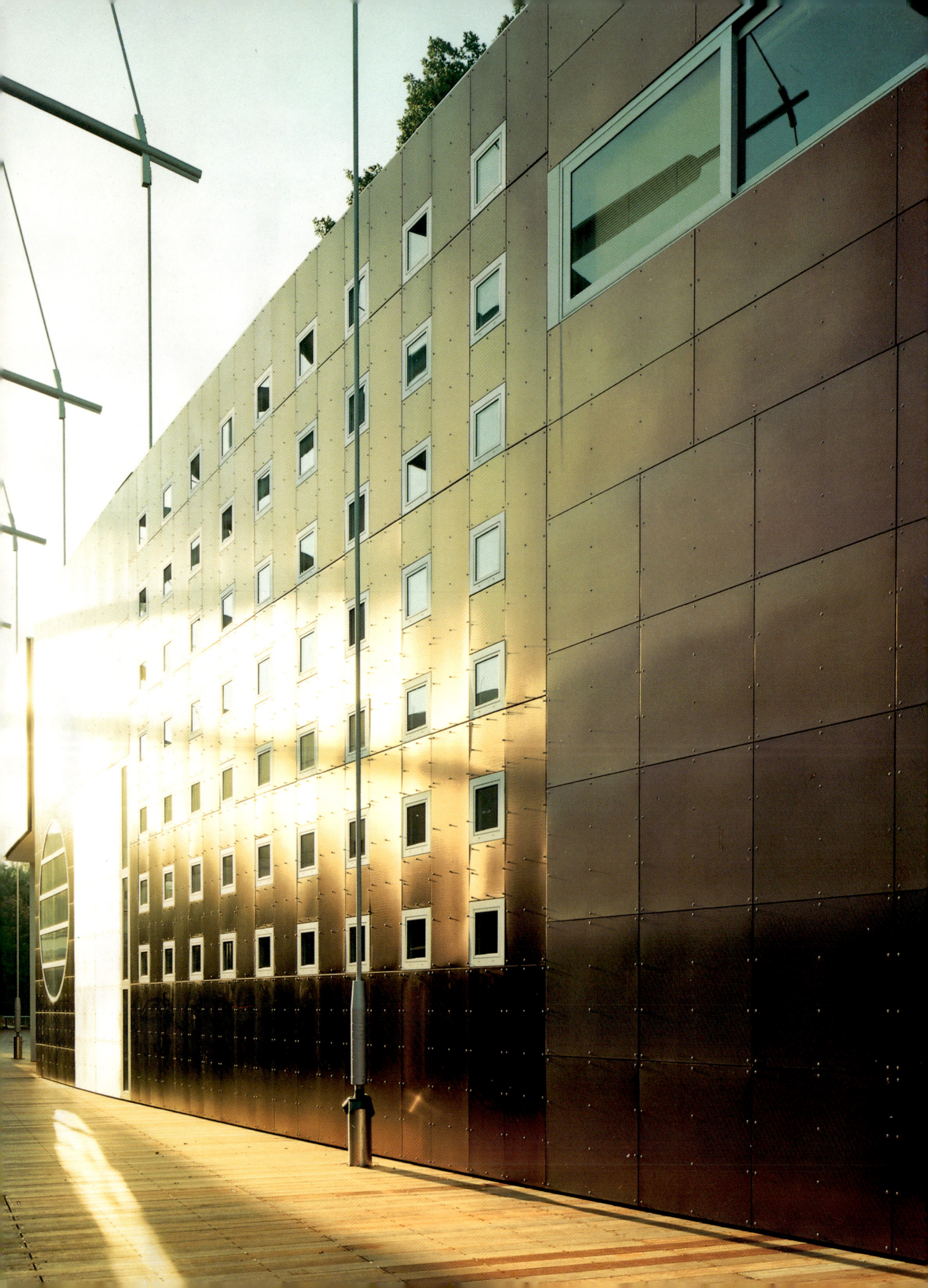

CHRISTOPH LANGHOF 175

ARNO LEDERER AND JORUNN RAGNARSDOTTIR

Exchange Office Addition • Stuttgart-Freiberg • 1990

A ventilation system and emergency power station had to be installed in the local telephone exchange office when its switching equipment was digitalized. At the same time, the building was slated for a design upgrade. The new building is simple. The diesel motor was installed in a concrete box, because it generates so much noise. A steel framework was placed on top of the box, to create an open space for the ventilation system between the concrete base and the flat roof. An enclosed facade was unnecessary; instead, wood laths protected by the large roof overhang serve as a visual barrier. The ventilation installation is reached from a stair pushed to the front of the building, and large ventilation pipes connect the annex to the old building. The concrete walls of the original building were restored, and then lined with corrugated aluminum, as a contrast to the annex. The remaining sand-yellow walls were painted gray.
Arno Lederer

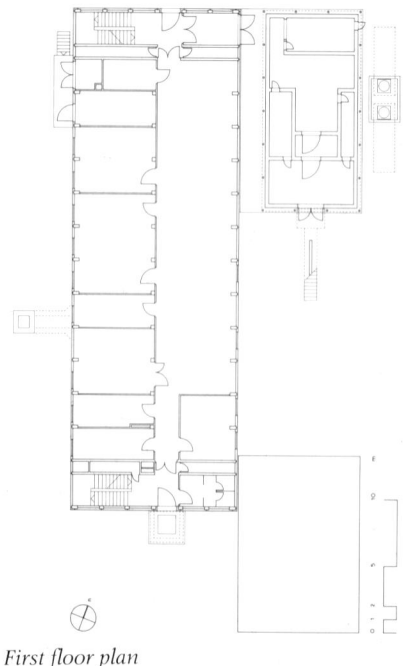

First floor plan

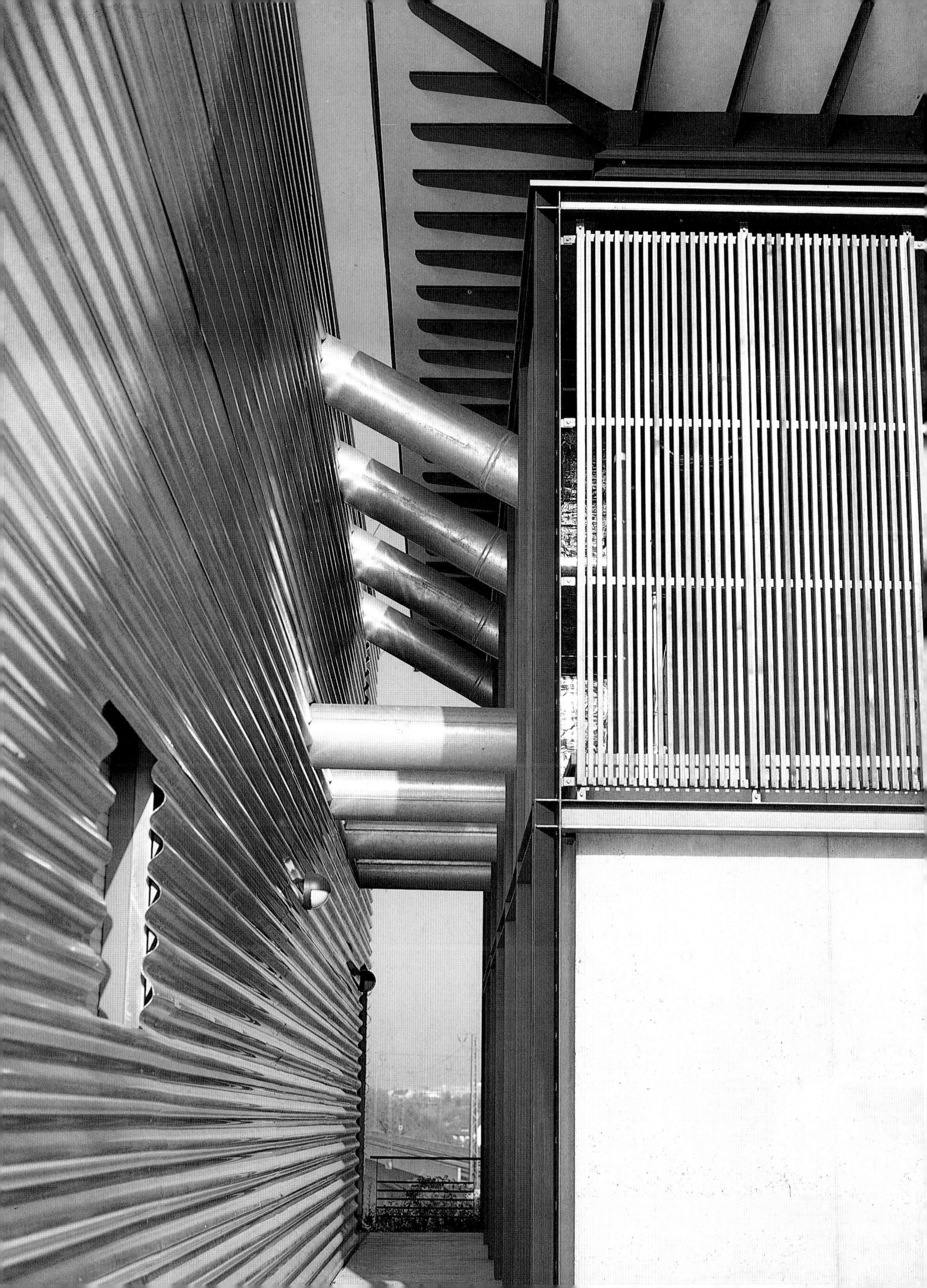

Tax Office • Reutlingen • 1987–91

This project was inspired by provisional buildings of the type erected after the war: simple architecture of often remarkable quality. The building design is simple: added next to early-1920s factory buildings, conventional double-loaded office wings supplement the overall complex.

The two new office facades, however, had to meet somewhat higher expectations: the fronts designed for the Kaiserstrasse and the Leonhardsplatz are important elements of the local urban fabric and were thus clad in anthracite-gray brick. At the entrance, necessarily located at the corner of Leonhardsplatz, the facade has been given a healthy bulge. Aside from emphasizing the corner and entry hall, it seems a fitting symbol for a government office that does nothing more than collect money.

The interior is more opulent. The entry hall is spacious, yet elegantly spartan: the floor is covered with Solnhofen tiles, which in former days were used in the entryways of private houses in the region. The building tries to strike a balance between poor and rich—white walls, tiled reception desk—appropriate for government offices. All floors are linoleum; doors are lighted by bathroom light fixtures. The pre-fab stairs are of white, exposed concrete; round overhead lights illuminate the narrow hallways. *Arno Lederer*

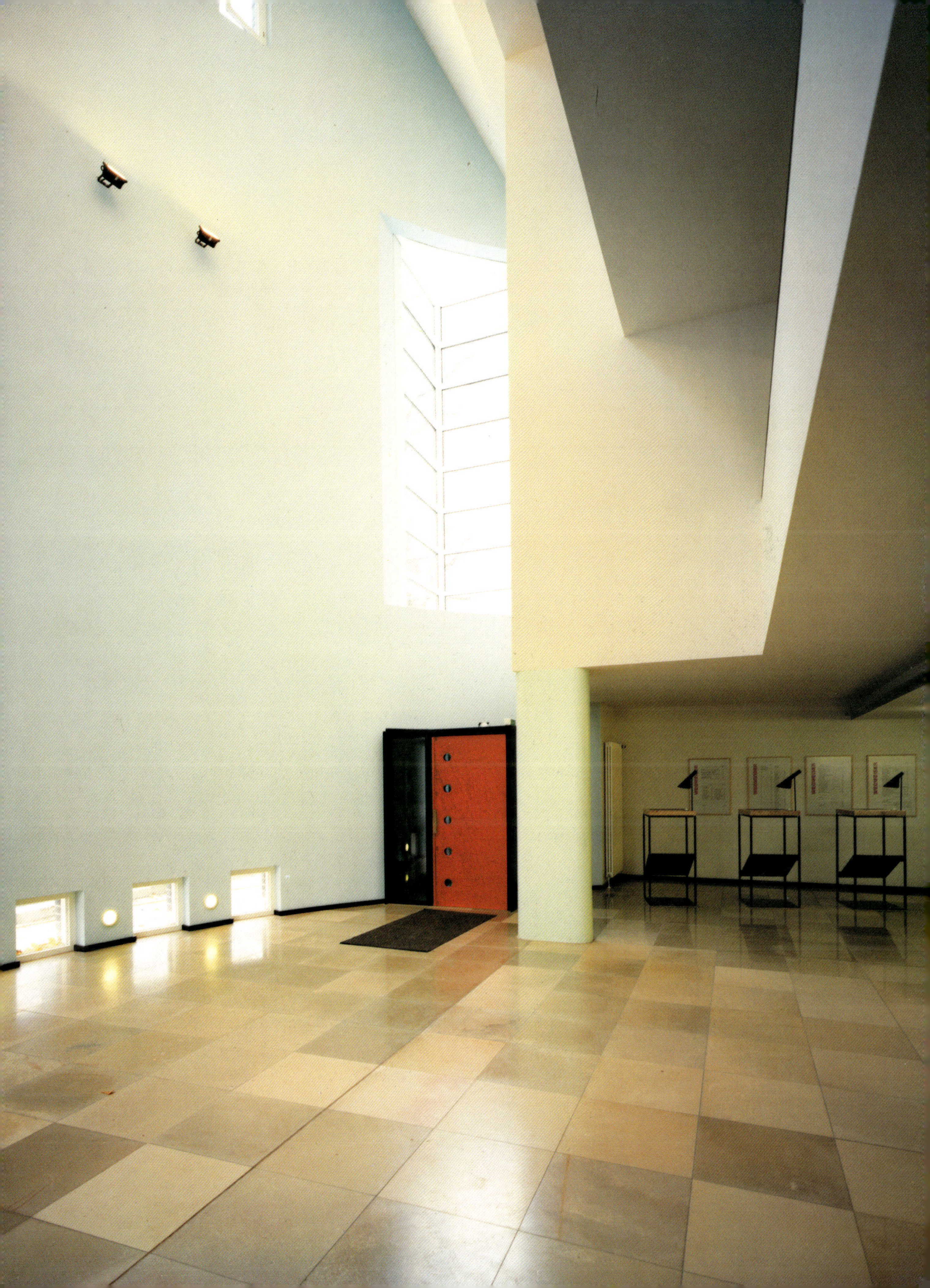

Southeast elevation

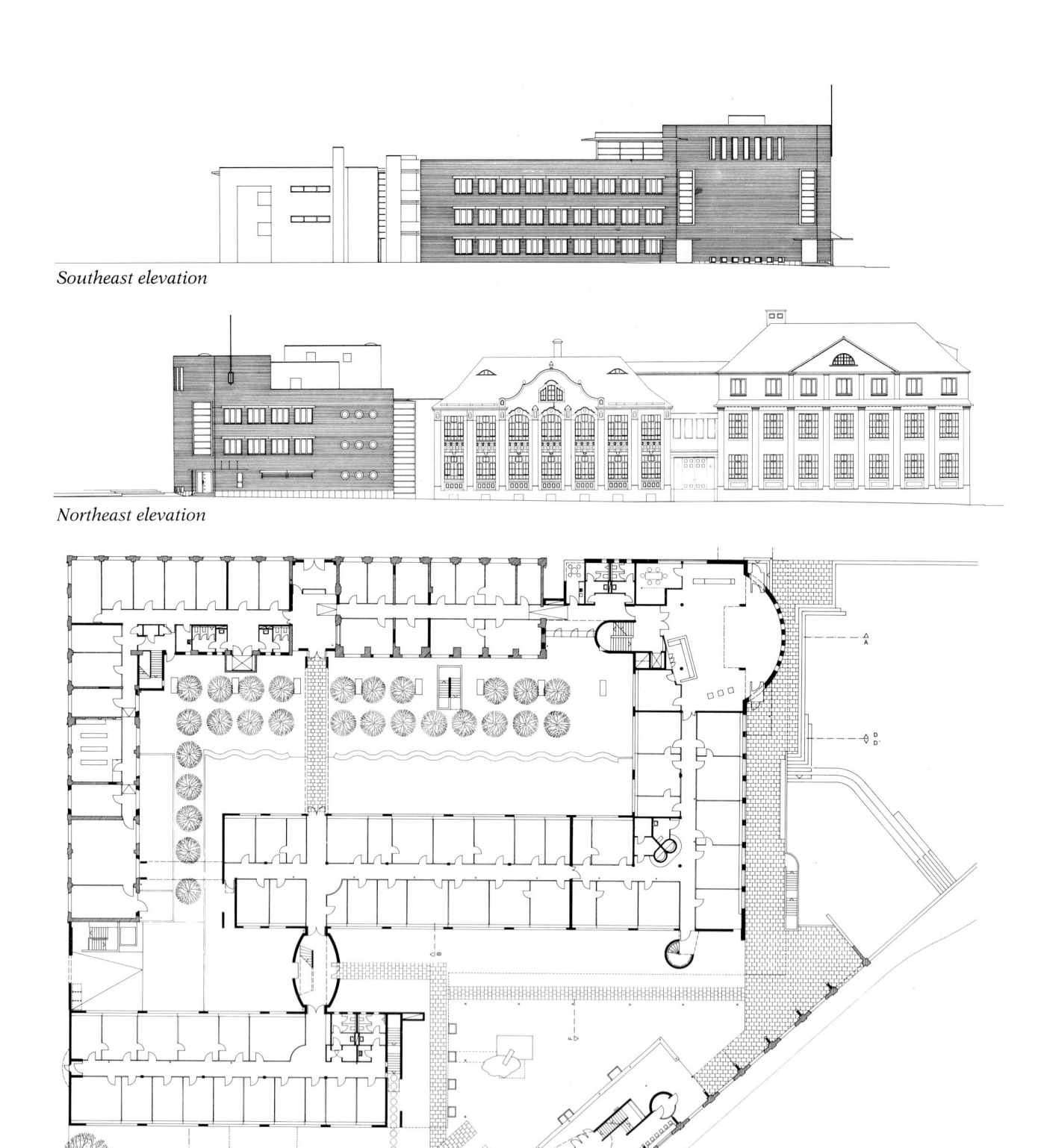

Northeast elevation

Ground floor plan, offices

Site plan

Ground floor plan, cafeteria

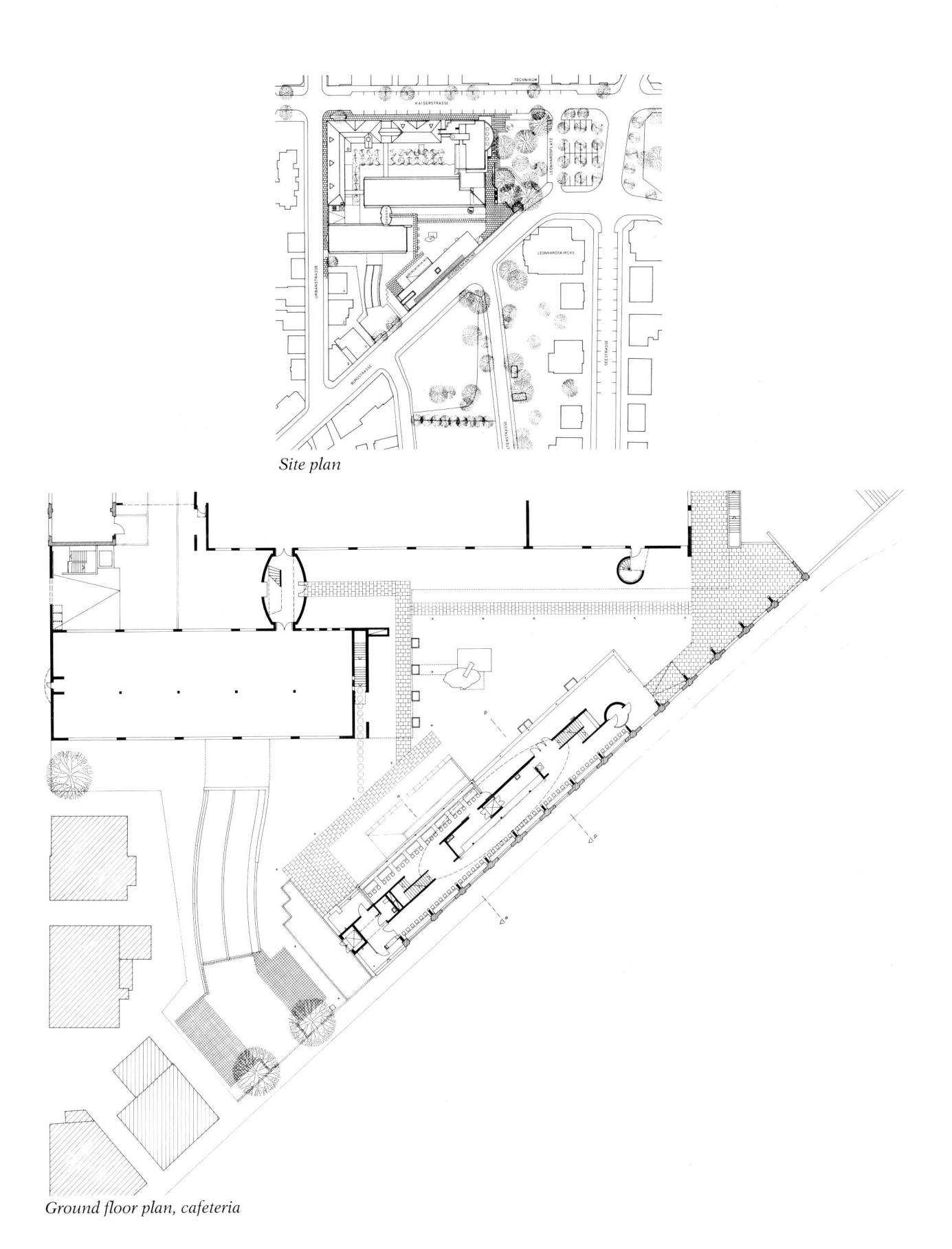

DANIEL LIBESKIND

Berlin Museum • Berlin • 1989–

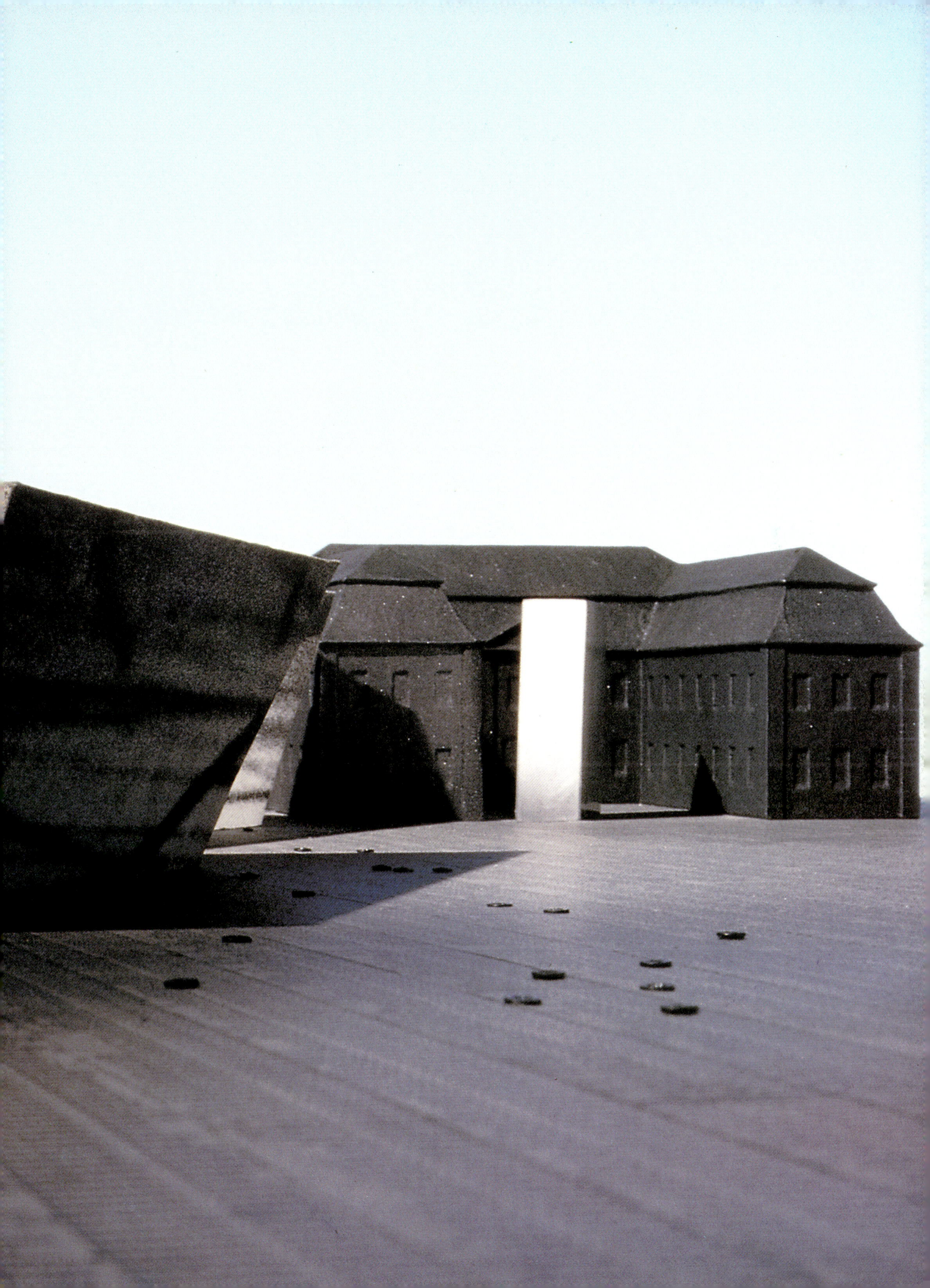

Ground level plan

The project, officially titled "Extension of the Berlin Museum with the Jewish Museum Department," is also called "Between the Lines" because it is a project about two lines of thinking, organization, and relationship. One is a straight line broken into many fragments; the other is a tortuous line continuing infinitely. The two lines develop architecturally and programmatically through a limited but definite dialogue. Yet they also fall apart, become disengaged, and are seen as separated. In this way, they expose the discontinuous void that runs through the museum.

The site is the Rondel, a famous baroque intersection of Wilhelmstrasse, Friedrichstrasse, and Lindenstrasse. In addition to recognizing this physical trace of Berlin, the design was inspired by an invisible matrix of anamnesis of relationships: The connection between Germans and Jews. The composer Arnold Schönberg, who in *Moses und Aron* created unresolvable relationships between the two title characters, between the revealed and unimaginable truth and the spoken and

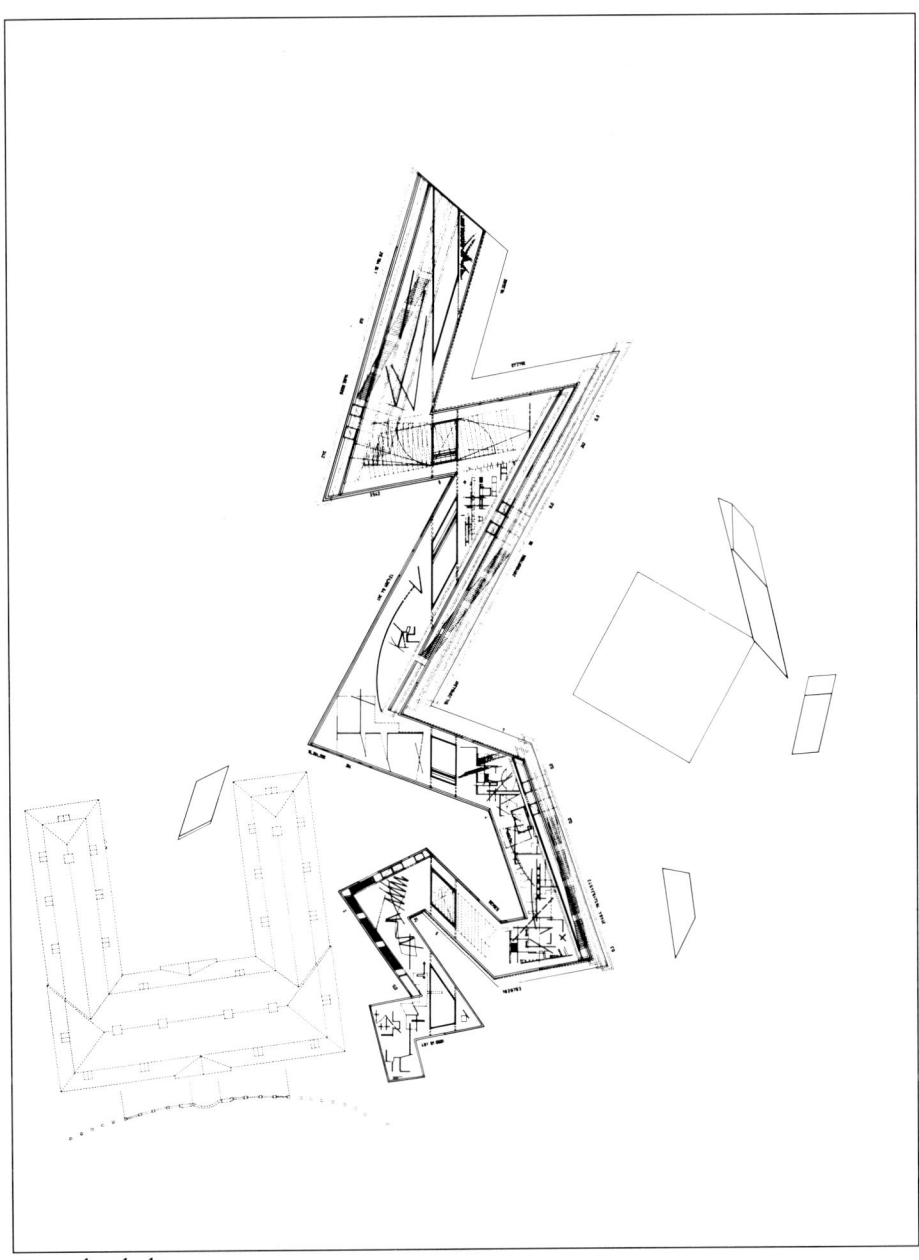

Upper level plan

mass-produced truth. The names of those who were deported from Berlin during the Holocaust. The text "One Way Street" by Walter Benjamin, which is represented in sixty sections along the zigzag, each standing for one of Benjamin's "Stations of the Star."

The new building, of more than 10,000 square meters, crosses under the existing museum and materializes independently on the outside. The two are joined underground, but simultaneously preserve the contradictory autonomy of both the old and the new on the surface.

Described simply, the museum is a zigzag with a structural rib; the structural rib is the void of the Jewish Museum, something every viewer will experience as an absent presence. The building is not simply a collage or a collision or a dialectic; it is instead a new type of structure organized around an absent center: the void, the invisible. And the void is, in fact, the collection of the Jewish Museum, reduced to archival and archaeological material since its former physicality has disappeared. *Daniel Libeskind*

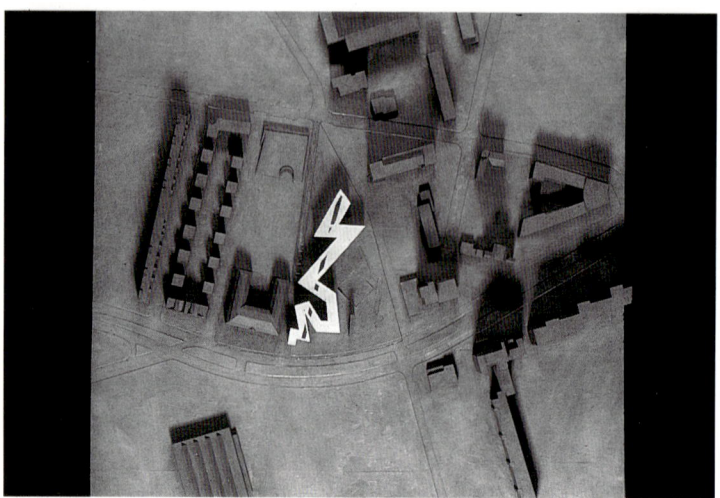

186 DANIEL LIBESKIND

DANIEL LIBESKIND 187

The Tenth Muse • Wiesbaden • 1992

The twenty-first century office complex will have to not only meet highly advanced energy, ecological, and technological requirements, but also radically reformulate the philosophy of the workday. The architecture will have to offer a new spatial, visual, and symbolic interpretation of the office environment.

In this project, work functions and ancillary social spaces have been fundamentally redefined by the introduction of an entirely new dimension of public activity and individual freedom. The seemingly autonomous office "crystals" are distributed in a free and dynamic configuration; the quality of interior, roof, and outdoor spaces offers a truly pleasing environment. "Muse Lines" related to the potential of the new offices cut across the old boundaries that divided routine from leisure, public from private, and work from pleasure, joining multiple diverse images from the spectrum of the intellect. The roof is no longer the boundary where buildings end; it extends the social life of the employees by changing their relationship to both city and nature, which is expressed at the foot of the building with a landscape grid that decomposes progressively and will give way by the end of the century to the forest, redressing ecological imbalance. The Tenth Muse—the Unexpected—leads the chorus that is condensing the post-contemporary city. *Daniel Libeskind*

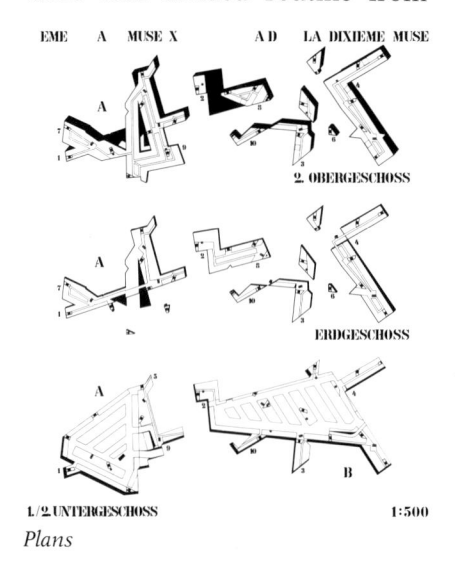

Plans

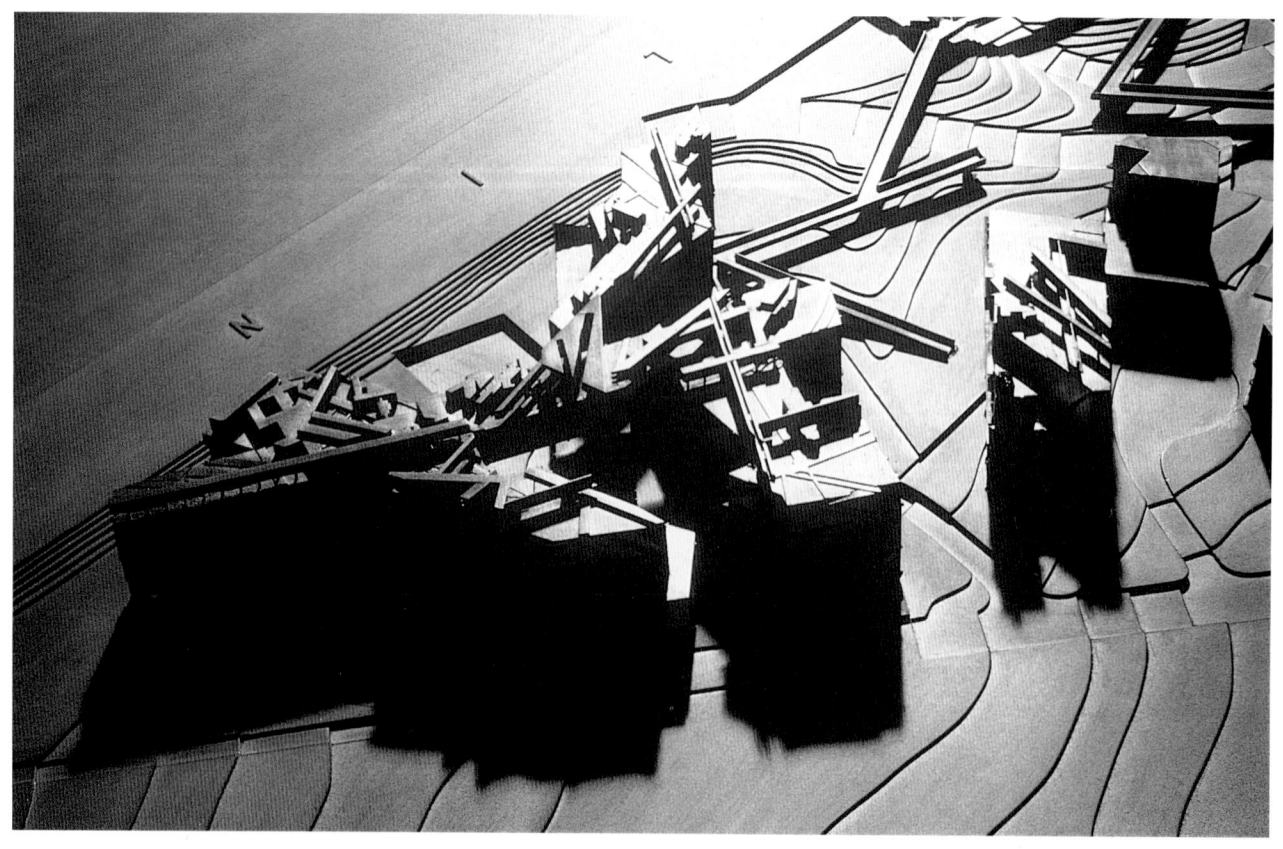

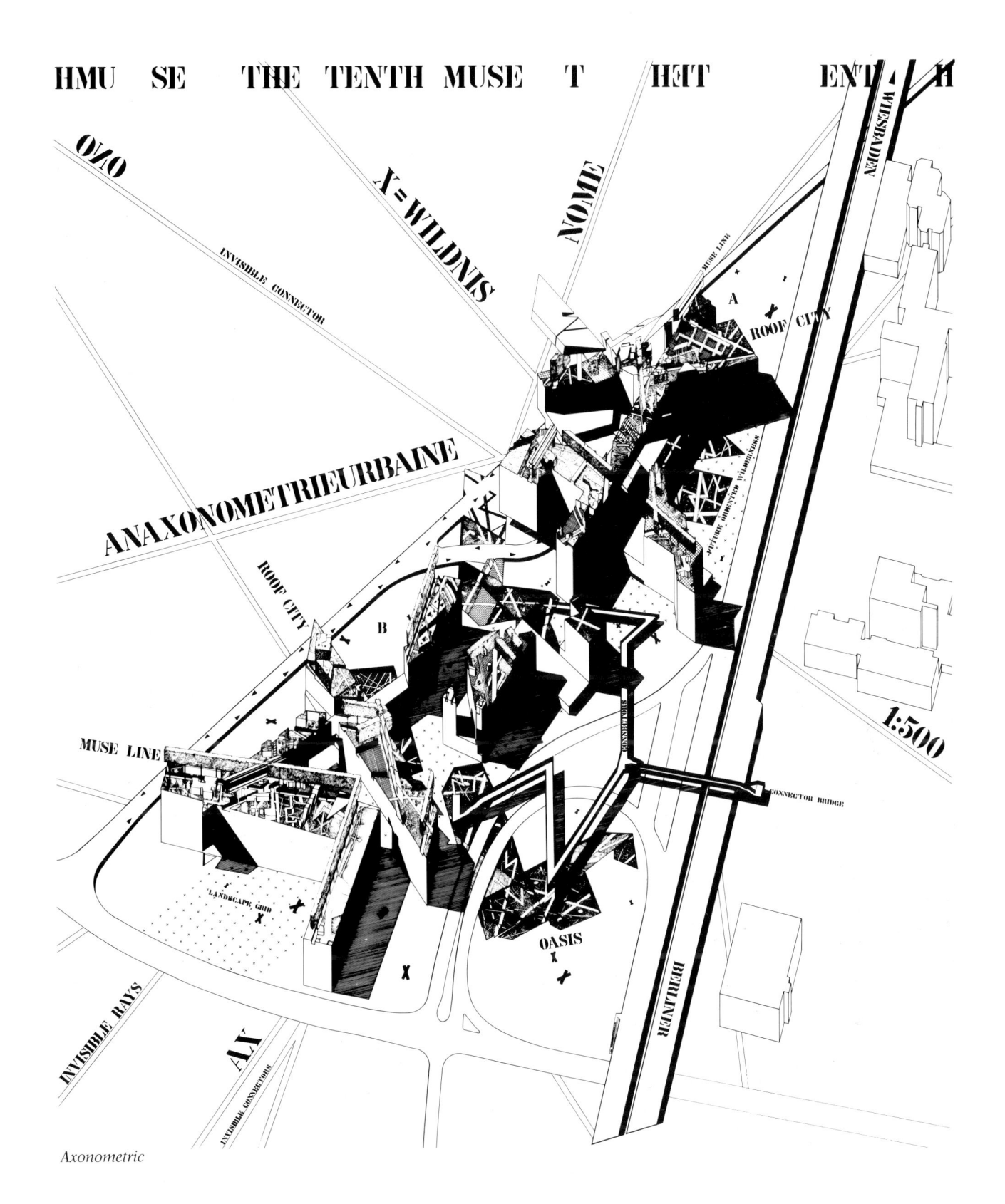

Axonometric

Private House • Berlin • 1990–

This urban villa seeks to demonstrate the complex possibilities of building and living in contemporary Berlin. As such the architectural design is one that replaces the traditional eighteenth- and nineteenth-century symmetrical villa typology with a different organization. The cube form is rearticulated with a set of distorted fragments; if they are reassembled through imagination and daily ritual, they make from the present disorder a future order.
Daniel Libeskind

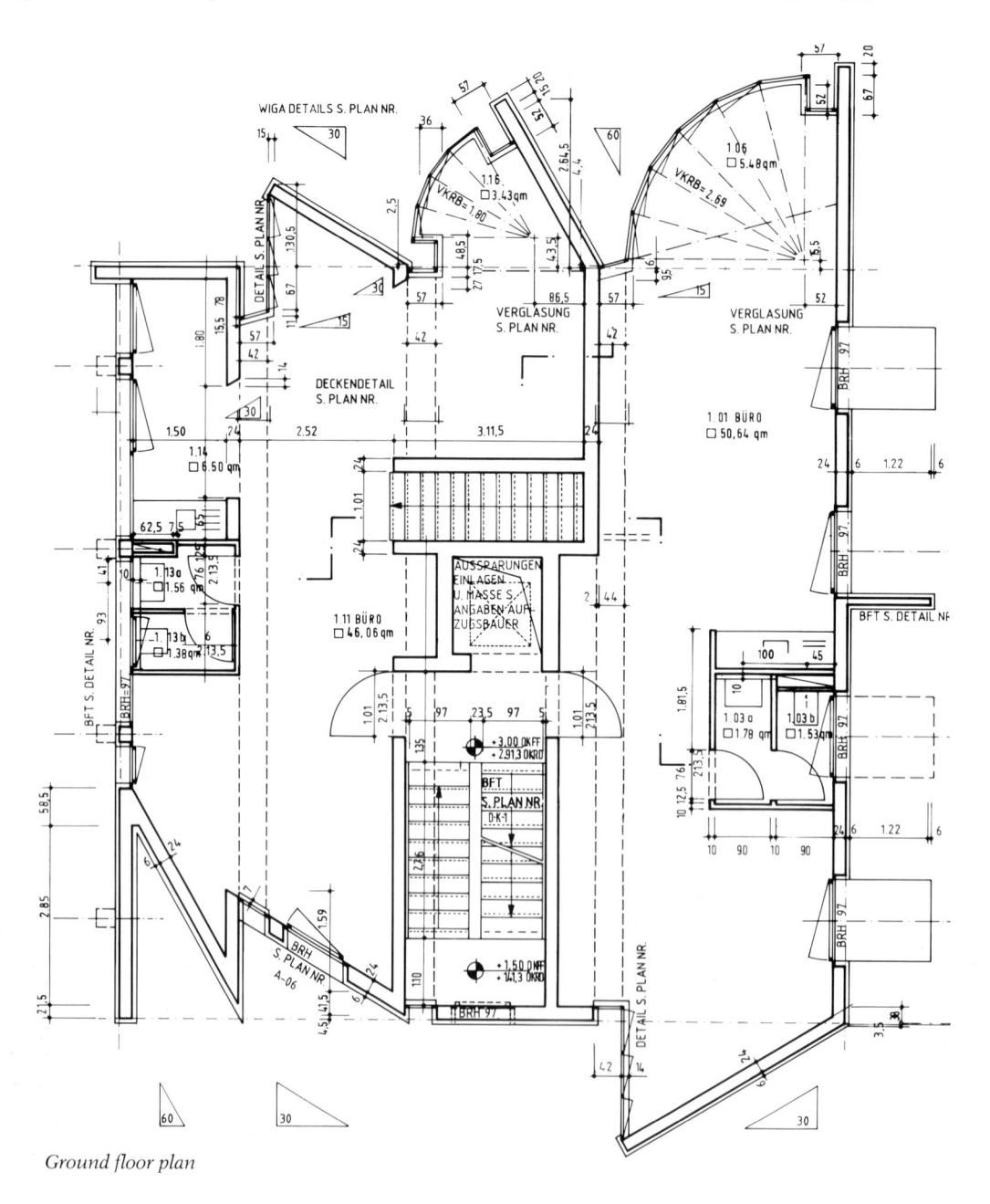

Ground floor plan

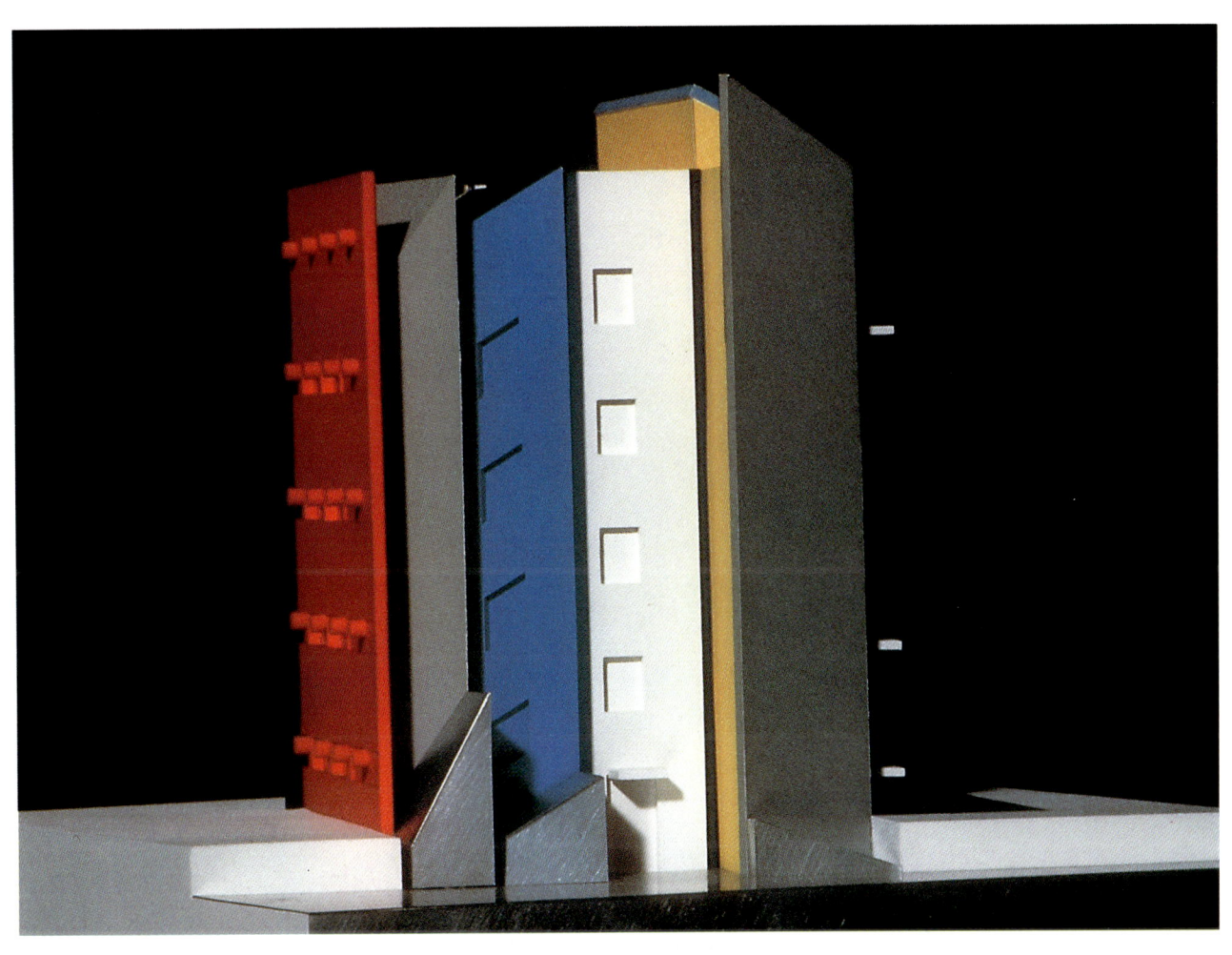

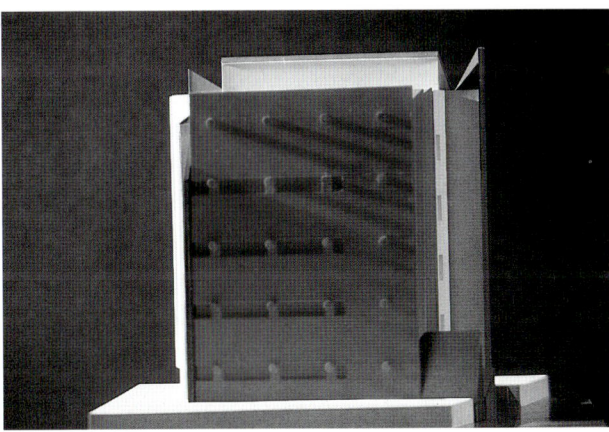

DANIEL LIBESKIND

KARLJOSEF SCHATTNER
Orphanage Conversion • Eichstätt • 1985–88

Cutaway axonometric

In the 1760s, the Prince Bishop established an orphanage to which a mayor of Eichstätt made a sizable donation. By 1985, however, the building could not have been in a worse state, and there were discussions about tearing it down. Fortunately, the local university's need for more space was the source of salvation; university institutes for psychology and journalism were moved to the location.

The orphanage is an imposing figure in the urban landscape, with a six-story facade extending along Ostenstrasse. The original designer, Maurizio Pedetti, united two three-story, sixteenth-century houses with a narrow connecting wing. With a summer residence on the opposite side of the street, the ensemble creates a strait of sorts, a gate. The resulting plan is a virtual rectangle with a small, open, interior courtyard.

In recent times, parts of the roof were missing, plaster had fallen off, moisture had penetrated the walls up to the second story, and trash lay in piles around the courtyard. The windows had been walled off in a makeshift attempt to salvage the structure, the wooden stairs had become dilapidated, and the original floors and doors had been used as heating materials by the tenants. For the university conversion, the eighteenth-century south, east, and west facades were restored. The north wall and the connecting walls between the two formerly detached houses, however, had to be torn down, and a new north front was designed, with unglazed openings, which functions as an ideal and typical abstraction of a facade.
Karljosef Schattner

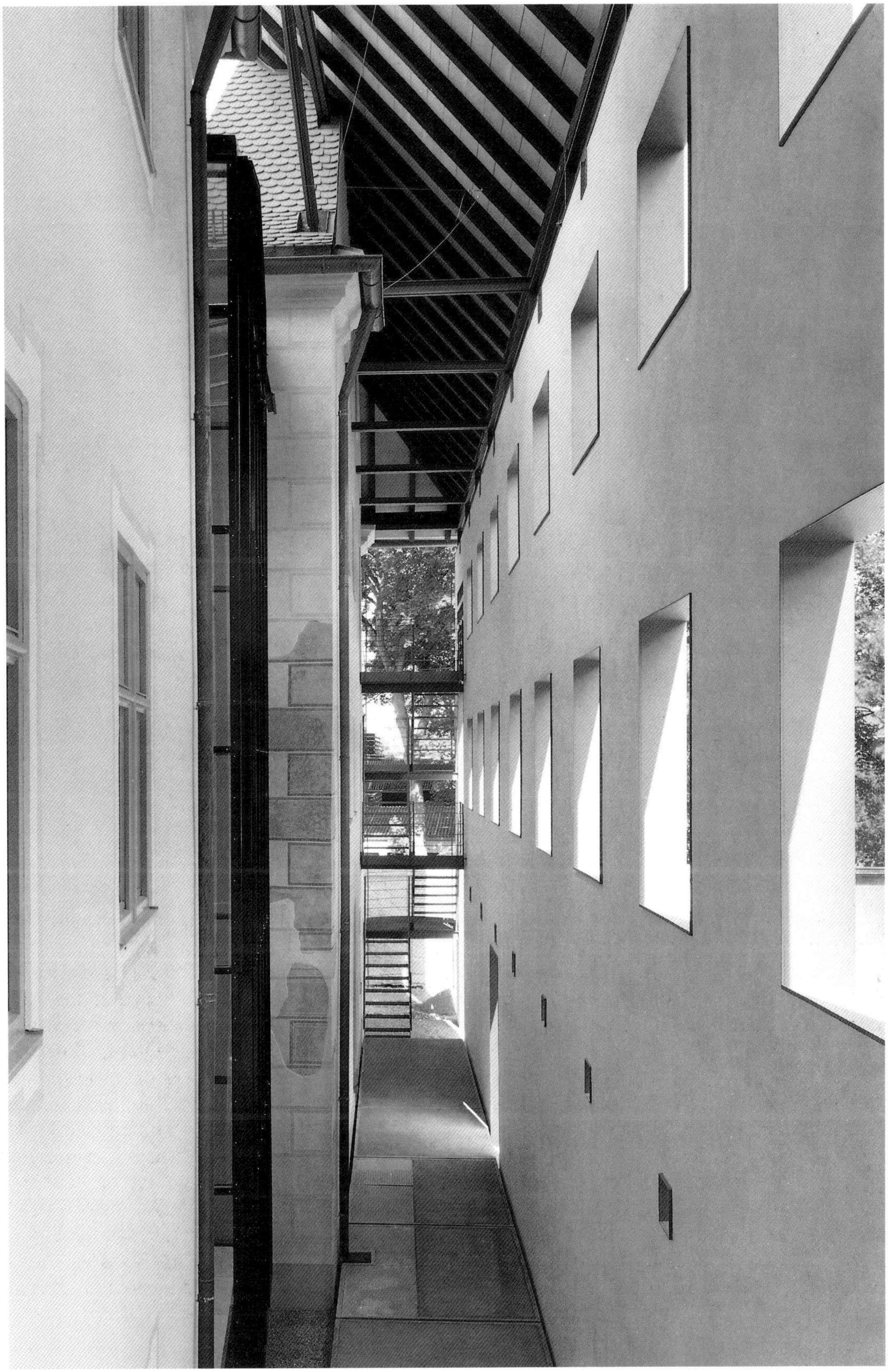

Castle Annex and Conversion • Hirschberg • 1987–92

The original commission involved the rearrangement of the Hirschberg Castle and the creation of new rooms such as a kitchen, dining halls, and cafeteria to accommodate a new educational center. The prerequisite was that the historical features of the structure be in no way affected. Initially, the new rooms were to be incorporated into the main axis of the complex under the bastion garden, which is situated in front of and to the east of the head structure. But when the vaults of the original Romanesque fortress were uncovered soon after construction work began, the design was changed.

The new rooms are now located in an annex off the south side. The height of the lower-level wall slabs changes with the slope of the hill. This wing also solved certain circulation problems in the castle. For example, both the castle's two-story chapel in the south wing and its third-story imperial hall in the head building extended the entire depth of the wing, interrupting the internal connecting passages. The annex now creates a lower-story bypass. At the same time, a new stairway in the south wing makes it possible to circumvent the imperial hall without leaving the building. In the north and south wings of the castle, the original layout—a single row of rooms along a naturally lighted corridor—was restored. *Karljosef Schattner*

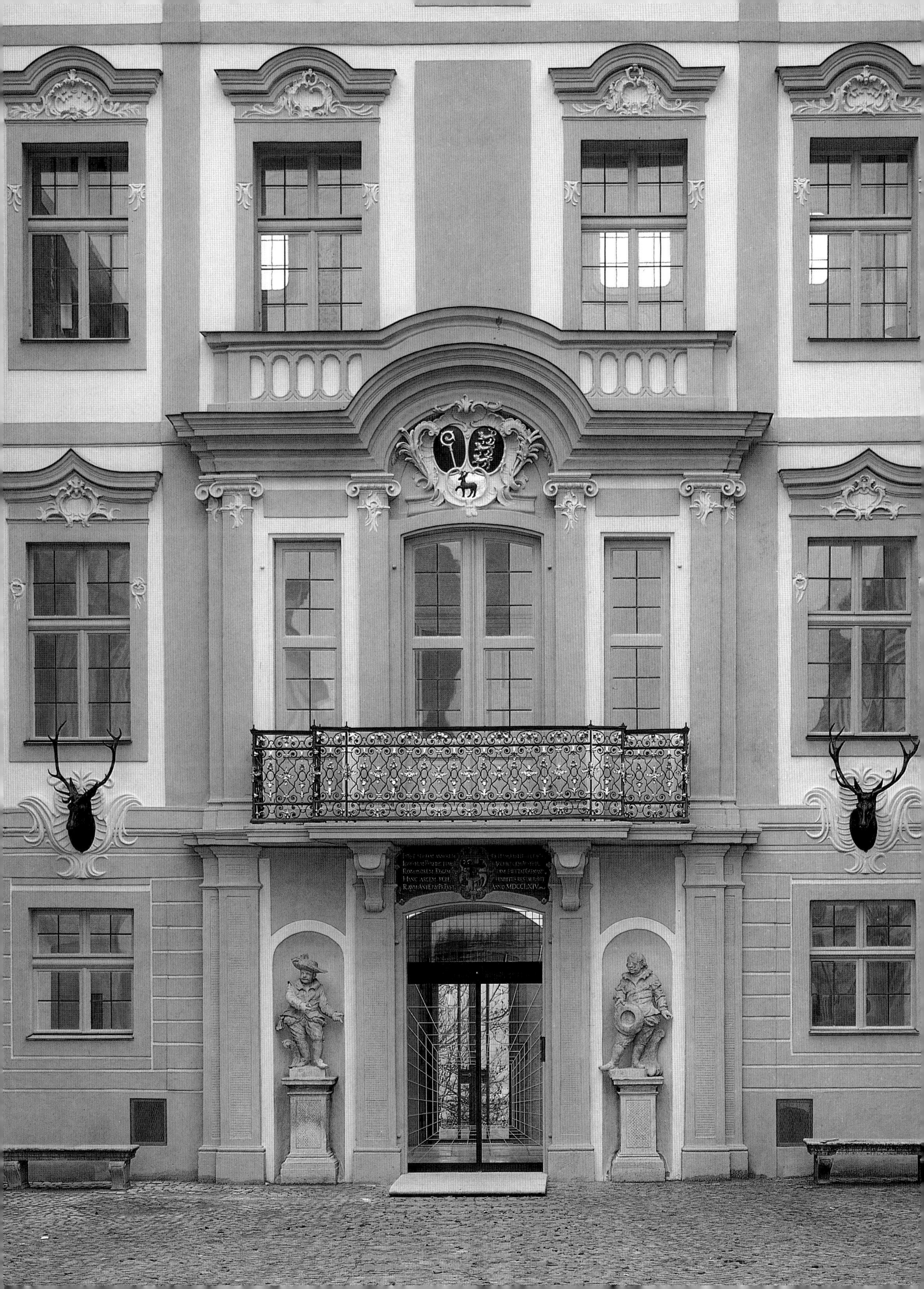
HANC ARCEM
ANNO MDCCLXIV

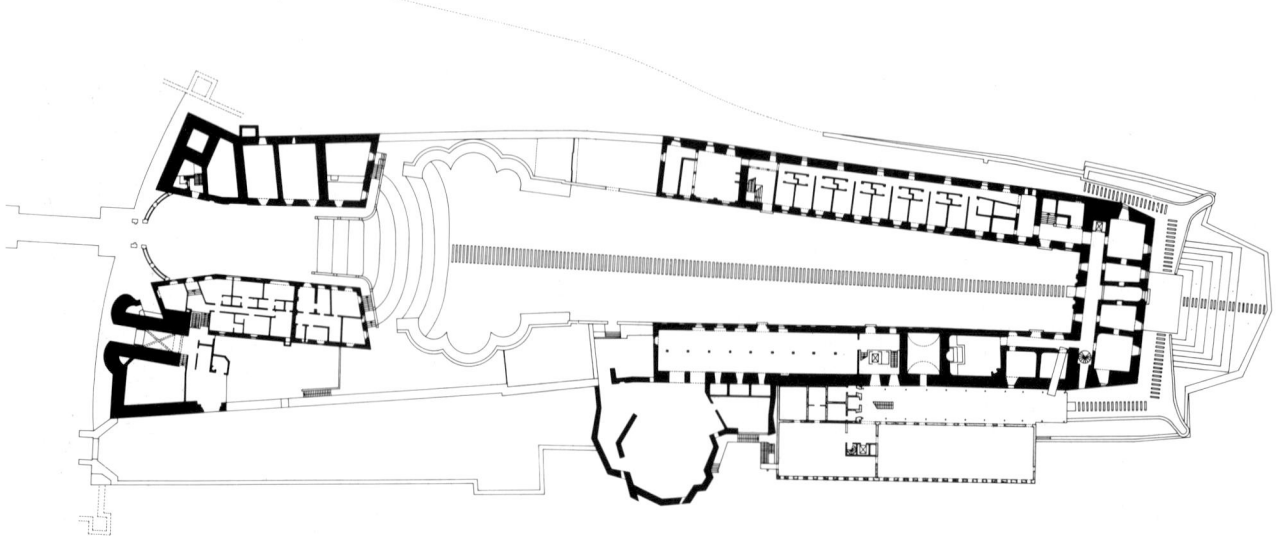

Lower level plan

196 KARLJOSEF SCHATTNER

KARLJOSEF SCHATTNER 197

Institute of Journalism • Eichstätt • 1985–87

East elevation

The building for the Institute of Journalism is located in the midst of other university buildings. As with nearly all new or reconstructed university buildings, it was essential to establish a dialogue with the historical structures in the immediate vicinity: in this case, a row of houses on Ostenstrasse, an adjacent baroque summer residence, and two parallel orangery gardens. To the west are two main parts of an office building, modern structures built by this architectural firm. When they were built, no one anticipated that this lot would become available.

The interaction of old and new at the Institute of Journalism has resulted in obvious conflicts and thus the development of a more aggressive language. Several attempts to divide the building mass into smaller sections and to refer to the gabled roofs of the neighboring Ostenstrasse buildings were in the end abandoned; even the corbel vault of the officers' casino once located on the site of the foyer and lecture hall building did not follow the lead of the orangery wing. Instead the interaction was depicted on a grand scale—grand by Eichstätt standards, that is. *Karljosef Schattner*

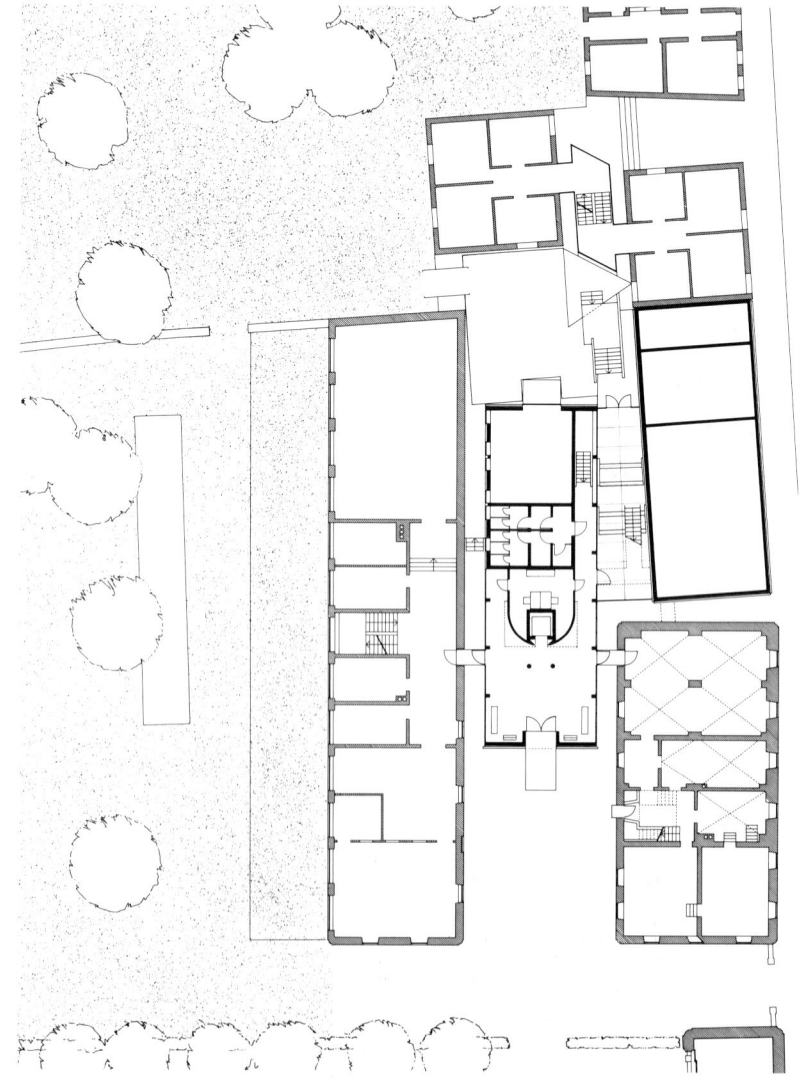

Ground floor plan

KARLJOSEF SCHATTNER 199

Library Addition and Conversion • Eichstätt • 1978–80

The original structure, the Ulmer Hof, was first built in Eichstätt in 1625 and completed to its current form in 1688. The building served as a residence until the early nineteenth century. In 1842, it was bequeathed to the state, which used it for a secondary school. In 1977, the Catholic University of Eichstätt acquired the empty building for the Department of Catholic Theology and its departmental library. Initially, the original three-wing structure was to be preserved and the interior courtyard was to be gutted to house a 90,000-volume reference library and reading rooms. Aside from opening up the ground-floor arcade, the original building was to be changed structurally as little as possible and was to provide space primarily for teaching staff and seminar rooms. The new library space in the courtyard was to be visible from the corridors on each level of the old building.

The three wings surrounding the library have plain, baroque facades with no vestige of ornamentation; during the course of construction it was decided to paint them with trompe l'oeil murals, first, to recall the historical building, and second, to indicate that the courtyard, while functioning as an interior space for the library, was originally an exterior space. The same intentions—to clearly differentiate the old and the new—were pursued throughout the design. The skylight in the library now separates the historical structure from the new insertion, which is also set apart in terms of materials and color.

The commission also called for uncovering the arcades in the interior courtyard. The unstable

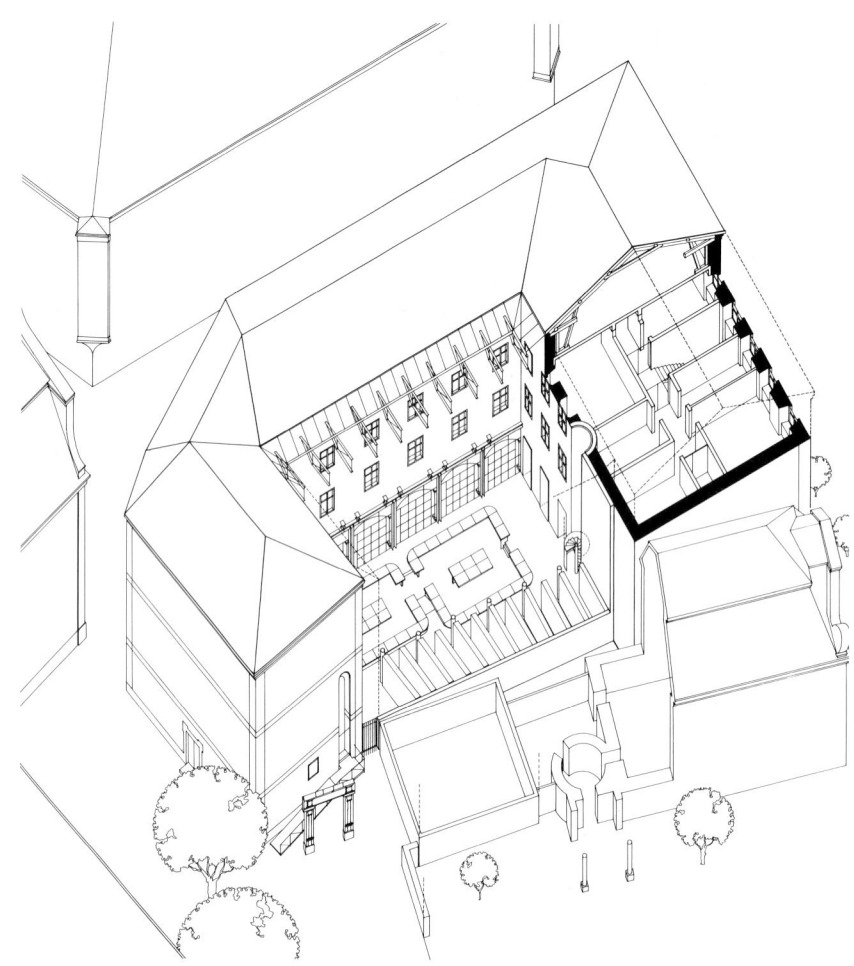

Cutaway axonometric

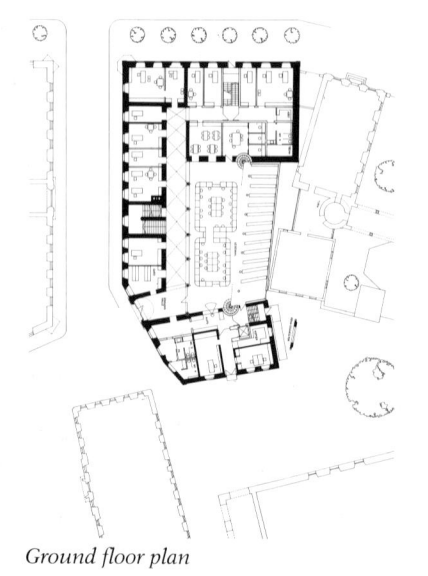

Ground floor plan

exterior wall, which would receive an additional load from the library roof, was secured with a steel construction at the arcade level. Here, too, the new structure was separated from the old without impairing either. The steel construction also houses the glazed area between the corridor and the library. The reading rooms were linked to form an uninterrupted area two steps below the rest of the room. Even the structure added for the fire stairs was distinguished from the original; the vaults were presented as though they were made of plate steel. *Karljosef Schattner*

KARLJOSEF SCHATTNER

AXEL SCHULTES
ORIGINATED AS BANGERT JANSEN SCHOLZ SCHULTES

Municipal Art Museum • Bonn • 1985–92

This museum shares a 100- by 300-meter site with a museum designed by the Austrian architect Gustav Peichl; the two buildings are set into a park-like landscape. The municipal art museum recalls features from a number of buildings—the Villa Imperiale in Tivoli, Le Corbusier's endless museum, a wharf in Barcelona, Cordoba's great mosque—without conforming to a particular type. These features create exhibition areas that are both individual and straightforward, appropriate for one artist and for many.

A wall along the Friedrich-Ebert-Allee both creates an urban space and acts as a backdrop for open-air sculpture; from different vantage points the space appears wide open or completely closed. The art hall is linked to the approach and the outside sculpture area by a glass-roofed, columned space; it acts as an open foyer and balances the loggia that runs the whole length of the building. A central foyer and the temporary exhibition areas define three diagonal circulation paths and in turn four other exhibition spaces.

Thomas Mann once said that "Art must become recognition"; this is almost a motto for the new museum. The tensions created by any such project—the political need for prestige versus the necessities of urban planning, the public nature of exhibitions versus the personal and private experience of art—force the building to achieve something almost impossible: the redefinition of convention to accommodate the new. It gestures toward the classical, while striking a balance between monumental and intimate, spirited and sedate, coarse and fine, solid and filigree: it is the living development of the building. *Axel Schultes*

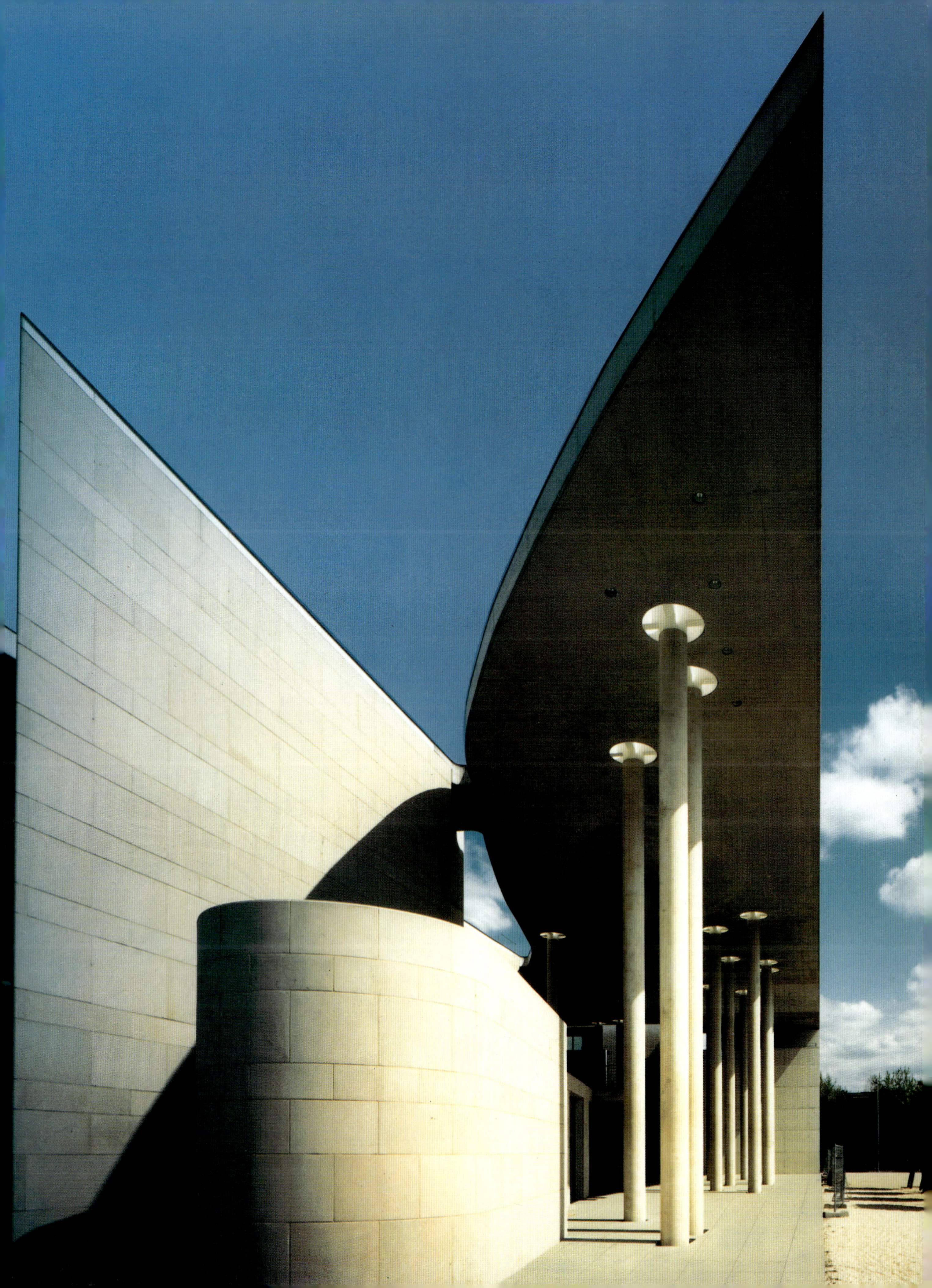

204   AXEL SCHULTES

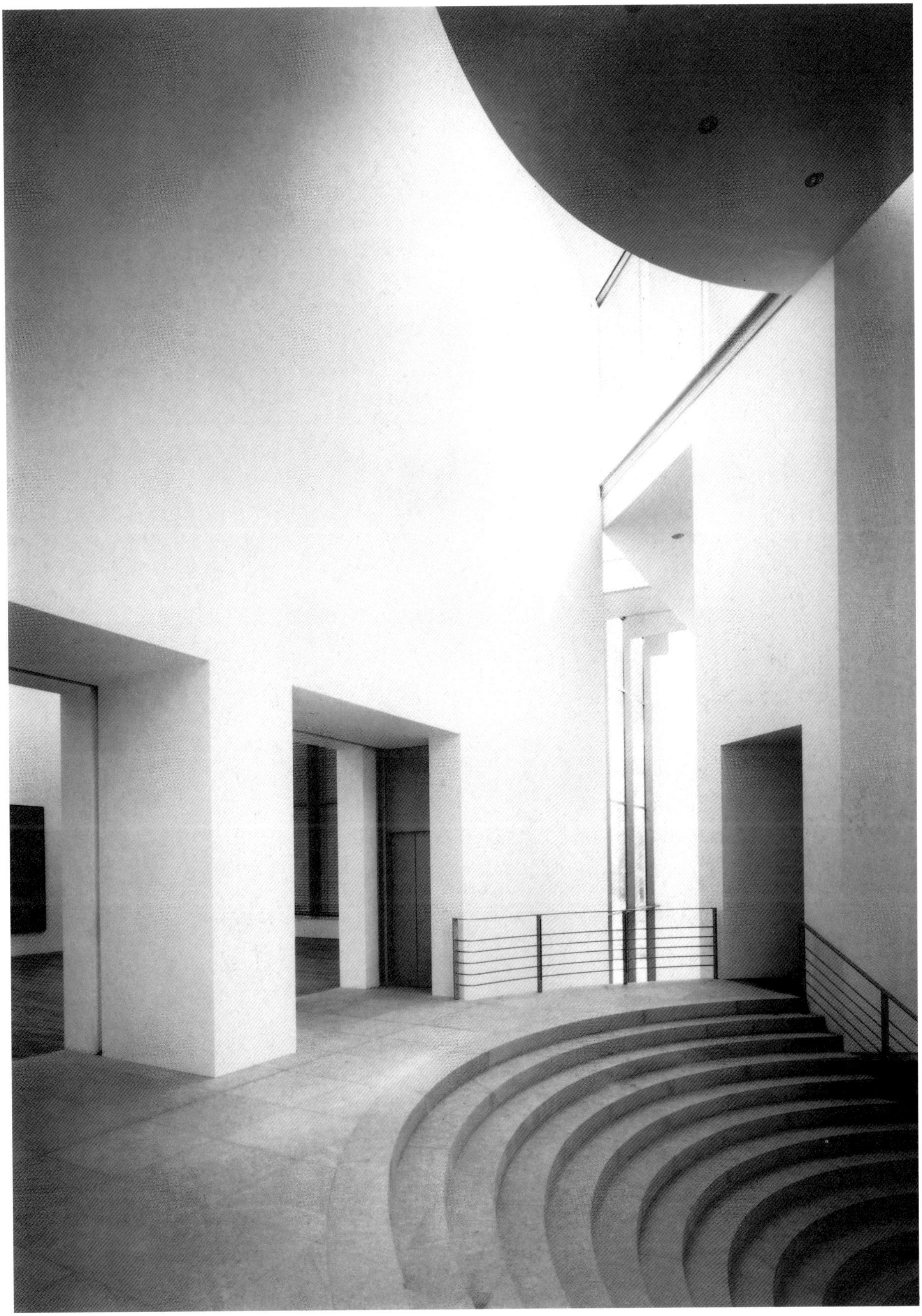

Potsdamer Platz Competition • Berlin • 1991

The competition for the Potsdamer Platz, touted as the new "Heart of Germany," raised a variety of issues. Should the site become something it never was: a square? Non-architects wanted to save it, to keep it the way it had become: desolate and empty. Architects had to consider how to create a space that is not really a space at all, how to relinquish the Euclidian box and preserve the space, or dole out new space to create a new present and future without eradicating the past.

This particular approach to the problem could not satisfy everyone; it explored unity and division, segment and continuum, impenetrability and permeability, narrowness and expanse, sharp and blurred edges. The structural plan for the four new blocks reverses the traditional relationship between street and inner courtyard: glazed, gallery-like interior courtyards, now called "malls," serve as the streets of the new quarter; narrow alley-like spaces between the mall sections provide service functions, like lighting, ventilation, and circulation. It would be exciting to see if this design approach could fulfill the varying wishes of the investors.

Axel Schultes

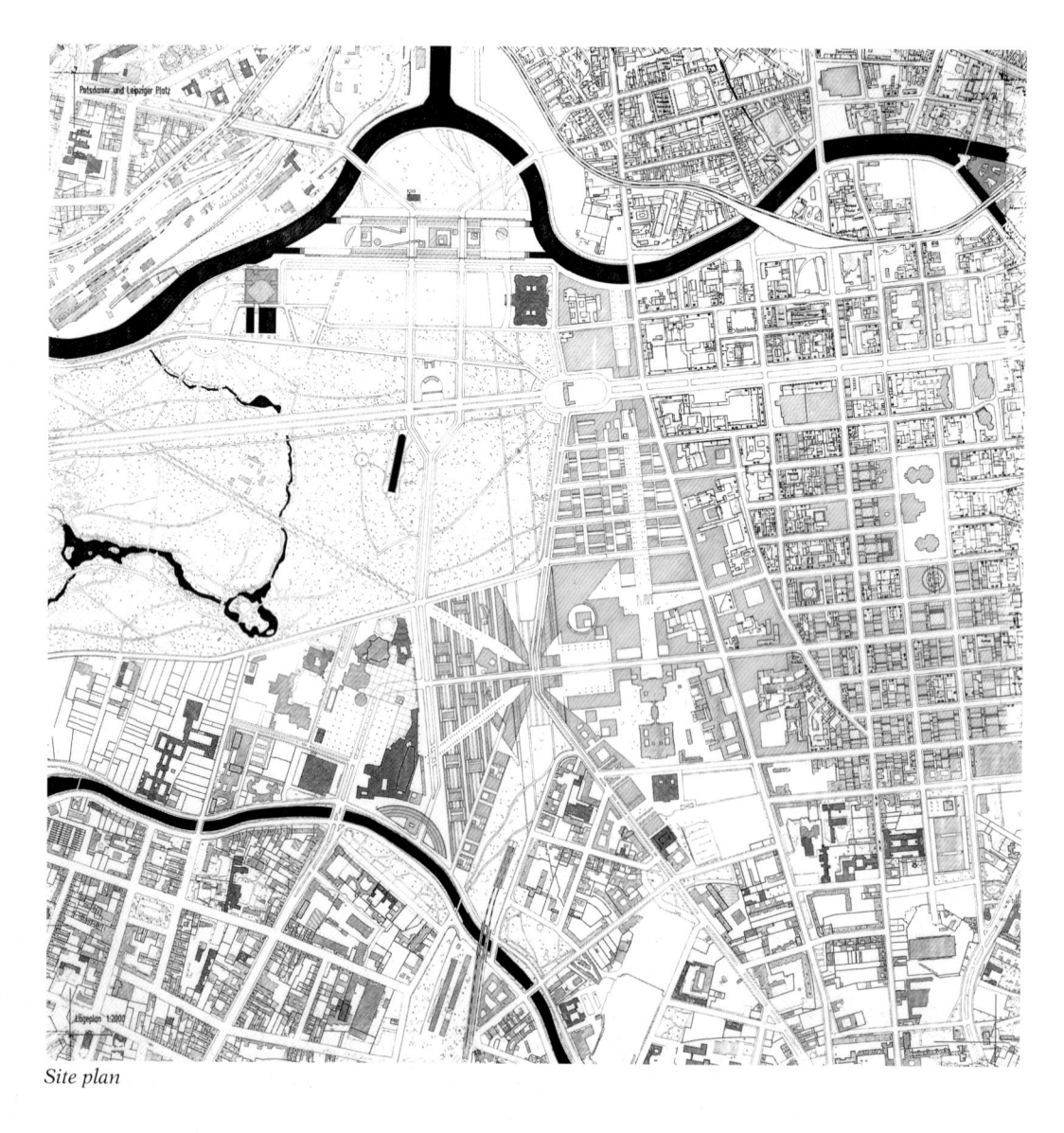

Site plan

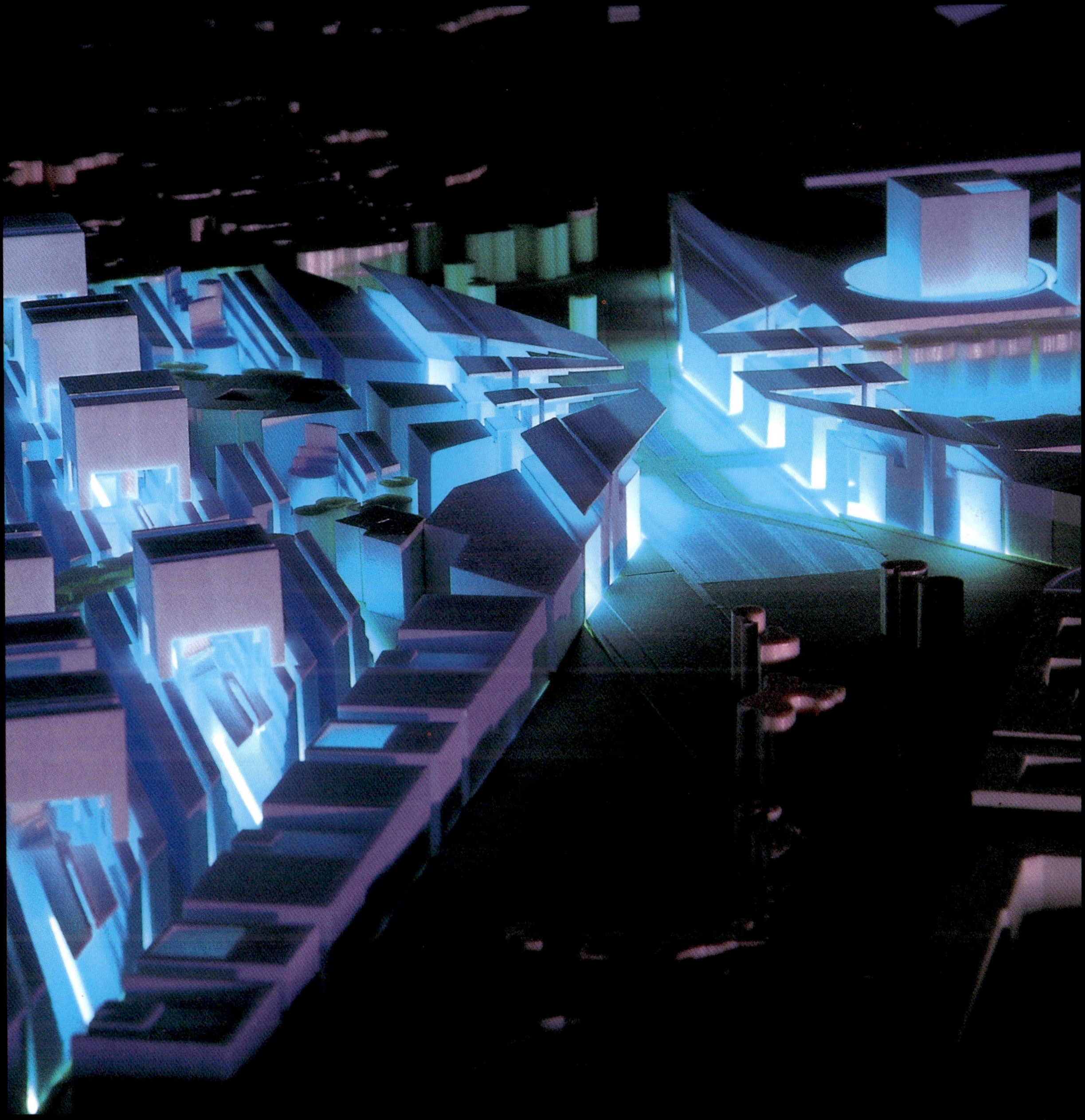

OTTO STEIDLE
Engineering Sciences University • Ulm-West • 1990–91

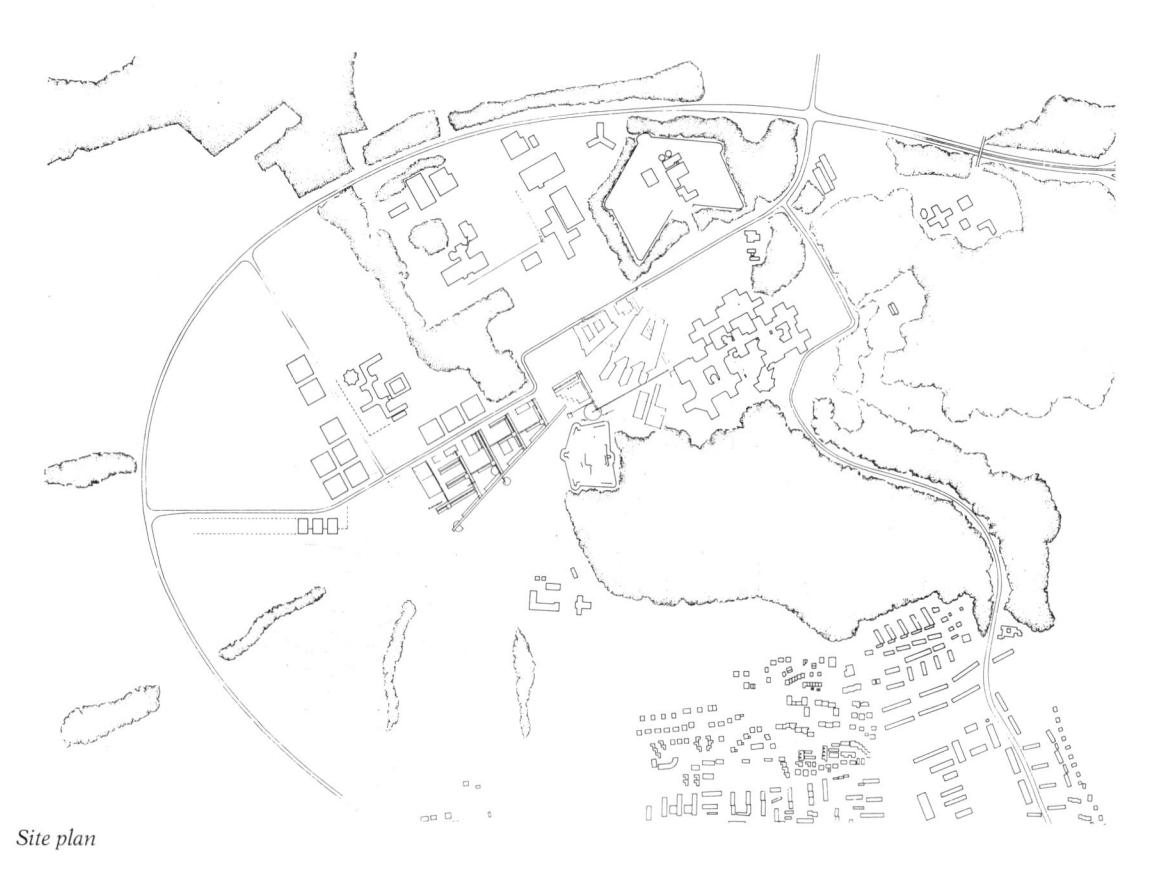

Site plan

A particular concept of urbanism —the ordered and structured city with paths and buildings, as opposed to the still wild countryside—was a major theme in the planning of this university. The defining element—in earlier times, the town wall—is here an elevated wood structure that connects the new university to an older one, making all of the individual areas accessible. But instead of the defensive town wall is a transparent promenade with an outside shell for plantings and second-story bridges which represent both functional and symbolic means of passage. Even the most fragmented academic facilities— lecture halls, seminar rooms, laboratories—are oriented toward this public, community-forming hub. Also adjacent to it are the individual living quarters and re-

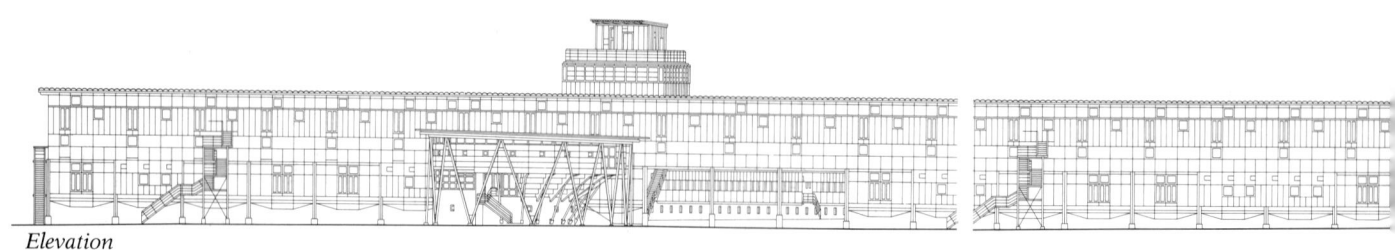

Elevation

search facilities. The elevated bridges create the necessary network without interrupting the landscape. The two-story building, its sodded roofs, and provisions for collecting and distributing rainwater ensure that the ecosystem is damaged as little as possible.

The two-story structure also enabled the development of a new type of structure, one without false floors and shafts. All research equipment is installed in the basement, which acts as a kind of horizontal equipment shaft; on the second floor are "thinking rooms." The open, gallery-like corridors are designed not only for circulation but as horizontal and vertical communications connections. Thus the structure becomes a multidimensional reality. Lights, shadows, spaces, zones, places, and passageways energize the building.

The generator for the facade design and color concept is the transparent promenade representing this urban energy. It was also based visually on a rhythmic diagram of Bach's Fugue in C Minor. All parts of the structure, joined through the idea of "city," interact yet retain their own distinctive features. *Peter Schmitz*

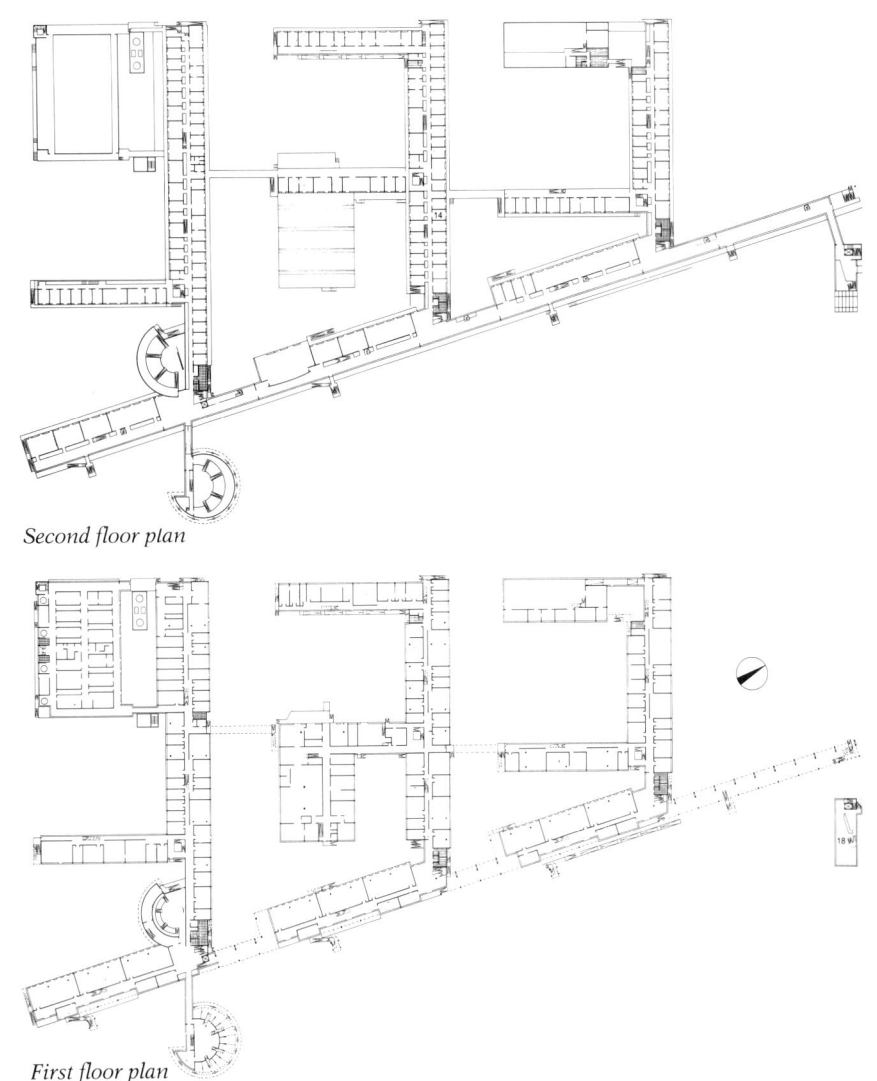

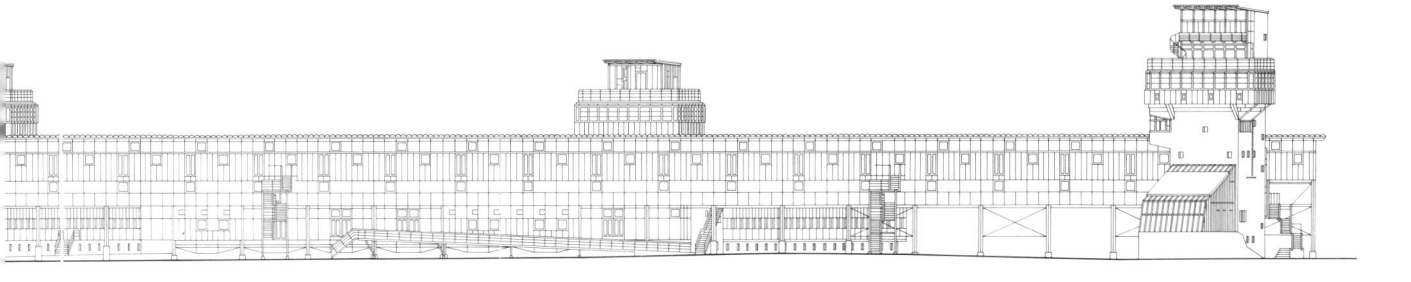

Second floor plan

First floor plan

210   OTTO STEIDLE

OTTO STEIDLE 211

OTTO STEIDLE AND UWE KIESSLER
Gruner & Jahr Publishing • Hamburg • 1983–91

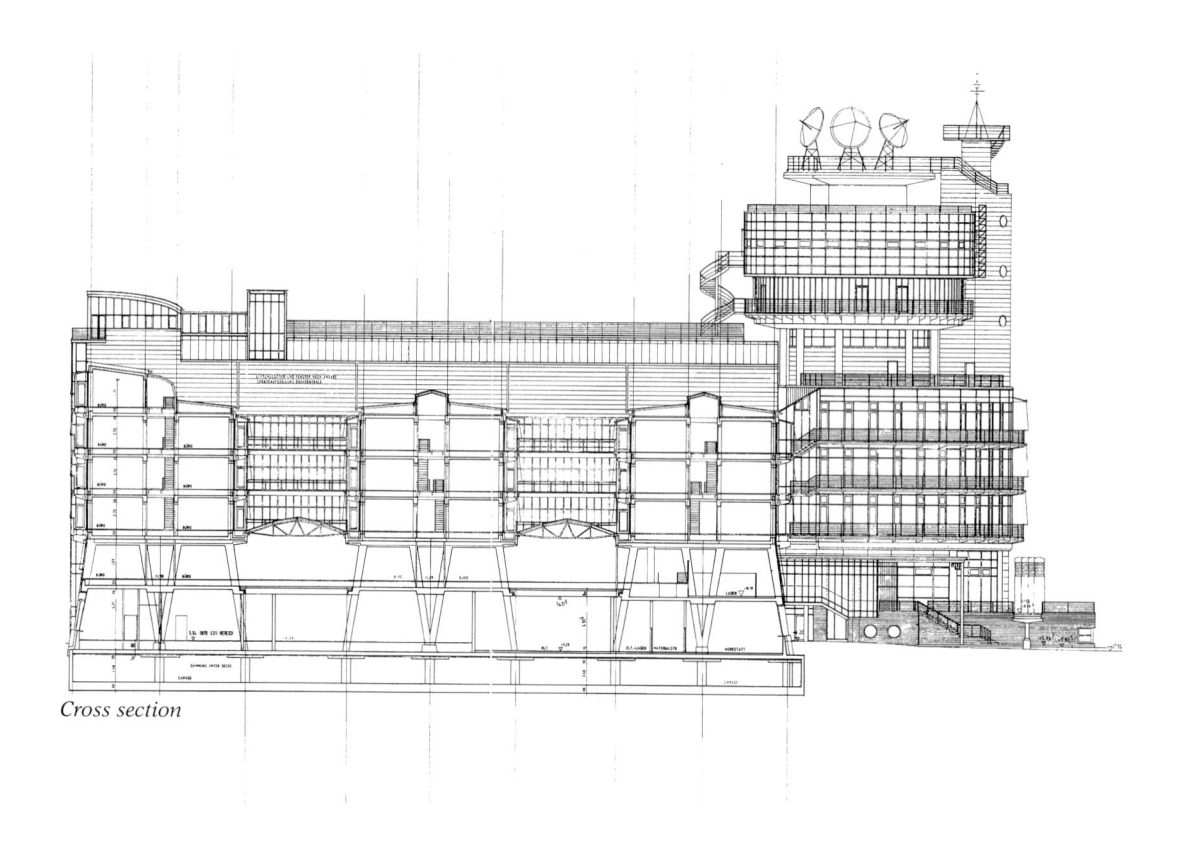

Cross section

A publishing house is for creative and productive editorial work, rather than administration. Architecture suitable for this purpose should not be based on typical office design, then, but should stimulate the imagination and promote communication. Some essential features are workshop-like rooms or studios and open, naturally lighted circulation areas. In this project, for a publisher of magazines, associations with shipyard architecture (cranes, ships, docks) and with specific local elements (the elevated railway, bridges) were planned. Translation of both these components and user needs into architectural features synthesizes the nature of the work and the building typology.

Stairs and gallery-like corridors in this building, as opposed to the usual elevators and enclosed hallways, are not just functional connections, but can transform routine errands and chance encounters into meaningful experiences, thus forming relationships and facilitating communication. This is one reason to make these areas light and airy.

A building as enormous as this cannot be integrated into the existing urban fabric as a hermetically sealed complex: its 2,500 employees represent the population of a small town. This was another important element in the design: to fit it into the neighborhood, the overall structure was developed on the lines of old buildings destroyed in the war. And this basic structure really did turn out to be flexible, producing an elegant building open to a great deal of variation. It is neither a high-rise office building nor a block development; it is more like a "horizontal skyscraper" or spatial city (after de Stijl-ist Frederick Kiesler).
Otto Steidle and Uwe Kiessler

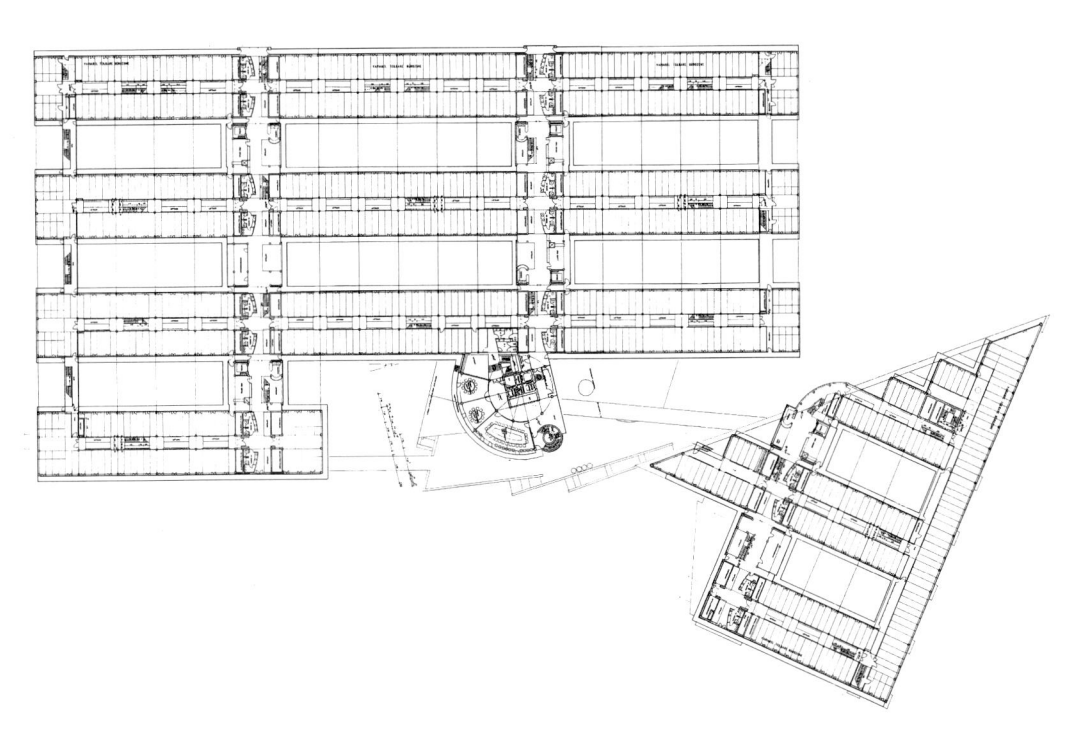

Typical floor plan

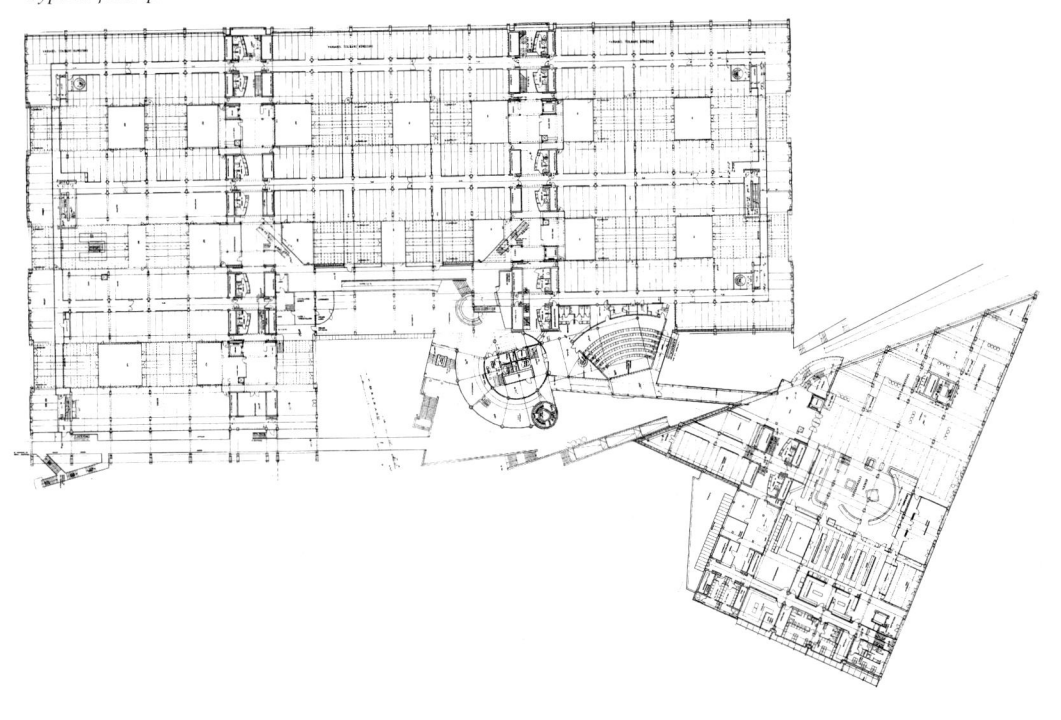

Main floor plan OTTO STEIDLE AND UWE KIESSLER   213

214 OTTO STEIDLE AND UWE KIESSLER

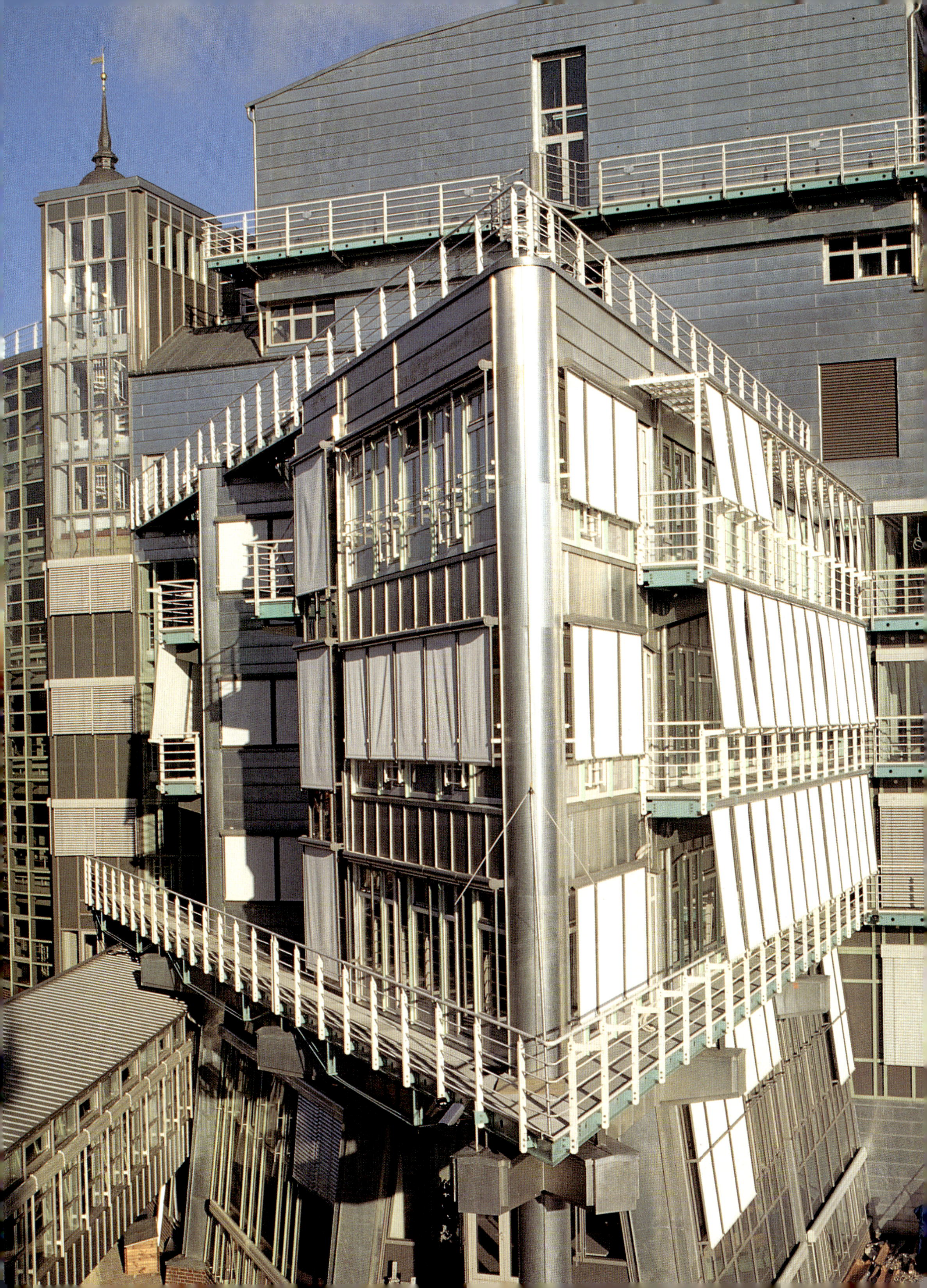

O. M. UNGERS
Town Portal Buildings • Frankfurt am Main • 1991

Two high-rises mark the western gateway into the city from the Theodor-Heuss-Allee: the Bosch Tower, for an electrical company, and the Trade Fair Tower. Both buildings are the same height and the same basic shape, but are different in structure and design. The distinct schemes were derived from the surrounding urban fabric, the varying functions, and technological conditions. Thus, the design results from a series of options for interpretation, all of which try to address the issue of gateway.

The Trade Fair Tower has offices on every floor. It has a solid structural core and an exterior shell of lightweight steel; inside the shell, the tower is climate-controlled throughout, including perimeter planting areas. The Bosch Tower has a variety of uses, including office and hotel space; the structural core is minimal and the building has exposed sanitation towers. The external shell is divided into three parts, each with its own mechanical system: The solid base course (picked up in the 35-meter-high building cubes of the overall complex) has an unspecified number of openings and is ventilated naturally. In the middle section—an articulated stone structure—the ventilation system is partly natural and partly artificial. The top section, with a steel framework, is totally enclosed and ventilated mechanically. *O. M. Ungers*

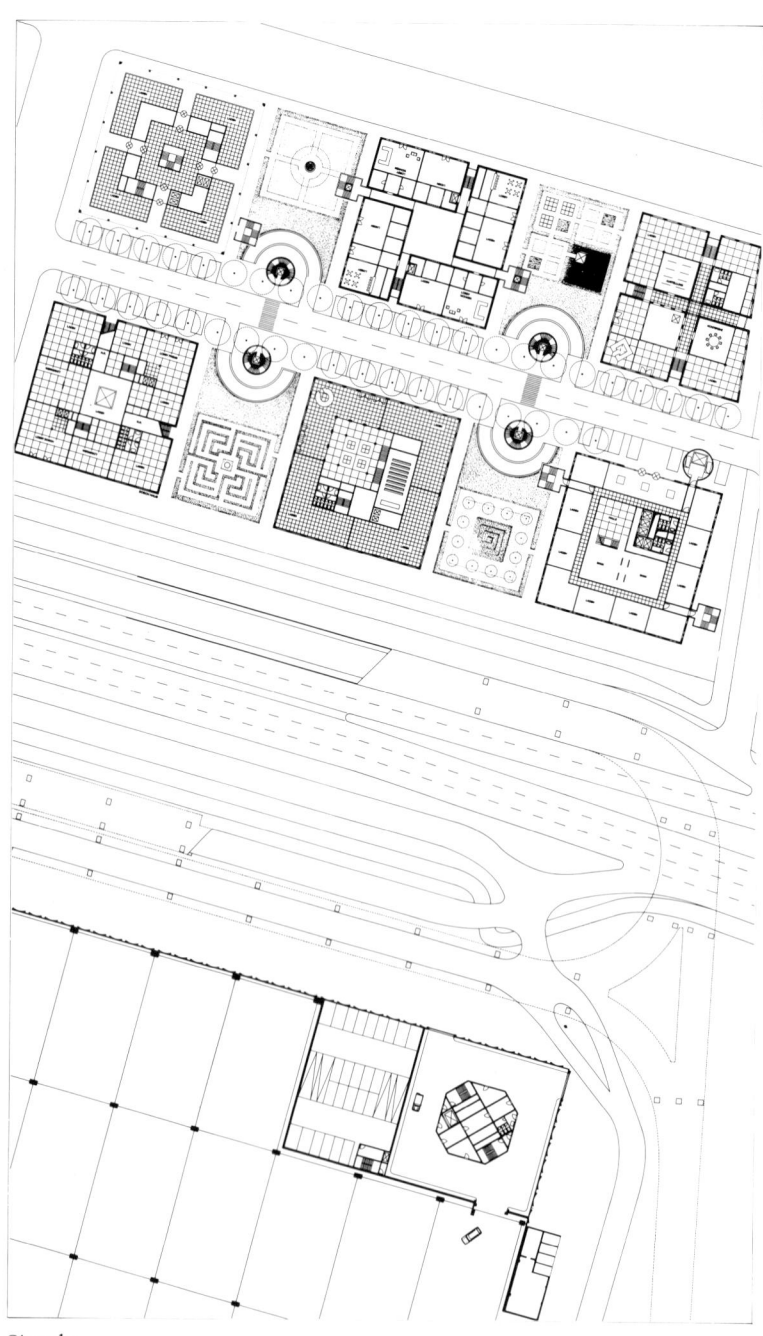

Site plan

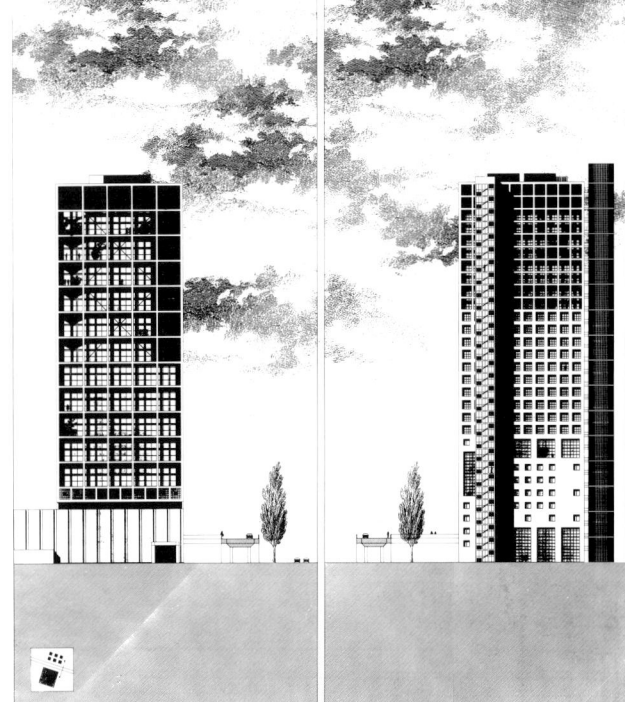

North elevation

East elevation

South elevation

West elevation

Cube House • Cologne • 1989–90

The Cube House on Quadrather Strasse is not merely an addition, but a complement to the main house on Belvedere Strasse. It is also a constructed manifesto for the 1990s. The brick house, dating from the 1950s, and the new, radical stone cube are related; like inhaling and exhaling, they are two parts of the same process.

The stone cube is lighted from above through four glass cubes; they dissolve spatial and material layers with their intermediate position. The interior structure consists of a painted skeleton, wood joined by ashlars, cinder blocks (which form the transition to the older structure), a carefully patched wall, and the surrounding stone walls.

The entire ensemble resembles a miniature city, a labyrinth of passageways, squares, towers, gates, entryways, niches, projections, and corners; it is a self-contained architectural world with revelations and surprises, a world of contradiction, illusion, and reality which runs the gamut from the image of architecture to fiction to the reality of function. It is an architecture of complementary opposites with historical references, embracing existential desire and real context.

O. M. Ungers

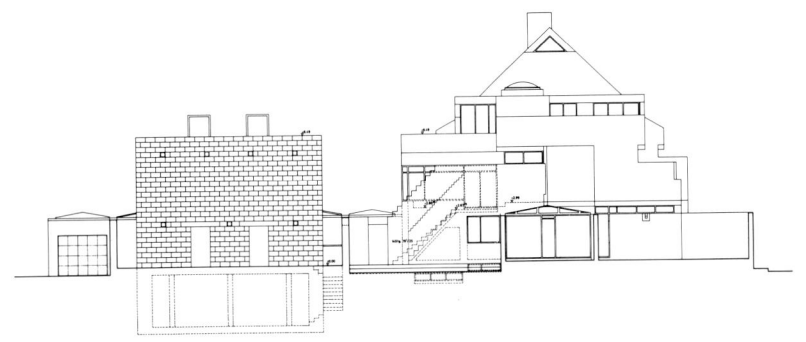

Cross section

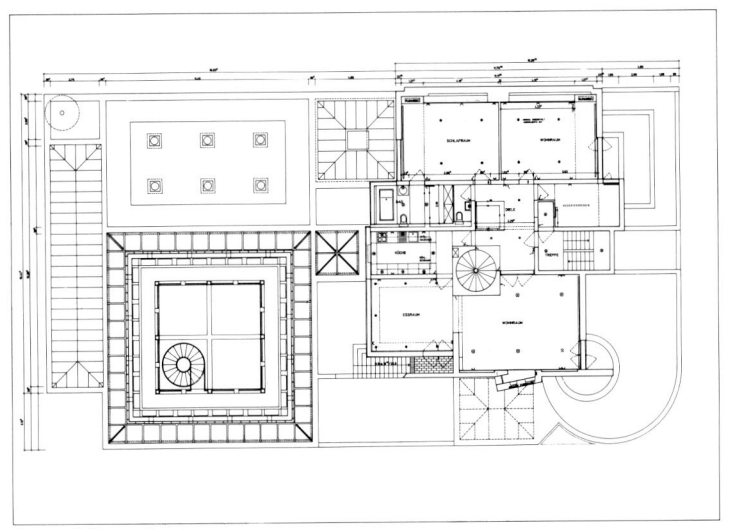

Second floor plan

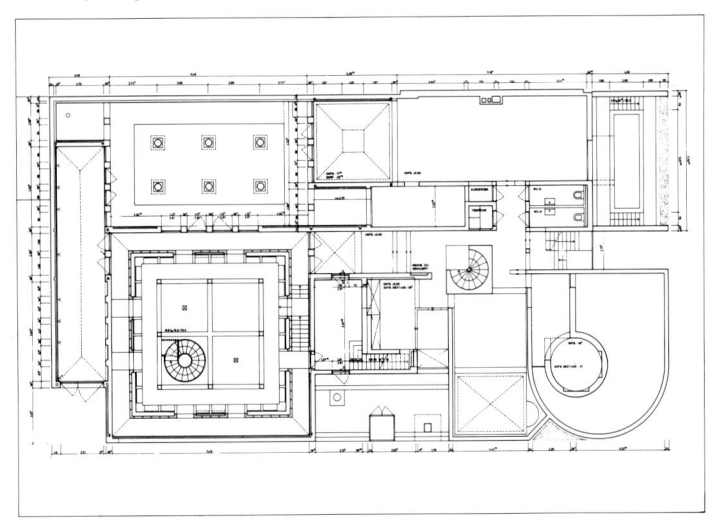

First floor plan

O. M. UNGERS

Baden Regional Library • Karlsruhe • 1980–92

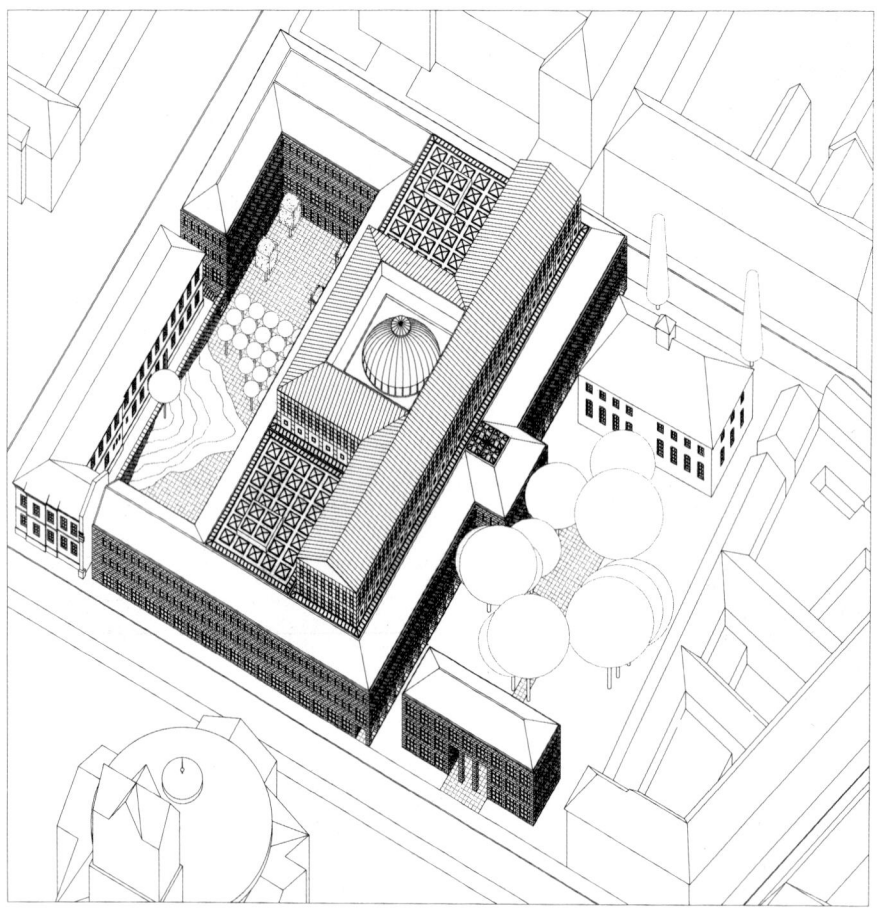

Axonometric

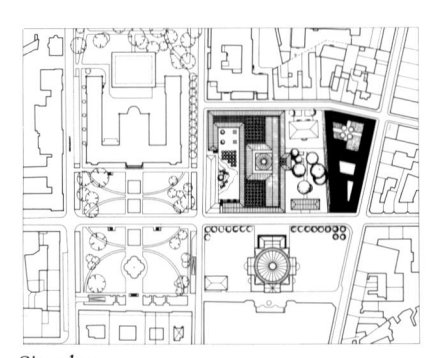

Site plan

The surrounding area determined the scale and formal language of this library. Of central importance were the incorporation of trees on the site, the dominance of St. Stephen's Church, and the primarily classicist architecture of Karlsruhe. Thus the library building consists of an external shell and an internal core: the shell reflects the scale of the structures on the block, including several historic buildings, and the core corresponds to St. Stephen's Church. The material, too, was selected in accordance with this concept: the shell is rough, made of stone and roofed with slate, and the core is of finer material, plastered and crowned with copper, to emphasize its relationship to the church. The two independent structural elements can be recognized as such in the interior of the building as well: shell and core are separated by a glass seam and by voids, some of which extend to full building height.

The structural dichotomy also arose from the program. The shell houses primarily support functions, such as administration and all uses not connected with actual library operations. The

Section

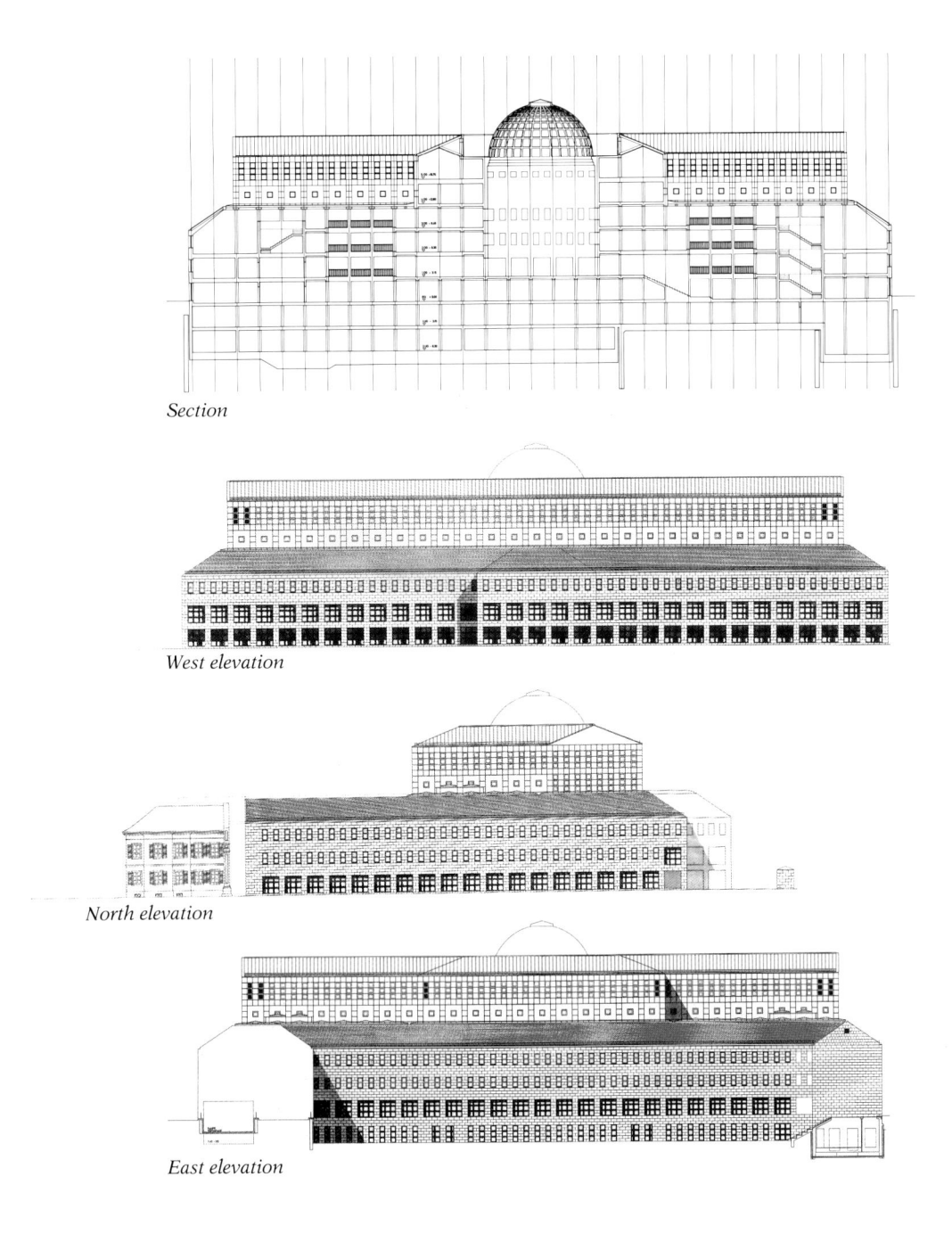

West elevation

North elevation

East elevation

core contains public areas, reading rooms, and stacks. The voids separating the two facilitate orientation within the library.

During construction, the emphasis was on traditional craftsmanship, in the execution of details, and traditional structural design, in the simple, column-load system. The architecture and the spaces are simple, cleanly and carefully proportioned volumes, differentiated by function. To keep with the classicist tradition in the area, there is no unnecessary or currently fashionable ornamentation or decoration.
O. M. Ungers

222 O. M. UNGERS

O. M. UNGERS

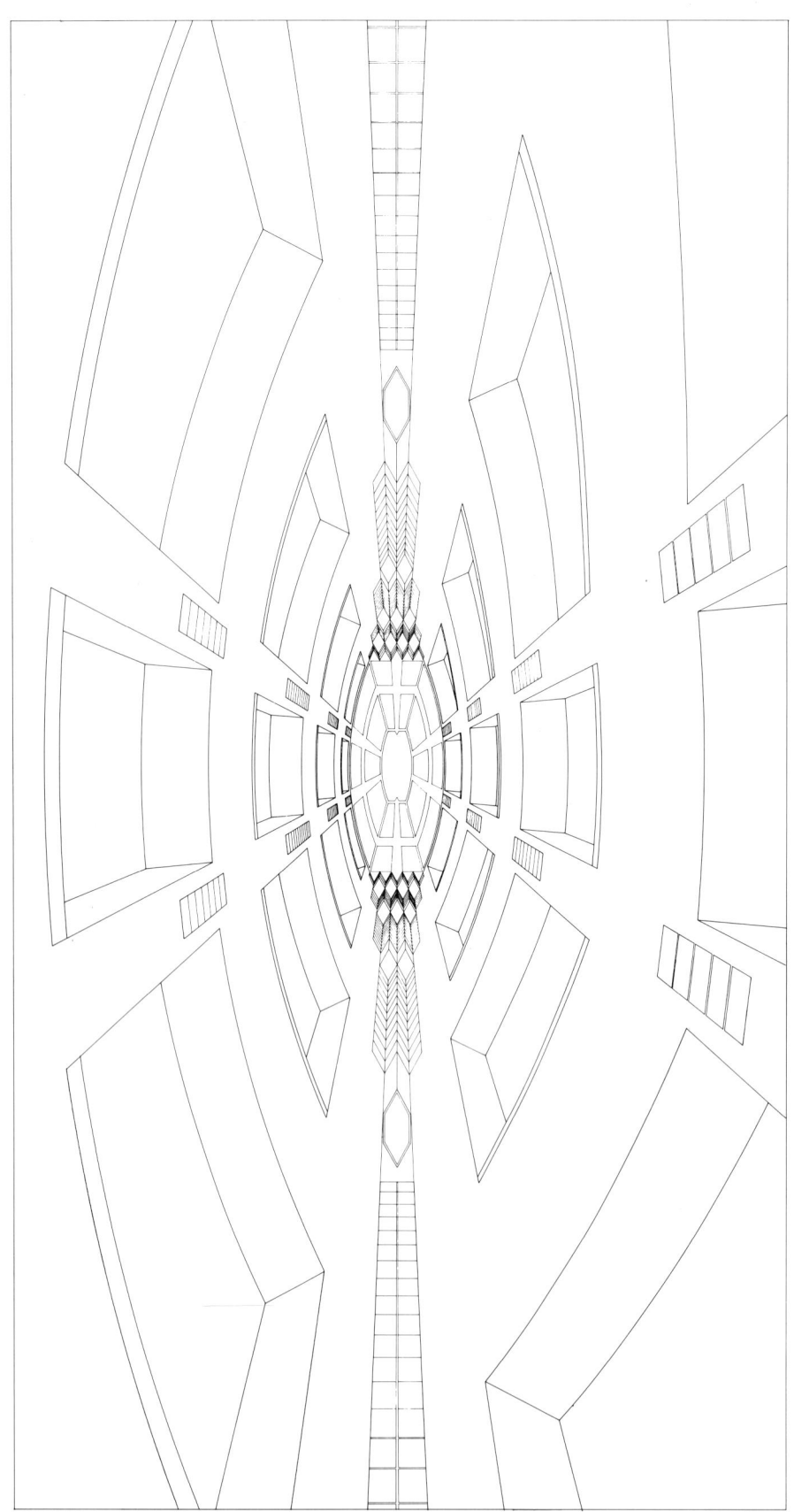

Jochem Jourdan, Landeszentralbank, Frankfurt am Main, 1978–80